'Group of cretins', *Journal of Mental Science*, vol. 41, 1895, p. 280.
By permission of the Bodleian Library, Oxford.

FROM IDIOCY TO MENTAL DEFICIENCY

From Idiocy to Mental Deficiency is the first book devoted to the social history of people with learning disabilities in Britain. Approaches to learning difficulties have changed dramatically in recent years. The implementation of 'Care in the Community', the campaign for disabled rights, and the debate over the education of children with special needs have combined to make this one of the most controversial areas in social policy today.

The nine original research essays collected here cover the social history of learning disability from the Middle Ages through to the establishment of the National Health Service. Together with the useful general introduction to the volume, they not only contribute to a neglected field of social and medical history; they also illuminate and inform current debates.

The research presented here will have a profound impact on how professionals in mental health, psychiatric nursing, social work, and disabled rights understand learning disability and society's responses to it over the course of history.

David Wright is Wellcome Lecturer in the History of Medicine at the University of Nottingham. **Anne Digby** is Professor of Social History at Oxford Brookes University.

STUDIES IN THE SOCIAL HISTORY OF MEDICINE

Edited by Jonathan Barry and Bernard Harris

In recent years, the social history of medicine has become recognised as a major field of historical enquiry. Aspects of health, disease, and medical care now attract the attention not only of social historians but also of researchers in a broad spectrum of historical and social science disciplines. The Society for the Social History of Medicine, founded in 1969, is an interdisciplinary body, based in Great Britain but international in membership. It exists to forward a wide-ranging view of the history of medicine, concerned equally with biological aspects of normal life, experience of and attitudes to illness, medical thought and treatment, and systems of medical care. Although frequently bearing on current issues, this interpretation of the subject makes primary reference to historical context and contemporary priorities. The intention is not to promote a sub-specialism but to conduct research according to the standards and intelligibility required of history in general. The Society publishes a journal, *Social History of Medicine*, and holds at least three conferences a year. Its series, Studies in the Social History of Medicine, does not represent publication of its proceedings, but comprises volumes on selected themes, often arising out of conferences but subsequently developed by the editors.

Life, Death and the Elderly
Edited by Margaret Pelling and Richard M. Smith

Medicine and Charity Before the Welfare State
Edited by Jonathan Barry and Colin Jones

In the Name of the Child
Edited by Roger Cooter

Reassessing Foucault
Power, Medicine and the Body
Edited by Colin Jones and Roy Porter

FROM IDIOCY TO MENTAL DEFICIENCY

Historical perspectives on people with learning disabilities

Edited by David Wright and Anne Digby

London and New York

First published 1996
by Routledge
11 New Fetter Lane, London EC4P 4EE

Simultaneously published in the USA and Canada
by Routledge
29 West 35th Street, New York, NY 10001

Routledge is an International Thomson publishing company.

Typeset in Baskerville by
Poole Typesetting (Wessex) Limited
Bournemouth, Dorset

Printed and bound in Great Britain by
TJ Press Ltd, Padstow, Cornwall

British Library Cataloguing in Publication Data
A catalogue record for this book is available from the British Library.

Library of Congress Cataloging in Publication Data
A catalogue record for this book has been requested.

ISBN 0–415–11215–X

CONTENTS

CONTRIBUTORS

Jonathan Andrews is a post-doctoral Research Fellow at the Wellcome Unit for the History of Medicine, University of Glasgow. He was the joint editor with Iain Smith of *Let There be Light Again: A History of Gartnavel Royal Hospital* (Glasgow: 1993). He is currently working on psychiatry in nineteenth-century Scotland, and in particular on the social and demographic profiles of patients admitted to Glasgow Royal Asylum, Gartnavel.

Pamela Cox is currently completing her doctoral thesis at the Department of Education in the University of Cambridge, where she also teaches. This research is funded by the Economic and Social Research Council and examines the experience of girls in the juvenile justice system in England and Wales in the early twentieth century.

Anne Digby is Professor of Social History at Oxford Brookes University and has published widely on the history of social policy and the social history of medicine, including *Madness, Morality and Medicine* (Cambridge University Press: 1985) and *Making a Medical Living* (Cambridge University Press: 1994). She is currently researching on general practitioners in Britain, 1850–1950.

David Gladstone is Director of Undergraduate Studies in the School for Policy Studies at the University of Bristol. A historian by training, his main interests are nineteenth-century and twentieth-century British social welfare. He has published widely on the history of social policy and has two books in press – *British Social Welfare: Past, Present and Future* (UCL Press: 1995) and (ed.) *Thomas Chalmers on Poverty and Political Economy* (Routledge: 1995). His current research is a study of the British Welfare State.

C.F. Goodey currently works at the Social Science Research Unit, University of London. He writes on contemporary issues concerning learning difficulties (see *Culture, Kinship and Genes*, edited by Angus Clarke, Macmillan: 1995), and has published early historical studies related to the present, one in *History of Psychiatry* (Royal College of Psychiatrists: 1994) and in *A History of Clinical Psychiatry* (G. Berrios and R. Porter (eds), 1995).

Mark Jackson is a Researcher and Lecturer at the Wellcome Unit for the History of Medicine in the University of Manchester. His doctoral thesis on new-born child murder in the eighteenth century is soon to be published by Manchester University Press. His current research interests include the social history of mental deficiency in the late nineteenth and early twentieth centuries, and a new project on the history of immunology and related biomedical sciences in the twentieth century.

Richard Neugebauer is a Research Scientist in the Epidemiology of Developmental Brain Disorders Department of New York State Psychiatric Institute and in the Gertrude H. Sergievsky Center, Faculty of Medicine, Columbia University. He has published articles on the history of mental illness as well as articles and books on psychiatric and perinatal epidemiology, neuroepidemiology and biostatistics.

Peter Rushton is Principal Lecturer in Sociology in the School of Social and International Studies, University of Sunderland. He has published widely on different aspects of early modern society in north-east England such as witchcraft, marriage and domestic relations, and the Poor Law, as well as on mental disabilities and social policy. He is currently working (with Gwenda Morgan) on a book on crime and punishment in north-east England in the eighteenth century.

Mathew Thomson is a lecturer and Wellcome University Award holder in the Department of History, University of Sheffield. He is currently revising his doctorate on mental deficiency for publication and researching mental hygiene in the first half of the twentieth century.

David Wright is a lecturer and Wellcome University Award holder at the University of Nottingham. His doctoral thesis, a study of the National Asylum for Idiots, Earlswood, will shortly be published by Oxford University Press. He is currently working on the economic and demographic origins of the institutional committal of the insane in Victorian England.

1

CONTEXTS AND PERSPECTIVES

Anne Digby

Historically, the social marginality of people with learning disabilities has been mirrored by their academic marginality. Even when the 'new social history' of the 1960s and 1970s had focused on 'history from below' and made visible a number of social groups previously neglected by historians, people with learning disabilities at first did not come into view. More recently some excellent, but as yet unpublished, doctoral theses have taken this group of people as their subject.[1] A Society for the Social History of Medicine conference entitled 'From "Idiocy" to "Mental Deficiency": Historical Perspectives on People with Learning Disabilities' attracted considerable interest at home and abroad when it was held in London in 1992.[2] This book is the outcome of papers given at that conference and will, it is hoped, stimulate further studies in the history of these individuals.

This introductory chapter provides a broad contextualisation and period perspective which aims to enhance an appreciation of the more detailed case studies in the volume. The chapter begins by looking at the language of difference, and earlier attempts to locate the nature of that difference. A discussion of the institutional response to learning disabilities from the eighteenth century to the twentieth century, of the social and intellectual climate in which this developed, and of alternatives in the form of familial or community care then follows. The chapter also highlights some human rights issues.

Pragmatic tests for idiocy (notably those in relation to property), were based on establishing orientation, intellect, judgement and memory. *Ad hoc* questioning ascertained whether individuals were aware of knowing where they were, what age they were, what day of the week it was, if there was an ability to count to twenty pence or do a simple literacy test, as well as determining whether there was an orderly weekly religious attendance at church.[3] As Richard Neugebauer indicates in Chapter 2, during both the medieval and early modern periods it is interesting to discover that naturalistic tests rather than demonological criteria were used to evaluate mental impairment in English court hearings that involved the Crown's incompetency jurisdiction over property. From the thirteenth century onwards there had been a legal dichotomy between idiocy and lunacy. Idiots (for a time also termed natural fools) were seen as having a disability that was permanent, a condition involving absence of understanding from birth. This was distinct from lunacy which was a postnatal event. By the seventeenth and eighteenth centuries, as Peter Rushton points out in Chapter 3, intermediate categories had been introduced. Legal decisions often effectively validated the viewpoint of families or endorsed the popular reputation of the individual as an idiot. A common-sense familiarity or lack of embarrassment towards eccentricity, lunacy or idiocy was indicated by the richly nuanced language describing them.[4]

Social negativity grew stronger as more widespread institutional care resulted in a distancing of idiots and imbeciles from the community. Closer social, medical, or educational attention was also focused upon these institutionalised individuals. At first this specialist focus was not necessarily associated with any great precision since, for example, those born deaf and dumb continued to be legally presumed to be idiots.[5] Idiots were seen as less able to reason than imbeciles, and an additional term, the feeble-minded, was borrowed from American writings in the 1860s. The fluidity of the latter enabled a variety of social problems to be conflated with it; late nineteenth-century fears of miscegenation and degeneration in Britain associated the feeble-minded with class and, in the Empire, with race.[6] In medico-legal terms the states of idiocy and imbecility were only gradually distinguished from lunacy. The Report of the Metropolitan Commissioners in Lunacy in 1844 recognised congenital idiots and congenital imbeciles as two of its nine categories of lunacy. Under the Lunacy Act of 1890 an insane person was defined as either an idiot, a lunatic or a person of unsound mind. Legally, however, it was not until the twentieth century that lunacy excluded mental disability. Twentieth-century legislation was interesting linguistically since successive mental health and education acts referred to feeble-mindedness, idiocy and imbecility (1913), mental sub-normality (1944 and 1959), and mental impairment (1983). In Britain, as in the United States, however, lay confusion of mental illness and idiocy/imbecility continued.[7]

Historically, therefore, the subject is confused by a multiplicity of terms, while current notions of political correctness and enablement have helped fuel an increasingly rapid change in nomenclature. For example, after forty years of existence as the 'Spastics Society' the organisation felt it necessary in 1994 to be renamed as 'Scope', with the subtitle 'for those with cerebral palsy', because it considered that the original name, 'spastics', had become a term of abuse.[8] With present-day equal opportunities policies, and with a more widespread adoption of a human rights culture, the stigmatising of people with learning disabilities – in which yesterday's definition becomes today's term of abuse – as in 'fool', 'idiot', 'moron', 'cretin', or 'imbecile' – may become harder. Today, it is society that the impaired themselves now perceive as disabling for the individual, and human potential will, it is thought, be achieved through anti-discrimination legislation. This may offer a better way forward than concern directed at stigmatised labelling. All too often debates over linguistic political correctness have produced semantic ingenuities – 'intellectually challenged', 'developmentally retarded', or 'differently abled' – which have done little to improve the actual civil rights of the disabled. It is this perspective which has informed the decision to use the terminology of the period under discussion in different parts of this chapter, as well as a belief that the language used historically helps us to understand past values and social attitudes.

Implicit in the language describing these individuals was, and is, the notion of the Other. 'The changing definitions of difference constitute the history of the mentally handicapped. These definitions have always been conceived of by others, never are they the expression of a group of people finding their own identity, their own history.'[9] The issue of their relative humanity or animality was the subject of discussion by early psychologists and philosophers.[10] Thomas Willis in a chapter on mental deficiency listed the physical insults to the body that predisposed parents to have imbecilic children.[11] Changelings, as the handicapped children of normal parents were called, aroused particular interest from Paracelsus onwards. Locke, in a famous and apparently unproblematic distinction between lunatics and idiots, argued that 'Idiots make very few or no propositions, and reason scarce at all.' But Locke's view of the idiot was far from unproblematic since this was based on a circular identification of idiots and changelings. In reviewing what it was to be human, it has been suggested that Locke provided a much more comprehensive exclusion of the idiot than the earlier one based on particular schema (such as the historical tests discussed above).[12] In Chapter 5 of this volume, Chris Goodey analyses the antecedents of Locke's thought in seventeenth-century theological debates that developed distinctions between natural and moral disability, probed the reasons why God should have created idiots, and pondered whether they could ever achieve salvation. Goodey demonstrates how Locke extended the discussion into the secular realm of the political nature of consent in a civil society, and so suggests the relevance – both past and present – of the relationship of disability to consent and civil liberty.

Idiocy was seen mainly as a domestic or family problem so that institutional remedies were thought largely inappropriate in the early modern period. The situation became a matter of public concern – and thus of Poor Law applications – only when care broke down, the burden of care resulted in family poverty, or if male adults (often the main productive members of the family), were concerned.[13] Peter Rushton argues in Chapter 3 that so far from indicating a pre-industrial golden age of social integration this situation suggests that the family was 'at the centre of the state-enforced system of care'. Thus the English parish only looked after a minority of individuals by subsidising care in neighbours' homes. And some parishes were so reluctant to shoulder the financial burden for this that payment had to be enforced by the magistracy. In contrast, in Chapter 4, Jonathan Andrews prefers to stress the compassionate nature of these kinds of parochial relief on the basis of his research into a sample of metropolitan parishes during the seventeenth and early eighteenth centuries. Whilst also emphasising the predominantly family-based and domiciliary locus of care he also finds that some idiots were sent out to surrounding counties for nursing or lodging. Boarding out with 'kindly guardians' was later employed in nineteenth-century Scotland for the mentally deficient. The official – and probably over-optimistic view – of these community-based strategies was that 'Being dressed like ordinary people … the old village fools seemed at once to disappear from the villages without having really left them.'[14]

Only a minority of idiots were placed in institutions. In Chapter 4 Jonathan Andrews suggests that whilst Bethlem Hospital was putting more effort into excluding the incurable, amongst whom were numbered the idiotic, from the late seventeenth century onwards workhouses privileged idiots above lunatics because of the utility of their labour. A process of institutionalisation gradually accelerated within an industrialising and urbanising society. This transition from life in the family or community (which was an almost invisible presence as far as the historical record was concerned), to that in institutions has led to more documentation and hence – for historians – to greater social visibility. But even in workhouses, asylums and prisons idiotic inmates were for some time outside the main focus of concern, not least because it was perceived only belatedly that they were a separate category. From the documentation it appears as if idiots and imbeciles had only 'walk-on parts' as criminals, paupers, or lunatics because they were not on the historical stage for long enough to be within the vision of eighteenth-century and nineteenth-century administrators and policy-makers. Ironically, in reality, they might be the longest-stay inmates. This failure to come 'under the spotlight' also derived from the circumstances surrounding institutional development. A burst of therapeutic and social optimism had created such establishments. But imbeciles and idiots were not the easiest people for whom to claim recovery or rapid discharge rates, and hence to publicise a 'successful' establishment which could then gain additional funding from a credulous public. A lack of understanding of their needs, and of a suitable typology in relation to those seen as idiots and imbeciles, led to them being housed in a variety of institutions. In this spectrum there was a hierarchy of cost as well as of social, educational or medical suitability; general workhouses were cheaper than any of the alternatives. The growth of Georgian and Victorian institutions was driven as much by the desire to safeguard the interests of society as to care for particular groups. Revealingly, the Quaker expert on psychological medicine, D.H. Tuke, stated in 1882 that:

> There may be times when, desiring to see the 'survival of the fittest', we may be tempted to wish that idiots and imbeciles were stamped out of society. But … there is a compensation for the continued existence of so pitiable a population in our midst in … that our sympathies are called forth on their behalf … those who are strong should help the weak.[15]

Once created, for whatever combination of altruistic and self-regarding motives, institutions both highlighted and themselves created problem populations. By the mid- and late nineteenth century the optimism of early reformers had been succeeded by a pessimism in which feeble-minded inmates were seen as inherently problematic. As long-stay, 'chronic' inmates they assisted in the silting up of the asylum through impeding its curative potential. At the same time, as recidivists in prison populations, they contributed to what was perceived as an alarming growth of Victorian criminality. In these circumstances it was predictable that the prevalence of the feeble-minded should become an important strand in contemporary debates on social degeneracy, and hence on eugenics. Henry Maudsley characteristically referred to hereditary degeneracy as culminating 'in the extreme degeneracy of idiocy'.[16] Within a wider focus of concern about the unregenerate poor 'who had turned their backs on progress, or had been rejected by it', there were groups who aroused particular anxiety; earlier this was the weak-minded criminal and later on, the feeble-minded fecund woman. A fear of the degenerate residuum or underclass, and of contamination arising from it, was part of a wider discussion of national efficiency, and of the coercive, disciplinary, or segregative social policies that might be involved in order to achieve it.[17] Although early Victorian asylum superintendents had discharged the weak-minded, without apparently seeing them as a threat to society, from the late 1860s by contrast there were demands for the certification and institutional isolation of the mentally retarded. And, during the late nineteenth century, rising statistics of 'feeble-mindedness' seemed to have attested more to increased social sensitivity than to any real growth in their numbers.

What were the English institutional policies or practices that had led up to this situation? Under the New Poor Law of 1834 it was only the practicalities of early workhouse administration that led to those of unsound mind becoming recognised as a distinct class of pauper: Poor Law orders between 1834 and 1847 referred variously to idiots, persons of weak intellect, mental imbeciles, and the mentally infirm. Other categories of disability were conflated with them, as were the deaf, or deaf and dumb, in Warwickshire workhouses.[18] Under later Poor Law orders of 1844 and 1852 idiots and imbeciles were allowed outdoor relief, but many found their way into the workhouses, some as short-stay inmates called 'ins and outs', and others as very long-stay ones.[19] A survey of long-standing inmates of workhouses in 1861 found that the idiotic and epileptic formed a principal category. In Norfolk, for instance, amongst indoor paupers who had been in the workhouse for over five years one-third were imbecilic or idiotic, including Rachel Dixon, 'an idiot' of King's Lynn, who had entered sixty-six years before.[20] Inside the workhouse there were no orders for the separation of lunatics and imbeciles from other inmates, nor any general provision of specialist accommodation. Indeed, the Webbs correctly referred to a 'paralysis' of Poor Law policy in regard to this group of people since circulars referred in passing to them, but not as a matter of central concern. For example, in 1868 the same diet was to be given to imbeciles as to the aged, whilst in 1895 there was a prohibition on care to workhouse children from weak-minded inmates. Otherwise, only an occasional inspectorial anxiety was raised about imbeciles and also about the group of senile imbeciles, with whom they were conflated. Concern was expressed about idiots' or imbeciles' impact on the sane in an institution rather than about any such individuals in their own right. In these circumstances few Poor Law unions built imbecile wards.[21] London was exceptional in that the Metropolitan Poor Act of 1867 led to specialist Poor Law accommodation being provided for idiots and imbeciles in large-scale institutions at Leavesden, Caterham, and later at a school for 1,000 pupils at Darenth.[22]

Until the late nineteenth century there existed at best only a blunted perception of difference between the imbecilic and the harmless or chronic lunatic, or between the congenitally handicapped and the senile demented. The English workhouse was the likeliest location for the imbecile, and local guardians found such imbecilic inmates useful – more especially as numbers of other able-bodied inmates soon declined to a point where they were insufficient in numbers for labour in the laundry or the kitchen. In many such cases the establishment gained more from the inmate in work, than did the individual from the institution through care. From 1845 the newly appointed Lunacy Commissioners were compliant with this situation, although they placed some pressure on the Poor Law authorities to improve facilities. But, at local level, little action was taken in response.[23] The cheapness of the workhouse in comparison to the asylum meant that Poor Law authorities preferred retention of all save violently disturbed lunatics whose troublesomeness outweighed the costs of sending them to an asylum. In Ireland, in contrast, certification at petty sessions meant that the law, and not the Poor Law administrator, was the primary determinant of the composition of asylum populations: here there was a clear distinction made between workhouses as the destination of idiots and imbeciles, and asylums as that of lunatics.[24]

Medical interest was much greater in lunacy than in idiocy and imbecility. Jonathan Andrews indicates in Chapter 4, that it was highly unusual to find references to medical treatment in seventeenth-century parochial records. And David Wright argues in Chapter 6 on the basis of an analysis of certification for the first Idiot Asylum in England, Earlswood, that so far from the Victorian medical practitioner having much expertise in the process of medical certification of idiocy, it was the family – who had had the experience of caring for the idiot child – who took the lead in specifying the 'indications' of the disability. Lay attitudes on what constituted idiocy, he suggests, involved a sense of difference in that the child was perceived as more dependent, and relatively backward because lacking meaningful speech, and being deficient in social skills. In Chapter 7 David Gladstone refers more briefly to the nature of initial assessments (by an honorary medical officer to the Western Counties Idiot Asylum in 1880), as being based very much on common-sense criteria. These indicated strong continuity with those which Richard Neugebauer and Peter Rushton suggested were used by lay people several centuries earlier. In linking the 'origins' of the children's idiocy to physical conditions such as epilepsy or physiological abnormalities, however, David Wright argues that certifying doctors did find medical models more useful.

It is important to recognise that advances in medical knowledge occurred only very gradually and episodically, and then often as the result of an individual doctor's interest. From the sixteenth to the nineteenth centuries there had been some discussion of cretinism, but it was during the late nineteenth century that the condition was discovered to have been the result of thyroid deficiency.[25] In 1866 John Langdon Down formulated his classic description of mongolism, and this led to it being renamed as Down's syndrome. It was not until the turn of the twentieth century, as Mark Jackson indicates in Chapter 8, that doctors constituted themselves as 'experts' in mental deficiency and wrote papers, articles and books discussing feeble-mindedness as a state which was likened to an organic disease. The diagnostic significance of physical aspects of mental defect, revealingly termed the 'stigmata of degeneration', was discussed by doctors in relation to what they saw as the distinctively pathological nature of the feeble-minded. This biological/medical model of mental deficiency as disease, in which clinical observations were coloured by moral judgements, influenced later social policies of segregation.[26] Differentiation in legal certification also derived from medical advances in knowledge. The Lunatics Act of 1845 had required two medical certificates for entry to a lunatic asylum, whereas there was medical discretion as to the certification of idiots. Under the Idiots Act of 1886 one medical certificate was required to send a child to a special school.

Creation of specialist accommodation for idiots, particularly for children, had come with five English provincial licensed houses for idiots; Earlswood, Surrey (1853), Eastern Counties (1859), Western Counties (1864), Northern Counties (1864), and Midland Counties (1868) which were registered under the Idiots Act of 1886.[27] The 1886 Act led to more children coming under institutional care, so that treatment and care of the idiot child assumed a new importance. David Gladstone discusses in Chapter 7 the interplay between broad national policy-making and local factors in the development of English institutions. More specifically, in the case of the Western Counties Asylum, he suggests that policy was directed increasingly at the industrial training of inmates, and at achieving economic viability through the recruitment of pauper inmates whose stay would be financed by the Poor Law. Institutionalisation also grew apace elsewhere. Scottish foundations included an Idiot Asylum in Edinburgh (1855), a Scottish National Institution for the Education of Imbecile Children at Larbert (1863), and a Special School for Mental Defectives at Paisley (1912).[28] In the USA there was provision in New York (1852), Massachusetts (1853), Philadelphia (1858), Ohio (1872), and Illinois (1872). Systematic training was developed from the 1840s by Edouard Sèguin, first at the School for Idiots at the Bicêtre in Paris, and later at the Massachusetts School for Idiots and Feebleminded Youths, while some further work was done by the medical psychologist, G.E. Shuttleworth, at the Royal Albert Asylum.[29]

Therapeutic optimism about the training of young idiots contrasted with much lower levels of concern about the adult with mental disabilities. In consequence relatively little is known about the lives of adult idiots and imbeciles in early asylums. During the Georgian period private madhouses had admitted imbeciles although they comprised only a very small group of patients. At the Bethel in Norwich two individuals were discharged in the late eighteenth century as 'unfit' because of being 'in a state of idiocy' or 'suffering from idiotism'.[30] At Witney and Hook Norton in Oxfordshire from 3 to 4 per cent of total admissions were those of imbecilic patients between 1725 and 1854. Their imbecility was only a part of a wider spectrum of presenting symptoms, including physical illness, and their duration of stay was short. In contrast, at the York Retreat, half of those termed imbecilic had treatment of ten years or more. Numbers of these patients declined from 10 to 1 per cent of the total patient population between 1796 and 1914, mainly as a result of a better knowledge of the clinical distinction between idiocy and lunacy which gradually led to a more discriminating admissions policy. As with Poor Law establishments, the work of imbecilic patients was useful to the asylum. One female imbecile demanded her release, stating that 'nothing ailed her mind' but that she had 'worked like a slave for seven years' in order – unsuccessfully – to earn her freedom.[31]

The allocation of an institution for the imbecilic adult was something of a lottery. Arbitrary decisions during the mid-nineteenth century showed that the police and magistracy were not particularly concerned to make a correct diagnosis of weak-mindedness, so that individuals might find themselves in prison, rather than an asylum. Sometimes a weak-minded person having been sent to prison was then transferred to an asylum.[32] The experience of male and female feeble-minded offenders was a differentiated one; the petty offences of feeble-minded women tended to get lesser punishments than the offences of mentally defective men, whose charges included more serious ones of sexual assault. Whilst the short sentences of the women often meant that their mental state was not detected by prison medical officers, those in prison for longer spells were more likely than men to be certified as insane and sent to an asylum.[33]

Prisons were the focus for the worst kind of stereotyping of imbecility, since here individual misfortune appeared most clearly as a social threat. The driving force for segregation from the 1860s to the 1880s came from prison surgeons, whose stereotypical view of the criminality and recidivism of the weak-minded arose from the small minority of mentally deficient prisoners with whom they came into contact. In 1870, an influential paper by J.B. Thomson, a Scottish prison surgeon, estimated that one in eight prisoners in Scotland were mentally weak, whilst in the previous year William Guy, Superintendent of Millbank, had highlighted the 'dark figure' of criminal imbecility and proposed transfer to lunatic asylums. This view was echoed in the Report of the Penal Servitude Acts Commission of 1878.[34] In any case a take-over of English local prisons by a central authority three years earlier had exposed large numbers of weak-minded individuals in prisons. This contributed to a widespread pessimism in penal and asylum circles about the ineffectiveness of institutional solutions for social problems and also fed into the contemporary debates about degeneracy. The numbers of weak-minded people in prisons thus caused concern, although the cost of implementing any system of segregation inhibited action, as it had done with Poor Law inmates. Only belatedly did a drive to provide segregated accommodation lead some prisons to specialise in this category of prisoner, notably Parkhurst for men and Aylesbury for women.

By the 1890s the focus of concern had moved from the weak-minded criminal to degeneracy more generally. In Chapter 8 Mark Jackson analyses the changed nature of the rhetoric that had fuelled such anxiety, and the influential role that Mary Dendy played in attempting to alter social perceptions of the feeble-minded. Depicting feeble-mindedness as a permanent, hereditarian condition that was essentially pathological, Dendy argued that it required permanent segregation, if it was not to result in degeneracy through pauperism and criminality. The Sandlebridge Schools and Colony were the practical outcome of this rhetoric, although Mark Jackson shows that – in its actual mix of educational and custodial methods, and in its failure to enforce permanent care – Sandlebridge was similar to earlier idiot asylums. At the beginning of the twentieth century, feeble-minded women in particular were seen as the source of a biological perpetuation of mental deficiency, and as a sexual threat to respectability and normal family life.[35] Traditional views on the animality of the idiot thus resurfaced in an interpretation of the unbridled sexuality of the subnormal woman. This gendered anxiety centred as much on moral as physical issues. A philanthropic concentration of female activists and their interest in women in asylums, workhouses, inebriate reformatories, magdalens and rescue homes, and lying-in hospitals also meant that institutional provision for feeble-minded women came to exceed that for men during the early twentieth century. Since its formation in 1897 the National Association for Promoting the Welfare of the Feeble-Minded had encouraged small voluntary homes for girls and women, but the Royal Commission on the Care and Control of the Feeble-Minded of 1904–8 was influenced by the contrasting American model of large state institutions for feeble-minded women. There, instead of conviction and prison, those on a criminal charge were given life-long care that effectively prevented breeding by those perceived as unfit.[36]

The gendered implications of social policy on mental deficiency during the early twentieth century are analysed in two chapters. Pamela Cox suggests in Chapter 9 that girls who were committed to mental-deficiency institutions were designated delinquent not only in terms of their perceived unbridled sexuality, but also in relation to their violent or disruptive behaviour, and their unemployability. And in Chapter 10 Mathew Thomson argues that the Mental Deficiency Act of 1913 was deployed by the London County Council as a 'tool of sexual control', so that long-stay institutional care was most likely to be given to females, whereas for males the legislation was useful at first in controlling delinquency through shorter periods of supervision and parole.

The construction of the feeble-minded as a social problem, and hence the appointment of the Royal Commission in 1904, had followed from a convergence of several debates. These discussions centred on not only the fecundity of the feeble-minded woman (and her threat both to morality and to the healthiness of the race), but on other issues, notably the educability of children with special needs, and the threat that a residuum of casual poor was seen as posing to the moral and physical welfare of society.[37] The resulting Mental Deficiency Act of 1913 provided for a division of those with congenital defects or impairment from a very early age, into idiots, imbeciles, and the feeble-minded. It proposed an institutional separation so that mental defectives should be taken out of Poor Law institutions and prisons into newly established colonies. While England accepted this principle, Scotland preferred a system of overlap between the Poor Law and lunacy authorities, and Ireland backed a transfer of mental defectives from all other institutions to the Poor Law.[38] That women were seen as a prime focus of the Act's provisions is suggested by a conspicuous presence of women (including Mary Dendy) on the Board of Control that succeeded the Lunacy Commission, as well as on the inspectorate.[39] But a lack of preventative powers, and still more of resources, meant that the Act's impact was blunted. At the local level Medical Officers of Health at first refused to accept such defectives because of the cost to local authorities, although more comprehensive provisions in the Mental Deficiency Act of 1927 aimed to expedite its implementation.[40] In Chapter 10 Mathew Thomson emphasises that the impact of mental-deficiency legislation should not be viewed in isolation, but should be placed instead within the context of an expanding welfare complex of penal, medical and educational provision, in which individuals might be shifted from one type of institution to another.

Matching the individual to an institution preoccupied policy-makers concerned with children, whether they were involved primarily with education or with health. Since the late nineteenth century the logic of the law requiring compulsory attendance for all children at elementary school had meant that great difficulty was experienced in determining those seen as educable and capable of attendance at ordinary schools, and those who required special schooling.[41] Special schools were first opened in London in 1892 and seven English School Boards soon followed this example. Legislation in 1899 permitted, and that in 1914 required, local educational authorities to provide special schools. From 1907 school medical inspections included a review of possible medical defect, and medical certification was then required before entry to special schools. But, despite concern over mental deficiency and feeble-mindedness there was no adequate measurement of the severity of mental defect. For example, in 1908 the Committee on Defective and Epileptic Children commented that, 'none of the witnesses were (*sic*) able to offer any verbal definition of the degree of want of intelligence which constitutes a defective child'.[42]

Intelligence testing appeared to answer that need. It was introduced within a historical social context of discussion about degeneracy, segregation and eugenics, so that it was predictable that a theoretical continuum in IQ became, in practice, a means to segregate and separate the 'subnormal' from the 'normal'. In 1905 Alfred Binet and Victor Simon had published the first set of French tests linking mental and chronological age, and the German psychologist, William Stern, then developed this work into the concept of intelligence quotient or IQ. Under Newman, its Chief Medical Officer, the Board of Education's early twentieth-century policies were informed by the concept of mental measurement. In 1924 the board's *Report on Psychological Tests of Educable Capacity* in part justified IQ testing as the 'sifting out of defectives and dull children by special educational methods'.[43] In practice, however, this approach was severely constrained by the financial strait-jacket which restrained government activity during the interwar years; the Mental Deficiency Committee found in 1926, for example, that more than three-quarters of these children were in ordinary rather than special schools.[44] Also inhibiting children going to special schools or mental-handicap hospitals were social and familial pressures. Families might see disability as a taboo area, deny its existence as far as possible, and be profoundly suspicious of any specialist institutional care because it was perceived to be stigmatising.[45] Within the climate of opinion created by the eugenics movement such suspicion was understandable.

In early twentieth-century Britain the eugenics movement's aims included voluntary sterilisation of mental defectives and birth control for unemployed workers. These objectives were impeded both by a lack of consensus (notably over whether mental defect was hereditary), and by a weak constituency of support. The movement attracted more support for its birth control policies,[46] but a policy that was perceived to be anti-working class was opposed by the Labour movement,[47] while any scientific legitimation of eugenics was much less apparent than in America.[48] In the USA between 1900 and 1940 the mental hygiene movement, backed by welfare officials and psychiatrists, and in the face of public apathy, succeeded for a short time in using state authority to back eugenic ideas on heredity. Indiana was the first state to pass a law for mandatory sterilisation of a group including idiots and imbeciles in 1907, and fifteen others emulated this in relation to those perceived as biologically undesirable.[49] There was sufficient ambivalence about sterilisation for such laws later to be overthrown by the courts, for state governors to veto the law, or to decline to release funds to institutions performing sterilisations. By the 1920s many superintendents of institutions for the mentally deficient were also having second thoughts about eugenics as a basis for sterilisation. Instead, they perceived a continued rationale for the practice in the mental hygiene movement's emphasis on social adjustment, and thus supported sterilisations for both men and women as a prelude to an inmate's parole and release into society.[50]

During the earliest years of the National Health Service, policy-making by default characterised the mentally handicapped in Britain since (as with earlier radical legislative changes in social policy), a restructuring of services was focused on the needs of other groups. Thereafter the relationship between institutions for the mentally subnormal and society came under greater critical scrutiny in the second half of the century. By the 1950s institutions were beginning to be perceived not as solutions as had been the case formerly, but as problems involving stigmatisation and depersonalisation. Within this context it gradually became clear that the institutionalisation of the mentally handicapped had helped exaggerate difference, and that this in itself then provided a self-sustaining rationale for institutional confinement.[51] A number of sociological studies exposed the negative features of mental handicap hospitals. These included professional seclusion leading to a 'corruption of care' (such that administrative convenience superseded social rehabilitation), obsolete training opportunities, and geographical remoteness which exacerbated the problem of maintaining contact between families and inmates.[52] Even in a late twentieth-century mental handicap hospital it was found that one in three patients was never visited within a year, and three out of four never left hospital to visit their families.[53] Hospitalisation thus might imply a profound isolation from normal life within society.

The Royal Commission on the Law Relating to Mental Illness and Mental Deficiency (1954–7) suggested that parallel services for community care should be developed by local authorities. In 1961 the Minister of Health, Enoch Powell, announced that mental hospital accommodation should be halved within fifteen years. But little practical action ensued so that the White Paper of 1971, *Better Services for the Mentally Handicapped*, found that only one in four English and Welsh authorities had so far developed this kind of residential provision.[54] Scandals in mental handicap hospitals, notably those at Ely and at South Ockendon,[55] caused further heart searching on the fundamental rationale and objectives of services for people with learning disabilities. Central to a rethinking of policy were two committees. The Warnock Committee into Special Educational Needs (1978) resulted in the Education Act (1981), which initiated a system of identifying, assessing and reviewing all children with special needs, and involving parents to a greater extent than hitherto. The Jay Committee into Mental Handicap and Care (1979) emphasised the human rights of the mentally handicapped to be treated as individuals and to live normally within the community.[56] The ensuing Care in the Community initiative of 1981 resulted in some transfer of resources to local authorities in order to effect the transfer of residents from hospitals into community care,[57] and this process found its logical culmination in the NHS and Community Care Act (1990), which transferred the entire responsibility for community care to local authorities.

Community care initiatives are often seen as a distinctive feature of the 1970s but more accurately should be perceived as the most common historical response to those with learning disabilities – as in parochial arrangements under the Old Poor Law in England, or in boarding-out arrangements in nineteenth-century Scotland. Mathew Thomson shows in Chapter 10 how the implementation of the Mental Deficiency Act of 1913 in London led to negotiation between families and the state to enable community- or family-based strategies to be worked out for the care of adolescents. (Significantly, he also indicates that families might be coerced into accepting medically or bureaucratically derived solutions.) In addition, prototypes for a different form of community may perhaps be found in the interwar English colony for mental defectives, which has been interpreted as 'a microcosm of the outside community', and one which embodied the fundamental work ethic of a wider society.[58] And James Trent argues that the farm colonies linked to institutions in the USA during the 1920s, and (to a lesser extent) the 1930s, aimed to provide an environment in which mental defectives could be prepared for work, and then for release on parole. Interestingly, in this case, the driving force was the urgent need to provide an economical mechanism so that inmates could be released into society, while grossly overcrowded institutions could be enabled to admit yet another cohort of inmates.

Later, during the 1970s, an unlikely alliance – between officials wanting to cut costs and humanitarians wishing to close down inhumane public institutions – resulted in a programme of de-institutionalisation in the USA. Drawing on Erving Goffman's ideas on deviance and labelling the psychologist, Wolf Wolfensberger, argued in an influential book, *The Principle of Normalization in Human Services* (1972) that existing state facilities had merely drawn attention to the negative or devalued qualities of mentally retarded individuals so that a new initiative was needed to provide an appropriate framework for human dignity. Publicity on early initiatives in Nebraska that implemented this kind of programme was particularly persuasive in helping shape English thinking at this time. Nebraska implemented a process of normalisation (sometimes called mainstreaming), through which the mentally handicapped lived in community housing. More generally an institutional bias remained sufficiently strong in the USA to ensure that the majority of mentally retarded people in 1988 were housed in community care units with more than sixteen beds, whilst a concomitant run-down of state facilities meant that these were predominantly private (often private for profit) establishments.[59]

In late twentieth-century Britain community care is a term whose apparent 'feelgood' resonance has helped conceal both its conceptual complexity and its parsimonious funding. A tension between optimistic labelling and harsh underlying economy then compounds practical problems involved in its implementation – such as moving resources from one sector to another, retraining staff, or co-ordinating educational, medical and social agencies. The Audit Commission discovered that in practice 'the care that people receive is as much dependent on where they live as on what they need'.[60] Integration posed problems, including those of financial costs, which were higher not lower than those of institutional care. It was significant that in 1976 a government consultative paper foresaw a 'continued development of community care with particular emphasis on low cost solutions'.[61] The Griffiths Report on Community Care of 1988 aptly referred to community care as 'a poor relation, everybody's distant relative, but nobody's baby'.[62]

Also relevant in the context of community care is the extent to which those with learning disabilities are/were perceived to be 'socially acceptable'. For adults with learning disabilities community care may involve varied mixes of life in the family alternating with professional care in day hospitals, or day care centres. When no longer distanced and invisible within an institution the presence within a neighbourhood of individuals with learning disabilities may make prejudice overt: 'All of us … have complex reactions when confronted by handicapped people. They arouse in us fears of our own possible abnormalities and dependencies. What if I were like that? How would I feel about myself? Would anyone like me?'[63]

In addition, there were important issues involved in deinstitutionalisation which concerned the nature of familial care. An empirical survey of the locus of community care for the mentally and physically impaired found that it had important gender implications, since 'the major burden of care falls on women – whether wives, mothers, spouses, siblings, or friends'.[64] As far as the mentally impaired child was concerned, the family was expected to assume responsibility. It did so in the vast majority of cases but, within the family, there was asymmetry in the responsibility assumed by parents, with mothers doing most domestic and child-related care.[65] This was a continuation of a long tradition in familial-based care since, as David Wright argues in Chapter 6, women were prominent in the mid-Victorian process of certifying idiot children, precisely because they had been responsible for their care.

Social integration and a developing culture of human rights have also raised issues concerning the sexual and reproductive rights of people with learning disabilities. The United Nations Declaration of 1971 on the Rights of Mentally Retarded Persons stated that, 'the mentally retarded person has, to the maximum degree of feasibility, the same rights as other human beings'. In 1990 the National Health Service and Community Care Act supported the principle of normalisation through integrating people with learning disabilities into the community. The logic of normalisation and of independence within the community, however, was that sexuality was no longer constrained automatically by social policies of segregation and/or involuntary sterilisation. Sex education for people with learning disabilities was needed, and concomitant human rights issues of informed consent to contraception or abortion were raised. Since there are likely to be growing numbers of parents with a learning disability, appropriate training, support, and assistance will have to be provided if the right of mentally impaired adults to be parents is to be balanced against their children's right to adequate care and protection.

'It remains to be seen whether changes will result which succeed in achieving the fine balance between autonomy and protection, rights and welfare, and self-determination and paternalism.'[66] Dynamic elements in this complex balancing act have included direct representation by the disabled (or their representatives) in decisions on service provision. This was prescribed in 1986 by the Disabled Persons Act. Also relevant here has been the growth of self-advocacy amongst people with learning disabilities; 'speaking up for yourself' and taking action, or 'saying what you like or don't like' and making choices.[67] This process of empowerment will need considerable momentum if it is to challenge deep-seated social assumptions and prejudices.

A House of Commons report urged in 1984 that, 'The great asylums signalled Victorian social concern [and] … an astonishing commitment of money … we are under a moral obligation at least to match the degree of commitment shown by earlier generations.'[68] Drawing attention to the vulnerability of levels of care to the amount of economic resources that society has considered to be appropriate historically was surely apposite. It was also interesting in that theoretical discussion of community care, relative to institutional care, has usually emphasised difference rather than similarity. Yet a comparison of recent practical problems faced in the services for those with learning disability – whether these were located in the community or in institutions – is instructive. Inadequate funding, stigma, social neglect, and a tendency to see those with learning disabilities as objects rather than subjects, have not immediately disappeared because the physical environment has altered. Changing the locus of care may be helpful in the longer term, in positively asserting the similarities between human beings, rather than in underlining a sense of difference by physical separation. But a radically revised social construction – a reinventing of social perceptions – of those with a learning disability is also needed if fundamental improvements in lifestyle are to be permanent. In its discussion of past perception and practice this book may make a modest contribution to that change.

NOTES

1 For example, M. Barrett, 'From Education to Segregation: an Inquiry into the Changing Character of Special Provision for the Retarded in England, c.1846–1918', University of Lancaster, Ph.D., 1987; H. S. Gelband, 'Mental Retardation and Institutional Treatment in Nineteenth-century England', University of Maryland, Ph.D., 1979; M. Thomson, 'The Problem of Mental Deficiency in England and Wales, c.1913–1946', University of Oxford, D.Phil., 1992; D. Wright, 'The National Asylum for Idiots, Earlswood, 1847–1886', University of Oxford, D.Phil., 1993; L. Zihni, 'A History of the Relationship between the Concept and the Treatment of People with Down's Syndrome in Britain and America, 1867–1967', University of London, Ph.D., 1990.

2 The SSHM also ran a conference in 1982 on 'Mental Handicap since the 19th Century: Medicine, Education or Politics?' The papers from this meeting were published as a special issue of the *Oxford Review of Education*, 1983, vol. 9, no. 3.

3 R. Neugebauer, 'A Doctor's Dilemma: The Case of William Harvey's Mentally Retarded Nephew', *Psychological Medicine*, 1989, vol. 19, pp. 569–72; M. Donnelly, *Managing the Mind: A Study of Medical Psychology in Early Nineteenth-Century Britain*, London, 1983, pp. 68, 70.

4 M. MacDonald, *Mystical Bedlam: Madness, Anxiety and Healing in Seventeenth-century England*, Cambridge, 1981, p. 34; R. Porter, *Mind-Forg'd Manacles: A History of Madness in England from the Restoration to the Regency*, Cambridge, Mass., 1987, p. 29.

5 N. Walker, *Crime and Insanity in England*, Edinburgh, 1968, I, p. 116.

6 J.T. Dunston, 'The Problem of the Feeble-Minded in South Africa', *Journal of Mental Science*, 1921; S. Dubow, *Racial Segregation and the Origins of Apartheid in South Africa, 1919–1936*, Basingstoke, 1989; J. Oppenheim, *Shattered Nerves: Doctors, Patients and Depression in Victorian England*, Oxford, 1991, pp. 276, 287.

7 N. Dain, *Concepts of Insanity in the United States, 1789–1865*, New Brunswick, 1964, pp. 45, 101.

8 The *Independent*, 4 November 1994.

9 J. Ryan and F. Thomas, *The Politics of Mental Handicap* (revised edition), London, 1987, p. 13.

10 K. Thomas, *Man and the Natural World: Changing Attitudes in England 1500–1800*, London, 1983, p. 44.

11 P.F. Cranefield, 'A Seventeenth Century View of Mental Deficiency and Schizophrenia: Thomas Willis on "Stupidity or Foolishness"', *Bulletin of the History of Medicine*, 1961, vol. 35, p. 311.

12 C. Goodey, 'John Locke's Idiots in the Natural History of Mind', *History of Psychiatry*, 1994, vol. 5, pp. 242, 249.

13 P. Rushton, 'Lunatics and Idiots: Mental Disability, the Community and the Poor Law in North-East England, 1600–1800', *Medical History*, 1988, vol. 32, pp. 34–50; A. Suzuki, 'Lunacy in Seventeenth- and Eighteenth-Century England: Analysis of Quarter Sessions Records, Part I', *History of Psychiatry*, 1991, vol. 2, p. 451.

14 *Criminal Lunacy Commission*, appendix A, p. 147, evidence of Arthur Mitchell, Deputy Commissioner in Lunacy for Scotland.

15 D.H. Tuke, *Chapters in the History of the Insane in the British Isles*, London, 1882, p. 318.

16 H. Maudsley, *Responsibility in Mental Disease*, London, 1874, p. 48.

17 G. Stedman Jones, *Outcast London*, Oxford, 1971, pp. 11, 285, 303, 331.

18 J. Saunders, 'Quarantining the Weak-Minded: Psychiatric Definitions of Degeneracy and the Late-Victorian Asylum', in W.F. Bynum, R. Porter and M. Shepherd (eds), *The Anatomy of Madness: Essays in the History of Psychiatry*, vol. 3, London, 1988, pp. 184, 289.

19 S. and B. Webb, *English Poor Law Policy*, London, 1910, pp. 49, 63, 80.

20 A. Digby, *Pauper Palaces*, London, 1978, pp. 172–3.

21 *Thirtieth Report of the Local Government Board*, London, 1900–1, Report of Mr Preston Thomas, pp. 122–3; H. Preston Thomas, *The Work and Play of a Government Inspector*, London, 1909, pp. 278–85.

22 *Eighth Report of the Local Government Board*, London, 1878–9, Report of Mr Courtenay Boyle, p. 120.

23 Webb, *Poor Law Policy*, pp. 138, 188, 221, 225.

24 M. Finnane, *Insanity and the Insane in Post-Famine Ireland*, London, 1981, pp. 87, 145–6.

25 M. Whitrow, 'Wagner-Jauregg's Contribution to the Study of Cretinism', *History of Psychiatry*, 1990, vol. 1, pp. 289–90.

26 P. Potts, 'Medicine, Morals and Mental Deficiency: The Contribution of Doctors to the Development of Special Education in England', *Oxford Review of Education*, 1983, vol. 9, pp. 181–95.

27 W. Parry-Jones, *The Trade in Lunacy*, London, 1972, pp. 70–2.

28 D.K. Henderson, *The Evolution of Psychiatry in Scotland*, Edinburgh, 1964, pp. 75–7.

29 I. Kraft, 'Edouard Sèguin and the Nineteenth-Century Moral Treatment of Idiots', *Bulletin of the History of Medicine*, 1961, vol. 35, pp. 393–418; G.E. Shuttleworth, *Mentally Deficient Children* (second edition), London, 1900.
30 M. Wilson, 'The Bethel at Norwich: An Eighteenth-Century Hospital for Lunatics', *Medical History*, 1994, vol. 38, p. 48.
31 Parry-Jones, *Trade in Lunacy*, pp. 219–20; A. Digby, *Madness, Morality and Medicine: A Study of the York Retreat, 1790–1914*, Cambridge, 1985, pp. 67, 196, 211, 216–17, 220.
32 J. Saunders, 'Magistrates and Madmen: Segregating the Criminal Insane in Late Nineteenth-century Warwickshire', in V. Bailey (ed.), *Policing and Punishment in Nineteenth-Century Britain*, London, 1981, pp. 229–30, 236.
33 L. Zedner, *Women, Crime, and Custody in Victorian England*, Oxford, 1991, p. 280.
34 Saunders, 'Quarantining', pp. 275, 277, 288.
35 H.G. Simmons, 'Explaining Social Policy: The English Mental Deficiency Act of 1913', *Journal of Social Policy*, 1978, vol. 11, p. 394.
36 Zedner, *Women, Crime*, pp. 270, 288–90.
37 Simmons, 'Explaining Social Policy', pp. 387–403.
38 Webb, *Poor Law Policy*, pp. 312, 355–6.
39 Zedner, *Women, Crime*, p. 293.
40 N. Walker and S. McCabe, *Crime and Insanity*, Edinburgh, 1973, II, pp. 24, 62.
41 H. Hendrick, *Child Welfare: England, 1872–1989*, London, 1993, pp. 21–3.
42 Quoted in G. Sutherland, *Ability, Merit, and Measurement: Mental Testing and English Education, 1890–1940*, Oxford, 1984, pp. 19–20.
43 Quoted in Hendrick, *Child Welfare*, p. 155.
44 Sutherland, *Ability, Merit*, pp. 53–6, 85.
45 S. Humphries and P. Gordon, *Out of Sight: The Experience of Disability, 1900–1950*, Plymouth, 1992, pp. 26–7, 88–9.
46 G.R. Searle, 'Eugenics and Politics in Britain in the 1930s', *Annals of Science*, 1979, vol. 36, pp. 154–69.
47 J. Macnicol, 'Eugenics and the Campaign for Voluntary Sterilisation in Britain between the Wars', *Social History of Medicine*, 1989, vol. 2, p. 168.
48 E.J. Larson, 'The Rhetoric of Eugenics: Expert Authority and the Mental Deficiency Bill', *British Journal of the History of Science*, 1991, vol. 24, pp. 45–60.
49 G. Grob, *Mental Illness and American Society, 1875–1940*, Princeton, 1983, pp. 171–8.
50 J.W. Trent, *Inventing the Feeble Mind: A History of Mental Retardation in the United States*, Berkeley, 1994, pp. 197–207.
51 E. Goffman, *Asylums: Essays on the Social Situation of Mental Patients and Other Inmates*, New York, 1961, pp. 9–12.
52 N. Korman and H. Glennerster, *Hospital Closure: A Political and Economic Study*, Milton Keynes, 1990, pp. 13–16.
53 Ryan and Thomas, *Mental Handicap*, p. 72.
54 A. Leighton (ed.), *Mental Handicap in the Community*, London, 1988, pp. 8–9; R. Lowe, *The Welfare State in Britain since 1945*, Basingstoke, 1993, pp. 184–5.
55 *Report of the Committee of Inquiry into Allegations of Ill-Treatment of Patients and Other Irregularities at the Ely Hospital, Cardiff*, London, 1969; *Report on South Ockendon Hospital*, London, 1974.
56 A. Alaszewski, 'The Development of Policy for the Mentally Handicapped since the Second World War: An Introduction', *Oxford Journal of Education*, 1983, vol. 9, pp. 227–31.

57 *Care in the Community: Moving Resources for Care in England*, London, 1981.
58 M. Thomson, 'Sterilization, Segregation and Community Care: Ideology, and Solutions to the Problem of Mental Deficiency in Interwar Britain', *History of Psychiatry*, 1992, vol. 3, pp. 487, 491.
59 Trent, *Inventing the Feeble Mind*, pp. 213–19, 261–5.
60 Audit Commission, *Making a Reality of Community Care*, London, 1986.
61 *Priorities for Health and Personal Social Services in England*, London, 1976.
62 *Community Care: Agenda for Action*, London, 1988.
63 Ryan and Thomas, *Mental Handicap*, p. 67.
64 G. Parker, 'Who Cares? A Review of Empirical Evidence from Britain', in R.E. Pahl (ed.), *On Work: Historical, Comparative and Theoretical Approaches*, Oxford, 1988, p. 506; S. Ayer and A. Alaszeweski, *Community Care and the Mentally Handicapped*, London, 1984, pp. 125, 150; P. White, *One in a Hundred: A Community-Based Mental Handicap Project*, London, 1984, p. 2.
65 Parker, 'Who Cares?', pp. 497–8, 501–6.
66 F. Painz, *Parents with a Learning Disability*, University of East Anglia Social Work Monographs no. 116, Norwich, 1993, p. 11.
67 J. Sutcliffe and K. Simons, *Self-Advocacy and Adults with Learning Difficulties*, National Institute of Adult Continuing Education, Leicester, 1993, p. 3.
68 *Second Report of House of Commons Social Services Committee: Community Care with Special Reference to Adult Mentally Ill and Mentally Handicapped People*, London, 1984–5, vol. 1, p. ii.

2

MENTAL HANDICAP IN MEDIEVAL AND EARLY MODERN ENGLAND

Criteria, measurement and care

Richard Neugebauer

INTRODUCTION

The early history of psychiatry is often viewed with a mixture of intense curiosity and dismay. Historical works produced by physicians generally assume that the period from the Middle Ages down to the seventeenth century was dominated by demonological beliefs about the etiology of brain disorders, with concomitant abuse and persecution or simple neglect of the insane.[1] Colp's account is representative:

> In the 1,000 years after the fall of the Western Roman Empire, 400–1400 AD ... there was a prevalence of religious beliefs in the understanding and treatment of mental illness ... Renaissance views of the mentally ill were influenced by a pervasive fear of witchcraft, which began in 1486 with the publication of a book, *Malleus Maleficarum* (Witches' Hammer) ... The *Malleus* ... suggested that almost any mental or physical affliction of a male or female could be a sign of witchcraft, and it prescribed inquisitorial procedures of mental or physical torture.[2]

This perspective, often propounded with reference to functional psychiatric disorders, has been extended to the mentally handicapped as well. According to Szymanski and Crocker, for centuries,

> mental illness and mental retardation (which were lumped together) were attributed to supernatural causes and considered in the province of priests and philosophers. Although a few retarded persons did have a career as 'court fools', others were exploited, persecuted and exorcised. The foundations of modern care of retarded people were laid in the nineteenth century.[3]

Note, too, the interesting presumption here that functional and organic disorders were not distinguished by pre-industrial Europeans.

This emphasis on demonology and persecution is often introduced to magnify further twentieth-century advances in psychobiology and humane treatment of mental disorders. However, by a wonderful sleight of a rhetorical hand, these same putative beliefs and practices have also been used to indict twentieth-century psychiatry, as Szasz and his epigones have done,[4] by seeing them as documenting the early ancestry of modern psychiatry's scapegoating and persecution of deviants. Thus, psychiatrists and antipsychiatrists agree on the nature of the evidence; they part ways only in their interpretation of its meaning for modern times.

Until recently, the evidence adduced in histories of psychiatry has been limited to printed texts, most often tracts on witchcraft or treatises attacking the practices and character of witch hunters.[5] Naturally, treatises on witchcraft are unlikely source materials for non-demonological interpretations of mental processes. In the last decade and a half, professional historians of science and of psychiatry have laboured strenuously to broaden the sources deployed in studies of pre-industrial European societies.[6] Despite these efforts, the passages from a recent comprehensive textbook of psychiatry cited above indicate that news of these fresh materials and perspectives has not travelled far.

The present chapter summarises findings from research conducted over the past twenty years on the history of (what we would today identify as) functional and organic psychiatric disorder in pre-industrial England. This account is based on records generated from the thirteenth century onwards by the Crown's legal incompetency jurisdiction over the mentally disabled. This legal incompetency jurisdiction, the records of which survive largely in manuscript form only, has enjoyed a virtually uninterrupted administrative history from the late thirteenth century to the present.[7] From the thirteenth century until 1540, this jurisdiction was exercised through the Court of Chancery. During at least part of this period, members of the King's Chamber, acting informally and often on an *ad hoc* basis, handled administrative matters associated with this jurisdiction.[8] In the sixteenth century, royal authority over the mentally disabled was vested in the Court of Wards and Liveries, a legal court created by two statutes in 1540 and 1542. As its name suggests, the primary purpose of this Court was to arrange for the guardianship and protection of underage heirs of deceased feudal tenants in chief of the king. However, the founding statute also established that the Court 'shall have authority by this act to survey govern and order all and singular idiots and natural fools now being in the kings hands or that hereafter shall come and be in the kings hands'.[9] Although only persons congenitally handicapped are mentioned, persons who developed disabilities and psychoses later were also included in this jurisdiction.

For over one hundred years Wards officials were responsible for all important judicial, financial, and administrative matters pertaining to the mentally disabled. In the mid-1640s the Court of Wards and Liveries ceased its operations because of the upheavals and instability associated with the outbreak of the English Civil War. The Court was officially abolished by statute in 1660[10] together with the feudal land law on which its jurisdiction over wards was based. Its jurisdiction over mentally disabled persons was transferred back to Chancery, where it has remained.[11] At present, the Court of Protection is in charge of such matters.

Records from the medieval and early modern period afford an entirely different picture of early European ideas and attitudes towards psychiatric illness from that advanced by Colp, Szymanski, Crocker and others. These documents provide incontrovertible evidence that medieval Englishmen employed naturalistic criteria in evaluating persons thought to be mentally ill or learning disabled. Furthermore, records from the sixteenth and seventeenth centuries indicate that under the Tudor monarchs efforts were made to enhance the humanitarian and beneficial features of this jurisdiction, a change that necessarily involved a loss of potential Crown revenues. The present chapter will show that the period from 1540 to 1640 witnessed an important transformation in the Crown's centuries-old rights and duties towards the mentally disabled, away from exploitation and towards benevolence. They also offer the social historian yet another opportunity to spare the human past, in the late E.P. Thompson's words, from 'the enormous condescension of history'.[12]

PREROGATIVA REGIS

Medieval English society was based on the preservation and stable transmission of landed wealth. Accordingly, the English Crown was seen as having both a paternal responsibility and the right to protect the person and property of individuals who were legally incompetent owing to mental disability. *Prerogativa Regis*, the first extant document pertaining to this issue, dates from the second half of the thirteenth century.[13] *Prerogativa Regis*, which was probably written by a Crown official, sets forth various royal rights and duties, including those over the mentally disabled. This document was erroneously represented as a statute in the medieval and early modern period and as a consequence, its statements on the Crown's rights over the mentally disabled served as the legal framework for the exercise of the royal jurisdiction in this area.

The mentally disabled are divided into two categories: natural fools or idiots[14] (Section 11); and persons *non compos mentis* (Section 12). *Prerogativa Regis* carefully differentiated these two categories both in terms of symptoms and mental functioning, and as regards royal responsibilities and fiscal claims. Section 11 read in part as follows:

> The king shall have the custody of the lands of natural fools taking the profits of them without waste or destruction and shall find them their necessaries … And after the death of such idiots he shall render it to the right heirs, so that such idiots shall not alien nor their heirs … be disinherited.[15]

According to a thirteenth-century legal document, a 'fool' was an individual of retarded intellectual development whose mental capacities never progressed beyond that of a child.[16] The more restrictive term 'natural fool' or 'idiot' referred specifically to persons congenitally handicapped[17] and, as the language of Section 11 suggests, their deficiencies were considered permanent. Natural, meaning from birth, contrasted, on the one hand, with types of natural mental impairment arising postnatally, for example, impairments developing with age,[18] and with disorders caused by 'accidents'. In legal writing, 'accidents' included such things as sickness and grief.[19] Strictly applied, this definition would exclude childhood cases of mental handicap that are now recognised as arising from encephalitis, meningitis, toxins and other environmental agents that could compromise cerebral integrity.

An early seventeenth-century legal dictionary summed up the meaning and synonymity of 'natural fool' and 'idiot', and alluded to ways of evaluating this mental state, as follows:

> Idiot is he that is a fool natural from his birth and knows not how to account or number 20 pence, nor cannot name his father or mother, nor of what age himself is, or such like easy and common matters; so that it appears he has no manner of understanding or reason, nor government of himself, what is for his profit or disprofit.[20]

By the end of the fifteenth century, 'idiot', rather than 'natural fool', had become the preferred term for persons congenitally handicapped in legal documents.[21]

The king was entitled to take possession of idiots' lands and to collect the revenues from their estate. Whatever the original intent of *Prerogativa Regis*, its language was interpreted broadly by later fifteenth-century authors so as to include custody of idiots' bodies and of all their personal property as well as of their land.[22] During the custodial period, the king recognised an obligation to protect the idiot's property from exploitation and to provide the idiot alone, not his family, with the bare necessities of life. However, any rents and profits collected by the Crown during the idiocy, in excess of the costs of the individual's upkeep, were considered a legitimate source of royal revenue. They were not turned over to the heirs at the time of the idiot's death. In short, custodial rights over wealthy heirs or heiresses who were judged to be severely handicapped from birth represented a potential source of substantial royal revenues.

Section 12 of *Prerogativa Regis* pertained to persons *non compos mentis*:

> Also, the King shall provide, when any that before time hath had his wit and memory happen to fail of his wit, as there are many *per lucida intervalla* that their lands and tenements shall be safely kept without waste and destruction and that they and their household shall live and be maintained competently with the profits of the same, and the residue besides their sustentation shall be kept to their use, to be delivered unto them when they come to right mind; so that such lands and tenements shall in no ways be aliened and the King shall take nothing to his own use.[23]

The term *non compos mentis* was more inclusive than 'natural fool'; all types of serious mental disabilities, except for congenital disorders, appear to have been subsumed under this rubric. Persons *non compos mentis* might have periods of temporary remission – lucid intervals – or experience complete recovery. By the fifteenth century the term 'lunatic'[24] replaced the phrase *non compos mentis* in legal discussions and in the administrative procedures that were developed to implement Section 12. Also, as with idiocy, by the end of the fifteenth century, the king's custodial rights were extended to the body as well as to the personal estate and land of the affected person.

From the subject's perspective and that of his family, lunacy was a more advantageous diagnosis. Royal guardianship of a lunatic's body and supervision of the lands had to be exercised solely for the lunatic's benefit. The king protected the lunatic's estate from waste and destruction and, at the same time, sustained him and his family with estate revenues. Any income not expended on the family's maintenance and estate repairs was returned on the lunatic's recovery. Thus, with idiots, the king acted as guardian but profited from the exercise of this responsibility. For lunatics, the Crown provided more extensive protection but at no charge to the individual subject.[25] Hence, we will generally substitute the terms mentally handicapped and psychotic, respectively, in the text, except where such usage unduly complicates the exposition.

In legal theory the Crown itself exercised these rights and responsibilities over mentally disabled persons. In administrative practice, the Crown's legal incompetency administration rarely, if ever, entailed direct royal supervision of the mentally disabled. Rather, the king transferred his custodial authority over the disabled to private individuals who entered into bonds with the Crown, obliging them to execute their trust responsibly. In fact, private individuals often notified royal officials of the existence of a mentally handicapped or psychotic individual in the hope of obtaining custody of them subsequent to an inquisition.[26] Hence, the Crown's legal incompetency jurisdiction served as a type of triage or clearing house for the arrangement of private but monitored guardianship of the mentally disabled.

This legal incompetency jurisdiction was created for the protection of property. As a consequence, only disabled individuals with personal or real estate were brought to the attention of the medieval Chancery or the Court of Wards and Liveries. Yet even persons with quite small holdings were referred to this jurisdiction. The Court of Wards' archives, together with contemporary Chancery files,[27] are sufficiently complete to afford valid estimates of the social class composition of the disabled individuals.[28] Only 40 per cent of its cases belonged to the landed classes, both the gentry and the great aristocratic families. Of the remainder, some were tradesmen and merchants; an occasional blacksmith and yeoman also found his way into the Court. Since widows and heiresses could hold property in their own right, approximately 20 per cent of all cases were women. Less extensive survival of medieval Chancery records makes it impossible to offer confident estimates of the social class distribution of cases from these earlier centuries. None the less, extant records indicate that the medieval jurisdiction also handled numerous cases below gentry rank.[29] It is important to keep this social composition in mind in the following discussion. It means that the measures of mental status and the etiologic theories we examine here were applied to persons belonging to various social classes and occupational groups in medieval and early modern England. They are not the ideas of an educated few constructed solely for the benefit of a privileged minority.

EXAMINATIONS AND CUSTODIAL ARRANGEMENTS

Examinations of persons thought to be mentally disabled, called inquisitions, were initiated by royal commissions, by local government officials known as escheators, who were drawn from the ranks of the county gentry, or by private persons seeking an eventual grant of custody.[30] After the founding of the Court of Wards, almost all such examinations were issued in response to petitions from individual subjects. Inquisitions were probably conducted along much the same lines, irrespective of their origin. The local royal official, or the commissioners, directed the sheriff of the appropriate county to summon a jury on an appointed day.[31] By statutory regulation, the sites for inquisitions were to be 'convenient and open places'[32] and the jurors to be 'good people and lawful, which be sufficiently inherited and of good fame, and of the county where the enquiry shall be'.[33] A minimum of twelve men were chosen as the jury,[34] although it was usual to include several more to insure agreement among the twelve.

The evidence taken by the government officials in the presence of this county jury focused on three basic questions. First, was the individual, alleged to be an idiot or a lunatic, in fact mentally disabled?; if so, then 'from what time, and how and in what manner, and [did he enjoy] lucid intervals'? Next, what land and other property did he possess and which of these had he given away during the time of his illness? Finally, who and how old was his next heir?[35] The inquisition findings were written on parchment and the document returned to Westminster within the month. Surviving evidence strongly suggests that the tests for mental handicap administered at the inquisitions remained essentially the same throughout the medieval and early modern period. They were designed to measure the subject's intellect and orientation at rudimentary levels. If a person met requirements in this regard, the examiners proceeded to evaluate reasoning and judgement in daily life.

The elementary test of mental status put forward in the early seventeenth-century dictionary cited above sounds remarkably modern in method and tone, however archaic the syntax. In the absence of manuscript records, we might imagine that this printed work heralded the beginnings of rationalism and the age of scientific enquiry. This interpretation quickly dissipates when we turn to the examination of a Cambridgeshire woman, Emma de Beston, for idiocy in July 1383:

> The said Emma, being caused to appear before them, was asked whence she came and said that she did not know. Being asked in what town she was, she said that she was at Ely. Being asked how many days there were in the week, she said seven but could not name them. Being asked how many husbands she had had in her time she said three, giving the name of one only and not knowing the names of the others. Being asked whether she had ever had issue by them, she said that she had a husband with a son, but did not know his name. Being asked how many shillings there were in forty pence, she said she did not know. Being asked whether she would rather have twenty silver groats than forty pence, she said they were of the same value. They examined her in all other ways which they thought best and found that she was not of sound mind, having neither sense nor memory nor sufficient intelligence to manage herself, her lands or her goods. As appeared by inspection she had the face and countenance of an idiot.[36]

Thus, rather than announcing the enlightened perspective of a new age, the seventeenth-century document merely described a practice that had been in place for centuries.

Similar questions were asked of persons alleged to be mentally handicapped two centuries later. Citing the ability to recognise coins, and to perform simple numerical functions in relation to these coins or in the abstract, was particularly common. At his examination in 1615, Thomas Pope was said to have been 'very well able to discern and know the difference of all pieces of silver of the Queen's coin and the perfect value of them from xiid to an half-penny'.[37] Similarly, the commissioners who examined the alleged idiot German Bradshaw in 1597 reported that he 'numbered 20 forwards and backwards and counted money and divided and discerned the same'.[38] Knowing one's own age or kin, for example, also formed part of these tests. Comments on the physical appearance and health of the individual were also introduced as the basis for arriving at a diagnosis.

By the time of the Court of Wards, literacy had been added to the criteria for determining intelligence, at least for some individuals. Katherine Tothill, for instance, was asked:

> whether she could read or had books read to her. She said she could and did read. We asked what book? She answered the Bible, which she said she could read well, all but the hard names. Then bringing her a Bible, we bade her turn to the Acts of the Apostles. She turned to the New Testament, and turning divers leaves over, she stuck upon one place. We asked her what that was. She answered, to the Romans. Turning further, she looked upon another place, and being demanded what that was, she said the first to the Corinthians, both which were true. At the last place we spoke to her to read where she read 2 verses. Then we turned to the Old Testament, and there she read another verse.[39]

By the late sixteenth century, if not earlier, examinations also explored the subject's daily life and habits. The commissioners who saw Thomas Pretyman in 1599 wanted to know, for example, if he was an 'orderly man' who 'keeps an orderly house and frequents the church and is admitted in the church to receive Holy Communion with the rest of his neighbours'.[40]

If an individual demonstrated an acceptable level of numeracy and performed well in other areas, the examiners appear to have pushed their enquiry further in an effort to assess the man's judgement and discretion regarding specific problems facing him in life. Ambrose Bennett's adaptive skills and behaviour were evaluated with the following questions in 1628:

> I … questioned him about several things for his estate. He directly informed me that he had £200 a year annuity or better out of the land conveyed to Sir Simon Bennett his brother, granted him during his life and a legacy of £2000 or £3000 in ready money. But said it was not fit for him to [manage] his whole estate. Myself inquiring how he did employ his estate he said that he paid his mother as I take it where he was last for his board after the rate of £120 a year and being asked what remained of his £200 annuity he said £80. Then what he did with that, he answered he maintained himself and a man, being asked what he did with his two thousand pounds legacy he said he put it out to interest, being asked how much interest of two thousand pounds would yearly yield him he said one hundred and three-score pounds a year, being asked what he would do with his estate growing so rich he said he would give it when he died amongst his friends that used him best and having many poor friends that he must do for I asked him what he paid now

> for his board, he said he told his brother if he did not pay him he said he had an entry upon his land if he paid not his half years payment at the day or within a quarter of a year, after I told him he was very skillful in his estate.[41]

The criteria employed in this jurisdiction to arrive at a legal verdict of lunacy are more difficult to establish. In contrast to examinations of mentally handicapped persons, the records from lunacy hearings lack any report of elaborate verbatim exchanges between the examiners and the allegedly disabled individual. Whether this omission reflects a true difference in Court practice, or is just an artifact of differential manuscript survival, is not clear. However, as a consequence, we possess only the following very general idea as to governmental criteria for psychoses. First, by definition, the condition had to commence postnatally to be considered psychosis. Second, references to lunatics, such as Beaton Norcott alias Norden, as 'somewhat defective in her memory and understanding by reason of sickness and old age',[42] indicate that these individuals, too, were evaluated for intellectual deficits. However, no extant records suggest that specific numeracy or literacy tests were administered. On the other hand, lunacy examinations do contain frequent references to the subject's possibly disturbed thoughts or behaviour, indicating a small difference in emphasis from examinations of mentally handicapped persons. John Davies' examination found him to be 'sometimes distempered in his mind and actions'.[43] Nicholas Goodridge was considered sane because 'upon sight of his sober and discreet carriage and behaviour' it appeared that he was 'a man of good discretion and understanding'.[44]

As we have seen, government officials used common-sense, naturalistic, rational criteria for assessing mental impairment. However, phenomenology and etiology are logically distinct. The use of naturalistic criteria could coexist with theories of demonic etiology. Mental retardation could be the work of the devil. Indeed, at Emma de Beston's idiocy inquisition her fourteenth-century examiners concluded that her impairment resulted from 'the snares of evil spirits'.[45] But in this regard Emma's examination is unique among surviving records. All other extant inquisitions treat mental handicap as a congenital condition whose occurrence required no appeal to the exercise or operation of supernatural forces. Moreover, in the case of psychosis, where we might expect that supernatural and demonic etiologies would be given greater rein, both royal officials and private individuals petitioning for custody advanced physical and psychological, never demonic, explanations for deranged behaviour.[46]

While the Devil may have exerted little influence on this legal incompetency jurisdiction, financial and political factors were very much in evidence in the deployment of its disability classifications. Since *Prerogativa Regis* linked diagnosis with issues effecting royal revenues, the diagnostic distinction between idiocy and lunacy was inevitably vulnerable to contamination by royal fiscal stratagems. The commission sent to examine a person for mental disability was initiated by a writ; selection of the appropriate writ required specification beforehand of the type of examination. Thus, several versions of a writ *de idiota inquirendo* were developed in the medieval period,[47] as was a writ for persons *non compos mentis*. One version of the idiocy writ makes plain that the medieval incompetency jurisdiction, in practice, played havoc with the distinction between congenital handicap and psychotic disorders arising postnatally drawn so carefully in *Prerogativa Regis*. The writ directed officials to enquire, 'whether the said I. be foolish and an idiot ... or not; and if he be then whether from his nativity, or from any other time, and if from any other time, then from what time and how and in what manner, and if he enjoys lucid intervals'. This writ employed idiot in a generic sense, subsuming Sections 11 and 12 of *Prerogativa Regis*. This contradiction in terminology may represent merely unintended confusion between legal theory and administrative practice. It is equally or more likely, however, that this apparent illogic reflects royal fiscal cunning. After all, a generic use of idiot would facilitate drawing into the Crown's profitable jurisdiction a very wide range of psychiatric disorders, thereby eluding the clear restrictions set forth in this regard in *Prerogativa Regis*.

That idiocy writs led to such results is evident from surviving inquisitions. For example, in May of 1359 Robert de Tothale was found to have been mentally handicapped since 1346, the year that his own son reached his fifth birthday.[48] From 1301 to 1392, and from 1485 to 1540, the mentally handicapped constituted 80 per cent of all extant officially examined cases of mental disability.[49] Solely from an epidemiological perspective, this ratio of congenital handicap to all severe psychiatric disorders is highly improbable and the internal evidence from de Tothale's examination establishes that some proportion of idiots in fact suffered from deficits of postnatal origin. Thus, despite equal billing in *Prerogativa Regis*, writs specifically for persons *non compos mentis* occupied at best a marginal position in the medieval period, probably because of the Crown's reluctance to handle non-profitable disability cases. However, a writ of this nature does survive from the thirteenth century,[50] and a few inquisitions held on the eschaetor's own initiative, known as *inquisitions virtute officii*, returned verdicts of *non compos mentis*.[51]

Before 1540, the custody of an idiot was purchased from the Crown by private persons for an amount known as a fine;[52] entry upon the land was given in return for an annual rent.[53] The amount of the fine and of the rent was based on the value of the individual's lands, as determined at the *inquisition post mortem*. However, the guardian was obliged to protect the mentally handicapped person, providing him, but not his family, with necessities and to maintain the estate and prevent its exploitation. The guardian was not answerable at the time of the person's death for surplus revenues, that is, for estate rents received above and beyond the rent owed to the king and the resources required to sustain the disabled person and his property.

Lunacy grants differed markedly from those for the mentally handicapped. Grants of such individuals and of their property were made to private persons without any fine and at no rent.[54] However, guardians were accountable for a more beneficial stewardship. The guardian of a psychotic individual was expected to maintain the disabled person and his family at an economic level commensurate with his or her social rank, not simply with necessities, and to preserve and protect the estate. Furthermore, the guardian was not entitled to any of the surplus revenues.[55]

SIXTEENTH- AND SEVENTEENTH-CENTURY TRANSFORMATIONS

The Court of Wards' jurisdiction over the mentally disabled underwent a radical transformation on two fronts from 1540 to 1640. The first change concerned the terms and conditions of idiocy grants; the second, a quantitative shift in the proportion of idiocy to lunacy grants. Each of these developments will be described in turn.

From its statutory inception the Court abandoned the practice of charging fines for grants of the handicapped.[56] Rents on their lands were also eliminated, although the timetable here is less certain. Numerous documents granting occupation of the lands of the mentally handicapped to guardians survive from Elizabeth I's reign (1558–1603) and none contain any reference to rents.[57] One extant document of this nature from 1541 also omits the rent.[58] Therefore, rent-free grants of lands of the mentally handicapped, which were the rule during Elizabeth's reign, may have been the order of the day starting in the 1540s. Unfortunately, the absence of this series of documents for the intervening years leaves this particular matter in doubt.

The elimination of fines and rents benefited both the guardian and the heirs of the mentally handicapped person. The guardian was now exempt from making large initial outlays of cash for the fine and from annual rental payments for the duration of his stewardship. Since the guardian was entitled to recoup his expenses from the handicapped person's estate revenues, this change probably meant lighter financial burdens on the disabled person's property. Under these new arrangements, however, the Crown had to abandon its claim to potential revenues.

These reductions in guardians' expenses, *vis-à-vis* the Crown, were yoked to increased responsibilities and obligations towards the mentally handicapped. This expansion is set forth in the founding statute, suggesting that this development may well have antedated the creation of the Court. After declaring that the chief officers of the Court should lease the lands of the handicapped for such rent as they thought fit, Section 26 required 'the finding and keeping of the said persons, their wives and children and the reparations of their houses always to be considered'.[59] An outline for an idiocy grant drafted in Easter of 1541 elaborated upon these terms as follows: 'The committee [i.e., the guardian] covenants (1) to find the idiot his children and family (if any be) with meat drink and apparel (2) to see them well governed, succoured, etc. according to their degree and estate.'[60] Thus, the committee was obliged to protect not only the mentally handicapped person, but his family as well. In addition, the handicapped person and his family were to be maintained not merely with bare necessities, as noted in *Prerogativa Regis*, but at a level consonant with their social standing. This expansion in guardians' responsibilities was characteristic of grants for the mentally handicapped for the remainder of the Court's history.

Items 3 and 4 of this outline for grants of the mentally handicapped reveal another important development:

> (3) in Hilary term next [the grantee] to account of the estate and profits (4) to stand to the order of this Court for allowance of his demands and disbursements and to answer the remain[der] of the estate to the use of the idiot, his wife and children, as the Court shall direct and yearly account.

In short, guardians of the handicapped were no longer entitled to the surplus revenues from the estate. Thus, on the one hand, guardians were obliged to make greater financial outlays on behalf of the retarded person and his family and, on the other, to account annually for any remaining surplus. With few exceptions, full accountability for guardians' handling of revenues from the estates of mentally handicapped persons became the rule in the Court of Wards and Liveries.[61]

In the Court of Wards, grants of psychotic persons were handled much as they had been in the medieval period. They remained free of fines and rents; guardians were expected to maintain the disabled person's entire family and were held accountable for all expenditures and income. Grants of psychotics, like those of the mentally handicapped, included covenants obliging committees to account annually for their receipts and disbursements. In summary, in the first twenty-five years of its existence, the Court of Wards and Liveries brought the terms of grants of the mentally handicapped closely into line with those previously reserved for psychotics. The solely protective royal jurisdiction over psychotic persons was extended thereby to the mentally handicapped as well. These administrative improvements may also reflect the growing admission by the Crown, and recognition by subjects, that many persons previously classified as idiots in fact did not meet the criteria for this classification but were more properly handled under the terms of Section 12 of *Prerogativa Regis*, that is, the section governing the jurisdiction over psychotics.

Changes regarding the disproportionate use of idiocy, relative to lunacy, grants were also underway during this period. As noted previously, prior to 1540, approximately 80 per cent of all grants of mentally disabled persons were for the mentally handicapped. The succeeding one hundred years witnessed a gradual reversal of this pattern. From 1540 to 1560, idiocy grants comprised 60 per cent of all mental disability grants; during Elizabeth's reign, idiocy grants dropped to 50 per cent of all grants. In James I's reign, which ended in 1625, this figure fell to 40 per cent, and by 1640 it was no more than 30 per cent.[62]

This secular change is too rapid to reflect a real decline in the relative frequency of mental handicap in England or a decline in the proportion of cases of handicap referred to the Court. In light of the fiscal consequences of lunacy and idiocy grants, the pace and direction of these changes point to underlying social and political rather than epidemiologic factors. This long-term shift suggests that the Crown was slowly acceding to a steady pressure from subjects to eliminate the use of idiocy grants. This quantitative shift is consistent with the other administrative developments noted earlier with regard to terms of idiocy grants. Both point to royal acceptance of reduced income from its jurisdiction over the mentally disabled and a new royal policy of offering increased protection to such subjects.

Tudor and early Stuart acceptance of these brakes on its prerogative income and solicitude for legally incompetent subjects were not limited to the mentally disabled. A somewhat parallel pattern prevailed on the far more extensive wardship side of the Court's jurisdiction. After a brief period of rising revenues from wardship in the period immediately following the Court's creation, the years under Elizabeth and the first decade of the seventeenth century witnessed little sustained growth in this source of royal revenues.[63] Similarly, instructions issued by Wards officials in the sixteenth and early seventeenth centuries urged that royal profits from wardship should not be pursued so aggressively as to impinge on the ward's welfare. 'Special care' was urged by royal instructions 'that our just and reasonable profits may be raised … and that neverthelesse our Tenants may be moderately charged, and our Wards may be educated'.[64]

This change in royal policies from aggressive fiscal feudalism to a type of Tudor paternalism was probably half willing, half coerced. On the one hand, the Crown may have wished to benefit those ascendant landed and commercial groups with whom it had entered into partnership through the course of the social and political struggles of the sixteenth century.[65] On the other hand, discontent with the exercise of the royal prerogative in the Court of Wards and elsewhere and with the feudal tenures on which this Court was based grew increasingly vocal by the turn of the century. It could be heard within the confines of the Court in the later sixteenth century[66] and was the subject of frequent and protracted debate when the Commons assembled in the early years of the seventeenth century.[67] Thus, the Crown's alliance with the groups represented in the Commons and clamours for fiscal reform voiced in the Commons very likely played a role in these changes in the Court's handling of the mentally disabled as well as of wards. These two components of the change in the legal incompetency jurisdiction may seem redundant. Why would prospective guardians continue to press for lunacy over idiocy grants when the terms of the two had become synonymous? The reason is probably that the alteration in idiocy grants remained an administrative change only. In law, idiots and lunatics were still sharply distinguished. That distinction was reiterated in legal tracts published after 1540[68] and remains intact today as part of the common law. Prospective guardians, consulting London solicitors before approaching the Court, were no doubt made aware of this distinction between law and practice. The beneficial terms under which idiocy grants were issued could legally revert to more exploitative forms under a king sufficiently desperate for funds. By contrast, the privileged status of a lunatic, an established part of the common law, represented a wall that the Crown would have greater difficulty in scaling than it would a simple administrative ruling. Once a man had been classified as a lunatic, the Crown could not legally require a fine or a rent at the time of the grant or at a subsequent juncture.

These efforts to erect hedges against royal incursions proved well founded. Starting in 1629, Charles I refused to call Parliament for eleven years. Free of parliamentary levies, he began to exploit his prerogative sources more vigorously. During this period of the so-called Eleven Year Tyranny,[69] fines and rents were systematically reintroduced for idiocy grants, but grants remained untouched.

Two additional features of the evolution of legal incompetency practice in the early seventeenth century deserve mention. Both represent an extension of the royal jurisdiction over the mentally disabled for the benefit of subjects. First, it was readily recognised by Court officials that the expenses associated with petitioning for custody and processing the custodial grant, all of which expenses were legitimately charged by the guardian against the disabled person's estate, could come close to bankrupting disabled persons of small means or deter prospective guardians altogether from seeking royal protection. During the early years of the seventeenth century, the Court created an informal system of monitored guardianship, installed without the full procedural panoply of commission hearings and jury verdicts.[70] As a consequence, Court costs were reduced to a minimum while at the same time Court protection was made accessible to nearly propertyless persons. This 'sliding scale' of Court fees facilitated the emergence of a small social welfare dimension to Court operations.

The jurisdiction's diagnostic reach was also extended. As we have discussed, given the language of *Prerogativa Regis* and the content of examination questions, it appears probable that only those suffering from profound or severe mental handicap present at birth were intended by the term idiot. However, Court of Wards officials recognised that certain individuals' intellectual capabilities could be sufficiently limited as to benefit from protection but not so incapacitated as to constitute idiots. Thus, John Ovenden was considered 'no ideot but a simple man of non sane memory'.[71] Similarly, John Styward was classified as 'simple but no ideot'[72] as were several other individuals as well.[73] For these individuals, as well as for persons with limited property, the Court created a less formal and less costly but none the less officially monitored type of guardianship.

GUARDIANS

Private subjects, usually the individual who first alerted the Court to the existence of the disability problem, received custody of the incompetent individual. The Court, unable to mandate good will, sought to choose guardians who were bound to the disabled person by affection or by the identity of their economic interests. Guardians were to be 'the nearest of kin … sound in religion, of good governance in their own families, without dissolution, without distemper, no greedy persons, no stepmothers'.[74] Whenever possible, the Court avoided handing over the disabled person to 'the mercy and power of a stranger'.[75] Moreover, even when the Court erred in this respect, the threat of being charged with abuse of trust by other family members, and the relative alacrity with which the Court acted on such charges, afforded some brake on physical or financial abuses by guardians.[76]

Occasionally, illustrious individuals requested custody of a disabled relative. For example, in 1637 William Harvey petitioned for guardianship of his nephew, William Fowkes, 'being an Ideot'.[77] Harvey was awarded custody, although apparently a niece had responsibility for Fowkes' daily care. In his will, Dr Harvey bequeathed money to this niece 'for the use and behoof and better ordering of Will Fowkes'.[78] Why didn't Harvey seek a lunacy grant, with its attendant fiscal benefits to the family – presumably an easy matter given his position as royal physician? It has been speculated elsewhere that Harvey's actions reflect his greater respect for his own medical observations of his nephew's true type of disability than for the family's purse.[79]

Physical supervision and care of the disabled party were frequently handled by retaining a live-in servant, a so-called 'keeper'[80] of the same gender as the disabled individual. Hours in attendance and the number of keepers fluctuated with the disabled party's degree of symptomatology and behavioural disturbance. In 1599 Jane Norris' maidservant was needed 'more than before because she grows old'.[81] A year later Jane 'was sometimes … very unruly whereby the (guardian) was enforced to have sometimes 2 sometimes more [servants] a whole weeke together to be with [Jane] and attend her day and night'.[82]

With or without servants, guardians' lives sometimes became an endless round of distributing reparations for their ward's misconduct. Amy Burton, guardian of Frances Dorrington, expended 60 shillings for 'messengers and for hiring of horses for seeking out [Frances, who had] often bene enticed away by evill disposed people', 20 shillings for 'redeeming at severall tymes [Frances'] … clothes laid out by him to pawne', 15 shillings 'for a sow with a pigge … which [Frances] killed by setting of doggs on her', and 10 shillings 'for making a disturbance in the Church in Coleman Street [London] in the tyme of divine service'.[83]

Placing the mentally handicapped or psychotic person in a private dwelling, together with a servant, was also common and in some respects anticipated the development of private madhouses in the eighteenth century.[84] Guardians' accounts recite a litany of the per annum costs of diet, lodging, and washing associated with the disabled person's upkeep in such a place,[85] together with 'wages, meat and drinke for persons' in attendance.

CONCLUSION

This incompetency jurisdiction of the English Crown is a far cry from the tired historical accounts of a medieval world rife with superstitious treatment of mental disorders and an early modern Europe swimming in the red tide of witchcrazes. This jurisdiction was premised on the government's responsibility to protect subjects who, by reason of mental impairment, were unable to protect themselves. Royal officials defined, measured and explained mental disabilities in entirely naturalistic terms, without reference to demonology. The legal disability categories of lunacy and idiocy describe these conditions in purely naturalistic terms. The questions administered at inquisitions evaluated impairment through entirely rational, pragmatic sense tests of intelligence, orientation, and socially appropriate behaviour. Etiological notions followed the same pattern. With the single exception of Emma de Beston, the mental illness of persons brought within the purview of this jurisdiction was presumed to be due to natural causes. Furthermore, these views of mental illness were not the monopoly of the ruling élites and reserved for members of their own class. The persons who entertained such views and the individuals to whom they were applied came from a wide range of social classes. Finally, whereas in the medieval period royal protection was linked with profit, in the sixteenth and early seventeenth centuries (at least until the reign of Charles I), this fiscal dimension gradually disappeared while the welfare aspects were significantly expanded.

While serving as a useful corrective to earlier histories of psychiatry, these records give rise to a variety of new, unsolved historical mysteries. Two may be mentioned. First, if both natural and supernatural explanations of bizarre conduct and ideation were available to medieval and early modern Englishmen, what factors, intrinsic to the behaviour or contextual in nature, determined the etiologic choice? Second, in this process of etiologic triage that went on in these centuries, roughly what proportion of mentally disabled individuals were judged incompetent owing entirely to natural causes? The incompetency archives do not provide answers or any hint of answers to either question.

Whatever the final resolution of these issues, the manuscript sources of this English legal incompetency jurisdiction demonstrate the serious hazards involved in the past and current neglect of manuscript sources, at least for the earlier periods in psychiatric history. If these legal incompetency archives are any indication, the real history of mental handicap and of psychiatry remains to be written.

NOTES

1 F. Alexander and S. Selesnick, *The History of Psychiatry*, New York, 1966; G. Zilboorg, *A History of Medical Psychology*, New York, 1941.

2 R. Colp, *History of Psychiatry*, ch. 50; H. Kaplan and B. Sadock (eds), *Psychiatry: Past and Future, Comprehensive Textbook of Psychiatry/V.* volume 2 (5th edition), Baltimore, p. 2134.

3 L. Szymanski and A. Crocker, *Mental Retardation, Comprehensive Textbook of Psychiatry/V.* volume 2 (5th edition), ch. 34; Kaplan and Sadock (eds), *Psychiatry*, p. 1731.

4 T. Szasz, *The Manufacture of Madness: A Comparative Study of the Inquisition and the Mental Health Movement*, New York, 1970.

5 Zilboorg, *A History of Medical Psychology*.

6 M. MacDonald, *Mystical Bedlam*, Cambridge, 1981; R. Porter, *Mind-Forg'd Manacles: A History of Madness in England from the Restoration to the Regency*, Cambridge, Mass., 1987; W. Bynum, R. Porter and M. Shepherd (eds), *The Anatomy of Madness: Essays in the History of Psychiatry* 3 vols, London, 1985–1988; P. Rushton, 'Lunatics and Idiots: Mental Disability, the Community and the Poor Law in North-East England, 1600–1800', *Medical History*, 1988, vol. 32, pp. 34–50; A. Suzuki, 'Lunacy in Seventeenth- and Eighteenth-Century England: Analysis of Quarter Sessions Records, Part I', *History of Psychiatry*, 1991, vol. 2, pp. 437–56; A. Suzuki, 'Lunacy in Seventeenth- and Eighteenth-Century England: Analysis of Quarter Sessions Records, Part II', *History of Psychiatry*, 1992, vol. 3, pp. 29–44.

7 N. Heywood and A. Massey, *Court of Protection Practice* (7th edition), London, 1954.

8 Public Record Office, Kew, Richmond, Surrey, Great Britain. (Citations from this collection of Crown-copyright records in the Public Record Office, as well as from other such collections cited below, appear by the kind permission of the Controller of HM Stationery Office.) Exchequer, King's Remembrancer, Various Accounts, E.101/415/3, memoranda 1 October 15 Henry VII.

9 Ibid.

10 A. Luders, T. Tomlins, J. France *et al.*, *Statutes of the Realm*, London, Record Commission, 1810–1822, vol. 5, part 1, p. 259.
11 W. Holdsworth, *A History of English Law* (3rd edition), London, 1922, vol. 1, pp. 473–5.
12 E.P. Thompson, *The Making of the English Working Class*, New York, 1963, Preface, p. 12.
13 A. Luders *et al.*, *Statutes of the Realm*, vol. 1, p. 226.
14 Hereafter, the term 'idiot' will be used without quotation marks.
15 A. Luders *et al.*, *Statutes of the Realm*, vol. 1, p. 226.
16 J. Whittaker (ed.), *The Mirror of Justices: Selden Society*, London, 1895, vol. 7, p. 138.
17 J. Cowell, 'Ideot' in *The Interpreter of Words and Termes*, London, 1701.
18 Whittaker, *The Mirror of Justices*, pp. 137–8.
19 E. Coke, *The First Part of the Institutes of the Laws of England: or, A Commentary Upon Littleton* (19th edition), F. Hargrave and C. Butler (eds), London, 1832, p. 247.
20 *An Exposition of Certaine Difficult and Obscure Words and Termes*, London, 1615, f.117.
21 Manuscript Collection, Cambridge University Library, Ee.5.22ff. 354 r–355 r.
22 Cambridge University Library, Hh.2.1.ff. 16 v–18 r.
23 A. Luders *et al.*, *Statutes of the Realm*.
24 Hereafter, the term 'lunatic' will appear without quotation marks.
25 H. Fisher (ed.), *The Collected Papers of Frederic William Maitland*, vol. 2, p. 182.
26 Public Record Office, Kew, Richmond, Surrey, Great Britain. Wards Archives. Wards 9/214–220. (Citations from this collection of Crown-copyright records in the Public Record Office, as well as from other such collections cited below, appear by the kind permission of the Controller of HM Stationery Office.)
27 PRO (Kew), *Chancery, Inquisitions Post Mortem*, Series II (Henry VII to Charles II).
28 R. Neugebauer, 'Application of a capture-recapture method (the Bernoulli census) to historical epidemiology', *American Journal of Epidemiology*, 1984, vol. 120, pp. 626–34.
29 Calendar of Inquisitions Miscellaneous (Chancery) Preserved in the Public Record Office (Henry III–12 Richard II), London, 1916–1957, vols 1–4. Calendar of Inquisitions Post Mortem and Other Analogous Documents Preserved in the Public Record Office (Henry III–15 Richard II), London, 1904–1974, vols 1–16. Calendar of Inquisitions Post Mortem and Other Analogous Documents Preserved in the Public Record Office, Series II (Henry VII), London, 1898–1955, vols 1–3.
30 H. Bell, *An Introduction to the History and Records of the Court of Wards and Liveries*, Cambridge, 1953.
31 Ibid., p. 140. After 1540, the Court of Wards' own local official, the feodary, who was usually a gentleman, joined these proceedings.
32 A. Luders *et al.*, *Statutes of the Realm*, vol. 2, p. 342.
33 Ibid. vol. 1, p. 368.
34 Ibid. vol. 3, Part 1, p. 4.
35 A. Fitzherbert, *Nouvelle Natura Brevium*, London, 1553.

36 Ibid.
37 Calendar of Inquisitions Miscellaneous (Chancery) (Henry III–12 Richard II), vol. 4, pp. 127–8.
38 Wards 9/86, f.299.
39 Wards 10/67, Examination of Mrs. Katherine Tothill, November 1626.
40 Wards 9/87, f.141.
41 Wards 10/51, certificates.
42 Wards 10/42, pt.2, certificate of 3 February, 1627.
43 Wards 9/93, f.103.
44 Wards 9/88, f.447.
45 Calendar of Inquisitions Miscellaneous (Chancery) (Henry III–12 Richard II), vol. 4, p. 125.
46 R. Neugebauer, 'Medieval and Early Modern Theories of Mental Illness', *Archive of General Psychiatry*, 1979, vol. 36, pp. 477–83.
47 Fitzherbert, *Nouvelle,* ff. 232–3.
48 Calendar of Inquisitions Post Mortem and Other Analogous Documents (Henry III–15 Richard II), vol. 10, p. 338.
49 Calendar of Inquisitions Post Mortem (Henry III–15 Richard II), vols 1–16; Calendar of Inquisitions Post Mortem (Henry VII), vols 1–3.
50 H. Hall, *Studies in English Official Historical Documents*, 2 vols, 1908–9 (reprint edition), New York, 1969, vol. 2, pp. 86–7.
51 Calendar of Inquisitions Post Mortem (Henry III–15 Richard II), vols 1–16; Calendar of Inquisitions Post Mortem (Henry VII), vols 1–3.
52 Exchequer, King's Remembrancer, Various Accounts, E.101/415/3, memoranda 1 October 15 Henry VII, f.298.
53 R.H. Brodie and J. Gairdner (eds), *Letters and Papers, Foreign and Domestic, of the Reign of Henry VIII* (2nd edition), rev. 21 vols. in 35 (1862–1910); (reprint edition), London, 1965, vol. 1 (2), p. 1463.
54 Cambridge University Library, Ee.5.22 ff. 354 r–355 r; Cambridge University Library, Hh.2.1.ff. 16–26.
55 Cambridge University Library. Ee.5.22 ff. 354 r–355 r; Holmes' Case, 1 Dyer 25b. English Reports (reprint edition), Edinburgh, 1900–1930.
56 Wards 5/1–52; Wards 9/102B–113.
57 Wards 9/105–110.
58 British Museum, Manuscript Collection, Lansdowne MSS 608, f.174.
59 A. Luders *et al.*, *Statutes of the Realm,* 3, part 2, p. 806.
60 Lansdowne MSS, 608, f.174.
61 Wards 5/1–52.
62 Public Record Office, Chancery Inquisitions Post Mortem, Series II (Henry VII to Charles II); Wards 5/1–52; Wards 9/105–110; Wards 9/148–151.
63 Bell, *An Introduction*, p. 47. This apparent paradox – strenuous royal efforts to create a special court to centralise and consolidate the royal claims over the heirs of feudal tenants-in-chief, followed by fiscal stagnation in this Court – awaits full explanation.
64 J. Ley, *A Learned Treatise concerning Wards and Liveries*, 1642, cited in ibid., p. 66.
65 Bell, *An Introduction*, p. 127.
66 Wards 10/50, deposition of John Birche.
67 Bell, *An Introduction*, ch. VII, 'The Agitation against the Court'.

68 W. Staunford, *Exposicion of the Kinges Prerogative*, London, 1590 edition, ff.33–7.
69 Bell, *An Introduction*; M. Ashley, *England in the Seventeenth Century*, Baltimore, Maryland, esp. ch. V: 'King Charles and the "Eleven Year Tyranny" 1625–40'.
70 R. Neugebauer, 'Social Class, Mental Illness and Government Policy in 16th and 17th Century England', New York, unpublished PhD thesis, 1976.
71 Wards 9/214, f.128.
72 Lansdowne MSS. 608, f.144.
73 Wards 10/22, Petition of John Mason concerning Mary Alsopp, 1605; Lansdowne MSS 608, f.197.
74 Public Record Office, State Papers, Domestic, 14/69.
75 Wards 9/93, f.322, 1620.
76 Wards 9/84–102, 1572–1645; Wards 9/527–558, 1600–1649.
77 Wards 10/45, 1637, part 1; R. Neugebauer, 'A Doctor's Dilemma: The Case of William Harvey's Mentally Retarded Nephew', *Psychological Medicine*, 1989, vol. 19, pp. 569–72.
78 G. Keynes, *The Life of William Harvey*, Oxford, 1966.
79 Neugebauer, 'A Doctor's Dilemma'.
80 Wards 9/87, f.188.
81 Wards 10/29, part 2, 1589–1599, The Account of William Wrey Committee of Jane Norris, Lunatic, 41 Elizabeth I.
82 Wards 10/29, part 2, 1599–1600, The Account of William Wrey Committee of Jane Norris, Lunatic, 42 Elizabeth I.
83 The Account of Amy Burton Committee and Guardian of Francis Dorrington, 2 December 1642.
84 W. Parry-Jones, *The Trade in Lunacy: A Study of Private Madhouses in England in the Eighteenth and Nineteenth Centuries*, London, 1972.
85 Wards 10/56, part 2, The Account of Raphe Smith Committee of Owen Saintpeer a Lunatic, Christmas 1638.

3

IDIOCY, THE FAMILY AND THE COMMUNITY IN EARLY MODERN NORTH-EAST ENGLAND

Peter Rushton

In the early modern period people with mental disabilities were the focus of both theoretical discourse and practical action. There was a detailed legal framework of concepts describing the nature of conditions such as 'idiocy' and, in the decisions of welfare and judicial authorities, a developing tradition of policies responding to the various social problems they presented.[1] While there is therefore much evidence of both the ideas and practices of the time, connections between the two are sometimes unclear. Some sources, particularly the rather cryptic administrative records of the Poor Law, are the products of a direct exercise of local power and rarely reflect a thoughtful or theoretical concern with those in need. Nevertheless, this managerial style of welfare can be revealing, for as has been pointed out, the reality of a discourse is often revealed through the 'content of the judgements' as much as in the logic of its theoretical arguments.[2] At this local level cases of people with what we might term learning disabilities were widely known and understood. Within the framework of the parish Poor Law, petitions because of illness, disability and poverty were common. Most of the officially accepted medical reasons for poverty concerned physical weakness, of course, the natural result of injury or ageing; but mental disabilities were understood to render people incapable of a normal economic and social life, making them equally dependent on others. In a typical request, Mary Jordan, of Corbridge in Northumberland, pleaded in 1711 with the local magistrates for assistance on the grounds that her husband had been known to them, and, she continued,

> now I am almost blinde and very hard of hearing, so I humbly entreate you to do something for me. I have two girls that's my

> grandchildren and the youngest is about thirty years of age and neither of them can tell to twenty … I am somewhat burthened with them because they are not capeable of service.[3]

The aim in this chapter is to examine cases of apparent learning disability like this as a means of exploring both the attitudes of families and communities and the policies which they and their governing authorities adopted.

The recent work on the English Poor Law has been provocative in its interpretation of welfare in the early modern period. One striking feature seemingly well demonstrated was the key role of the local community in maintaining the elderly, the sick and the disabled (of various kinds). Public aid for these categories of need seems to have been relatively unquestioned if not generous. Unemployed men, by contrast, seem to have suffered at different historical periods from a more fickle official sympathy, as the usual victims in recurrent attempts at cutting costs and forcing them back to work.[4] Interpretations of the Poor Law have consequently attempted to combine an examination of the lives of the poor and the role played by public relief in ensuring them a minimum of comfort, with an exploration of the apparent theoretical and political context of official policies. Most modern studies have concluded that the nineteenth-century accusations of arbitrary generosity and irrational self-defeating subsidy of a pauperised underclass (as we would express it today) were not valid for the early modern period, but neither was there an uncaring dark age of welfare. The overwhelming evidence suggests that there existed much more careful and organised policies of relief than has hitherto been recognised.[5] The issue which tends to dominate much discussion of the early modern elderly or physically disabled is one which is redolent of modern concern, that is, whether the family or the local community was the more crucial source of both financial and practical care. With cases of the different types of mental disability, too, this is the question central to much of the analysis of the evidence provided by the Poor Law, together with the additional problem of the role of specialised caring institutions in the eighteenth century. Most studies suggest that with those deemed mad, local authorities were willing to resort to expensive incarceration in gaols, houses of correction, workhouses, or other safe places. But this was not an exclusive or uniform policy, with many 'lunatics' as well as idiots left in the community, usually with their families, with or without public financial support. Institutions such as Bethlem, supplemented by private asylums, played a part in providing specialised care, and were better managed than their later reputations suggested. The growing asylum framework seems to have provided a licence for the separation of the 'mad' from the 'bad', and their founders usually specifically forbade the presence of idiots. The impression from most studies is that the local officials attempted to diagnose the nature of the mental disabilities consistently and carefully, but because of the huge number of managing authorities (more than 10,000 parishes), we have no clear overall national picture of the situation before 1800.[6]

The sources on particular individuals in need fall into two categories: those provided by the parish and its officials on the one hand, and those court records left by the county magistrates when the responsibility for care had become subject to dispute between either individuals or parishes. The basic information at parish level, of levels of relief, and of its recipients and purpose, is supplemented by legal discussions of responsibility when the family or the parish abrogated their duties. In this process supervision of all the mentally disabled was in fact ultimately accountable to the justices long before they had a formal requirement to be specifically responsible for the custody of lunatics.[7] The first task, therefore, before examining the details of many individual cases, is to place the local practice within the contemporary legal framework. As has been frequently noted, the early modern English population was both intensely litigious and remarkably legalistic in its behaviour, to the point where law may indeed have been a far greater force for social integration than religion. Yet the letter of the law may be a poor guide to actual decisions and principles, for a divided society may be compelled to allow rival interpretations of the same statutes. The legal framework therefore provides an important starting-point for any examination of the policies directed towards the mentally disabled, but should not be taken as the final word. Coherence in theory does not necessarily imply consistency in policy.[8]

THE ORIGINS OF THE LAW ON IDIOCY

It would be very odd to begin a history of the legal definition of the mentally disabled with the suggestion that, on the whole, there is no history to consider. Yet in some ways this might be a tenable view, for when the first detailed handbooks were produced in the late sixteenth and early seventeenth centuries to aid justices and others to administer the law, they embodied almost unchanged a simple dichotomy between the idiot and the lunatic which had shaped medieval law since the thirteenth century. Since this also provided the intellectual background to the developing medical and welfare policies after 1600, this language, used to diagnose, treat or otherwise deal with those who displayed unusual mental functioning remained virtually unchanged for centuries. In law, philosophy, and policies of poor relief, the distinction between idiocy, an irrecoverable condition, and lunacy, a temporary illness, was a recurrent dichotomy.

The legal implications of these definitions were serious, involving potential loss of legal rights to property, compulsory incarceration, both private and public, and general reduction in social rights. For example, in the thirteenth century, among those forbidden from becoming judges were 'Women ... serfs, and those under the age of twenty-one, open lepers, idiots, attorneys, lunatics, deaf mutes, those excommunicated by a bishop, criminal persons'. This dichotomy between genetic and temporary disabilities remains strong today, as recurrent Mental Health Acts testify. Whereas the Middle Ages dealt with 'lepers, lunatics and idiots', the eighteenth century with 'lunaticks, ideots and drunkards', the modern police are advised against handling the 'mentally handicapped' and 'mentally ill' (and juveniles) without outside assistance. This could suggest, to the jaundiced eye, that the only change that has occurred since 1300 is that suspected juvenile delinquents have replaced lepers and drunks in the ranks of the untouchables.[9]

This consistency down the centuries in basic terminology and definitions of mental disability is extraordinary. Yet the circumstances of application, have, of course, changed considerably. The legal theory was further elaborated in textbooks designed for a national (that is, English and Welsh) educated public in the early modern period, and at the same time definitions of mental competence became subject to an increasing philosophical as well as medical concern. By the eighteenth century, therefore, there was a background of ready-made concepts and tested legal policies towards those deemed lunatic or idiot. Moreover, there was also a limited growth of acknowledged expertise in dealing with awkward individuals which, though it did not amount to the equivalent of a modern profession, was nevertheless essential to local communities. While, therefore, there were no real 'experts' in mental disabilities before the eighteenth-century asylums, there were many constables, gaolers and keepers of workhouses and houses of correction who were trusted to deal with the persons allocated to them. In villages and families, too, there may have been those with accepted skill.

The deep-rooted character of these concepts is perhaps surprising, but may indicate a thorough penetration of early modern popular culture with the language of the law courts. As Michael MacDonald points out, mental conditions that had become problematic socially or legally were initially discovered by the neighbours or family of the afflicted, and only then was their judgement validated by official legal authority. This process will be discussed later in this chapter, but it is interesting to note that few examples exist to suggest that popular ideas differed radically from those of the legal culture.[10]

EARLY MODERN LEGAL THEORY

The essential concepts were thus apparently fixed before the end of the thirteenth century, but the methods by which the distinction was established in practice in this period were imprecise. Neugebauer's astonishing figures from the Court of Wards (80 per cent of cases before 1540 comprised allegations of idiocy) suggest a serious confusion in reality if not theory. Examiners had to investigate whether the condition had persisted since nativity or if not, when it had developed or struck. Neugebauer suggests they were conflating many postnatal conditions into one concept of idiocy, and even talked of 'lucid intervals', which theoretically were the quality of the mad. It is possible that the relative clarity of the methods of testing for idiocy resulted in the neglect of the potentially more difficult lunacy cases, or, perhaps, the courts simply found 'idiocy' the easier judgement to reach.[11]

In the early modern period, however, when magistrates bore the brunt of most decision-making about all the mentally disabled, the concepts were apparently clearly outlined for them in legal handbooks, and the impression is that the distinction between lunatics and idiots was generally maintained consistently. By this time, among the cases of mental abnormality, problems of lunacy dominated the local courts statistically, as far more allegations about madness or 'distraction' were heard than imputations of idiocy. Commentators in the seventeenth century such as Michael Dalton provided a clear and detailed scheme to assist magistrates and others, proposing three kinds of people classifiable as *non compos mentis*:

> [1] A fool natural, who is so (*a nativitate*) from his birth; and in such a one there is no hope of recovery.
> [2] He who was once of good and sound memory, and after (by sickness, hurt or other accident, or visitation of God) loseth his memory.

> [3] A Lunatick, who enjoys lucid intervals, and sometimes is of good understanding and memory, and sometimes is *non compos mentis*.[12]

The second category seems to have been deliberately vague, suggesting that loss of memory could be both physical and mental, a state perhaps midway between idiocy and madness, and may in practice have been conflated with straightforward lunacy. A similar tendency to complicate the medieval dichotomy with intermediate categories is displayed by Swinburne, whose work on the validity of wills also included a discussion of those unfit to make them. Even if a 'fool' made an intelligible testament, his will was not acceptable, for 'a naturall foole doth not understand what he saith, although he seeme to speake wisely'. But also, even if a man was not an idiot, 'yet if he be so simple that there is but small oddes betwixt him and a natural foole, such a person cannot make a testament'. But nevertheless Swinburne in apparent self-contradiction concedes the remote possibility of idiots making wills, for, he says, 'a fooles Testament wisely conceived is sometimes good in law'. This kind of careful legalistic vagueness implies that much was still left to the court to decide.[13]

More than a century later, Blackstone repeated much the same definitions, observing that with regard to criminal prosecutions 'a total idiocy, or absolute insanity, excuses from the guilt, and of course from the punishment'. The lawyers thus talked constantly of temporary loss of memory when discussing lunacy, but seemed to regard idiocy as simply failure to learn: 'the idiot is one that hath no understanding from his nativity'. In other areas of congenital disability, too, legal thinking supposed no possibility of learning. Blackstone, displaying the influence of Locke's psychology, propounded that

> A man is not an idiot if he hath any glimmering of reason so that he can tell his parents, his age or the like common matters. But a man who is born deaf dumb, and blind, is looked upon by the law as in the same state with an idiot; he being supposed incapable of understanding, as wanting those senses which furnish the human mind with ideas.[14]

Swinburne, however, asserted that anyone who could make a sign of intelligent intention, whatever their disabilities, could make a will. By the early modern period, therefore, in legal circles at least, idiocy, failure to become a normally learned adult, together with the other forms of mental unreason, seem to have been seen as an involuntary loss of judgement, an 'involuntary ignorance' in contrast to faults such as drunkenness which was regarded as inexcusable behaviour because it was 'voluntary'.[15] Nevertheless the law (at least as embodied in the advice in legal textbooks) was not concerned with the origins of the disability unless it was the outcome of a criminal act, but only with the fact of its existence. Where it occurred, learning disability, whether of physical or mental origin, debarred people from legal responsibility.

ANIMALITY AND HUMANITY

This basic framework of ideas remained apparently unaffected by philosophical or medical questioning. Indeed, Locke merely provides an extended gloss on the pre-existing legal concepts rather than a critical challenge to them. Lunatics, he thought, lacked none of the basic mental skills, but applied them wrongly, 'for they do not appear to me to have lost the Faculty of Reasoning: but having joined together some Ideas very wrongly, they mistake them for Truths'. But he speculates inconclusively about whether idiots and beasts are of the same species, since both share a complete lack of intellectual faculties.[16]

This association of animality and abnormality, was, as Keith Thomas notes in a very Foucauldian manner, common in the seventeenth and eighteenth centuries, particularly in connection with vagrants, lunatics and the Irish. This element of revulsion may have justified the use of severe restraints and punishments, for example imprisoning lunatics in barns and having to have their quarters 'cleaned out' like horses' stables. There are some indications that idiots were popularly supposed to be closer to animals in the way that, in north-east England and elsewhere, parents reported the uncontrollable physical appetites of their children. In 1720, 23-year-old William Batey was described by his mother Jane as 'an idiott and has been so from his Birth, and never able to putt on his own cloaths … and is always very glutinous and desirous of meat'.[17] In a later account, this time from early nineteenth-century Somerset, John Skinner came across a group of gypsies,

> with a little child which was tied to the back of an ass, surrounded by a variety of tent equipage, being very clamorous, … On enquiring of its mother whether it ailed anything, its chief cries were so piercing, she replied that it ailed nothing more than it had always done from the time of its birth, as it was unfortunately an idiot, and although seven years old was not near so

> large as its brother who was not four; that it was accustomed to make that horrid yelling, and was so importunate for food it would regularly eat a small loaf a day and not be satisfied.[18]

Apparently, in these instances a healthy appetite was confirmation of a lack of self-control, perhaps of animal greed, rather than an indication of normal childlike needs.

Interestingly, there are no accounts of a dangerously uncontrolled sexual appetite associated with idiocy, even among mature and adult victims. Some literary images seem to dwell on the possibility of enhanced sexual appetite among 'fools', but one legal authority felt that the capacity to have (actually to 'beget') children was proof of normality rather than idiocy.[19]

TESTS AND DIAGNOSES OF REASON AND KNOWLEDGE

The medieval period had developed tests for the central courts that were to dominate discussions of 'idiocy' for the next three centuries. Even today, Walker comments, the tests do not seem unreasonable, if rather crude. They followed the legal definition of idiocy in exploring whether the individuals had developed the socially necessary skills of numeracy and everyday language use. People were asked to add up sums of money, describe objects or animals, and count numbers forwards or backwards. One fourteenth-century victim was asked if she preferred twenty groats to forty pence (a groat was a fourpence piece), and in a famous case Henry Roberts in the early eighteenth century was asked what a lamb and a calf were called at one, two and three years old. Normality was defined in terms of someone who knows 'what shall be for his Profit or what for his Loss', a calculative rationality that any competent person could exercise in a highly monetarised and increasingly capitalist society. In addition, the competent person was supposed to have everyday knowledge: as Swinburne put it at the end of the sixteenth century,

> An Idiot, or a naturall foole is he, who notwithstanding he bee of lawfull age, yet he is so witless, that he can not knoweth who is his father, or mother, nor is able to answer any such easie question.[20]

Lunacy, by contrast, was viewed far less as the loss of a technical expertise and seems to have lacked any comprehensive tests except the public opinion of specially convened juries in both criminal and civil trials. In such trials the juries do not seem to have received any instructions as to how to proceed.

However, there are few instances of this kind of testing for the conditions of idiocy outside the central courts at any time in the early modern period. Blackstone assumed that only in civil cases would the issue of idiocy have required testing or examination by a jury, for neither type of the mentally disabled could be prosecuted in criminal law. In civil courts, if a plaintiff's idiocy could be established by the defendant, the suit could be dismissed. On these occasions, as in allegations of lunacy, the everyday knowledge of normal mental states was thought sufficient to diagnose the abnormal, suggesting that, as Neugebauer notes, those manifesting these signs, to the popular mind, 'lived next door' and were part of ordinary acquaintance. The use of friends and neighbours as witnesses suggests that a general popular reputation was taken as evidence in many instances. There was certainly nothing resembling the Lord Chancellor's testing of Henry Roberts, who wrote a bitterly resentful pamphlet about his investigation. There were no cases of panels or even taking of 'expert' opinion, although magistrates and Poor Law officials made frequent use of doctors to treat the poor from the 1720s onwards, and in the cities for many decades before.[21]

PETITIONERS AND POOR RELIEF

How did cases come to official notice, and what shaped the response? The evidence here is largely derived from north-east England, with glances at the data from published sources from elsewhere. Some cases derived entirely from disputes between parishes over their responsibilities to care and pay for people's welfare. Here, the cases appear as typical Poor Law disputes over maintenance or removal, a parish objecting to a payment imposed by the court, or demanding the removal of the recipient to another parish entirely. Most recipients, of course, would never have been the subject of a court hearing, though widely known in their parishes where the patchy survival of records makes them hard to trace. 'It should be borne in mind that the court naturally took no cognizance of those cases where no dispute arose.'[22] But local records are even more cursory when giving precise details about the nature of those receiving poor relief. Even comprehensive listings of the poor, such as those for Elizabethan Ipswich and Norwich, can provide only tantalising glimpses of the mental condition of the poor: interestingly, only Ipswich lists 'innocents' amongst its recipients, while Norwich, with a far larger survey, found none. Consequently, two-thirds of the cases known in north-east England appear in the quarter sessions disputes or pleas rather than in the parish records. We have too few regional studies yet to know if this is typical of the evidence available.[23]

There is something very suspect about the kinds of people recorded. The majority were male (four-fifths, 25 male to 6 female) and, where the age is known or implied, adult (11 out of 18): the oldest was 50 years old. This suggests that a disproportionate amount of attention was paid to those who should in 'normal' life be independent and caring for others rather than dependent and cared for. As Suzuki suggests in his study of lunacy cases in a similar context, the failure of the mature male was the occasion of much greater anxiety and public attention: patriarchy depends on men being at the very least reliable. However, idiots may not have been regarded as being completely incapable of earning a living: one Ipswich man in the 1597 census of the poor was regarded as 'abell' to work, though in want. Both Suzuki and Andrews stress that this was also a factor in the policies adopted in some instances. In several of these Elizabethan urban surveys the presence of a mentally disabled person is a recognised element in the family's poverty. The failures deemed more important than employability may have been managerial in nature, concentrating attention on men who were not able to perform with masculine authority. One Northumberland wife described her husband as 'a simple man, and not in a capacity to manage their concerns, and to order and take care of their husbandry'. Significantly, her parents-in-law had married him to her, their servant girl, to ensure a steadier future for the whole household, a plan that disintegrated when the young woman was disabled (physically) in an accident. She was ejected from the house, and consequently petitioning for relief.[24] It is also an interesting aspect of these cases that while, in law, the individuals were usually defined as idiots, the language of the petitioners showed much greater variety of terms, possibly reflecting a heightened sensitivity or tact. The most commonly used alternative term was 'innocent', as in one heartfelt plea by Margaret Williamson to the Northumberland justices in 1702:

> She hath an innocent son twelve yeares of age uncapable of knowing any by name or face, yea his own mother (your petitioner) that bore him is a stranger unto him. And further this her innocent is so unruly and past Government that without a continuall eye had unto him she is in daily fear of some ill to be done either to her, himselfe or some others.

The neighbours had asked her to watch him carefully, and her husband, the child's stepfather, whose own disability had not allowed her to be 'idle', was nevertheless willing to become her 'fellow helper' in this caring task.[25] The word 'innocent' or 'simple' occurs in a quarter of the north-east cases, especially in the parish lists (in 8 of the 33). It may be significant that all the Elizabethan cases in published sources use the term, but archival research may revise this.[26]

In the eighteenth century, by contrast, one elderly petitioner tried for credibility in court by using legal jargon, describing her daughter as '*non comptis mentis* (sic) worse than an Idiot', and another petition for aid attracted the footnote from the clerk that 'the said James Twizell was borne a foole which is the cause of his poverty'. The law perhaps encouraged a more determined bluntness in dealing with these social problems, aided by the published handbooks discussed earlier that became popular guides by the end of the seventeenth century.[27]

The character of petitioners, and their reasons for coming to court, reveal much of the dilemmas of the individuals in need. Petitioners' identities are not always known, but, where recorded, they are overwhelmingly family – mostly parents, siblings (or siblings-in-law) or spouses.[28] The majority were women, the largest category being mothers of the needy persons. Their reason for requesting aid was largely their own poverty, frequently the result of age or injury. One friend, for example, petitioned on behalf of Julian Mauther in 1708, 'who, lame and not able to goe abroad and beg bread, has an innocent to her daughter who is twenty years old, yet cannot put on her cloaths or stirr out'. One father was described as 'a poor infirm man', and a mother (of William Batey, above), said 'she is become old and very failed and not able (as she used to do) to maintaine either herselfe or him'. In one instance there was a curious distinction drawn between husband and wife: 'to James Hedley's wife for his innocent son, two shillings', as though it was recognised by the parish that the woman, who presumably was not the mother of the child, was the actual carer in practice. In other cases, the substitutes for deceased parents were, at least initially, refused help: Matthew Robinson petitioned for help in looking after James Twizell, 'the said James relations dying but his sister, wife to your petitioner, was forced to take him and hath kept and maintained him for the space of forty years without being burthensome to any person'. But, 'being old', he and his wife had to petition twice for help, the second time to force the parish to pay the one shilling and sixpence per week ordered by the court.[29]

DECISIONS OF THE COURT

It is worth noting that this couple had no legal obligation to care for a sibling under the Poor Law of 1601, but were 'forced' to do so. Probably the justices encouraged, or enforced, this kind of familial support, especially where male relatives had money, as a couple of North Riding cases suggest. In one, a Helmsley man was paid one shilling a week to care for his son-in-law, 'an ideot … incapable of providing for himself', while in an order of very dubious legality, three brothers (one in fact probably a brother-in-law) had to pay three pounds a year between them for the care of Richard Wardell, an 'impotent ideot'. The absence of legal justification was sometimes challenged by these male relatives, but it may be that, in the seventeenth century at least, magistrates took a wider view of family obligations than the narrow span of linear duties (parents, children and grandchildren, but not siblings or grandparents or in-laws) specified in the law. Possibly siblings were compelled to care: in a long case in the Essex quarter sessions of 1660–1, a brother was forced to provide for his sister with his 'competent sum of money' after he had abandoned her in a conveniently empty cottage in Cold Norton. After five parishes had become involved, and the woman removed to two of them where she had been at various times or had family connections, she was sent back to Cold Norton to be maintained by her brother. It is notable that there are no instances of the transference of family property from the victim to the kin who would finance the care: it seems likely that the strict letter of the law was followed and idiots, once defined, did not inherit or accumulate property, unlike many lunatics. So, in the absence of an available female carer, the magistrates were seeking specifically male relatives in the family network with sufficient resources and close enough in kinship to justify the imposition of a considerable burden. Probably local opinion had already concluded that this was the right policy, and they merely were reaffirming this in court orders.[30]

In other cases the practical care was provided from outside the family entirely. George Bell in 1711 was receiving one shilling a week from the parish for maintaining 'an innocent child of one Richard Thompson deceased', and in 1727 Jacob Grieve was being paid for keeping an 'innocent'. The use of men as guardians has an interesting parallel in their role in assessing and looking after lunatics, where men thought to be mad were often watched over by male relatives or friends. This could be dangerous: one man in 1792, afraid to sleep by himself, murdered one of the two men who joined him at night. With parish care of idiots, the substitute for the family is sometimes not specified, as in 1735 when the 'inhabitants of Wingates' had agreed to receive and maintain Peter Mather. Only one apparently professional carer, a man, with whom an infant had been 'tabled' (that is, boarded at parish expense) some distance from her home, appeared in court in the North East complaining because the promised payments from her family had not been forthcoming – fourteen pounds having been left for her 'diet'. But in one sense these are not exceptions, for in a society where the primary care was familial or communal, the problems only came to the notice of the county officialdom when the private caring system disintegrated, through death or poverty.[31]

The petitions suggest that many parishes resented the orders to pay for this kind of care: about a third were brought to enforce payments previously ordered, suggesting that parish overseers had ignored orders from the previous hearings of the court. Whether local officials were more likely to try and avoid their responsibilities in this kind of case compared with those involving more routine Poor Law candidates, it is impossible to say. On occasion, the courts did not allow any debate about the responsibilities to obstruct the provision of care: in a Durham case, it was ordered that:

> the inhabitants of West Herrington and the Inhabitants of Offerton be summoned to appear at the next sessions to show cause who ought to maintaine Robert Childon an Ideot and in the interim the ideot to be kept by the whole parish.

Eventually the people of Houghton-le-Spring were allocated responsibility, and had to reimburse the other parishes. But this parochial reluctance may have been based on a realistic assessment of the time such care might go on. Some parishes paid for the mentally abnormal year after year. Corbridge, for example, found funds from its special charity for five years for Matthew Rowell after 1714, and Gateshead in 1815 listed Deborah Cloughton among its 'out-poor' (receiving relief outside the workhouse), having commenced receipt thirty-five years earlier in 1780. It is therefore not surprising to find both initial requests for aid and subsequent petitions for increased help resisted or, at least, obstructed, by parish officials who could appeal against the allocation of responsibility to their parish or, more rarely, request removal to another.[32]

These efforts resulted in a situation where, to judge from the quarter sessions cases, the majority of individuals in north-east England were cared for by their families, with or without assistance, but a minority were looked after by the parish in the homes of neighbours. The information in the parish lists is more vague, as the majority of individuals are just listed as recipients of their own relief, 'out of the house', as Matthew Montrose of Berwick was in 1763, but the contexts of care were probably similar. Some were clearly on their own, as John Forster was in 1745, when his parish awarded him one shilling and sixpence a week after the death of his mother.[33] Unlike other parts of the country, the North East does not seem to have adopted institutional care for idiots, in marked contrast to the pattern found for lunatics. This does not mean that institutions did not maintain idiots: at least one was on the lists of ordinary recipients of relief from Newcastle-upon-Tyne's Holy Jesus Hospital at the end of the seventeenth century, but does not seem to have been resident. Elsewhere, in London in particular, there is evidence that in workhouses idiots were sometimes lodged and employed around the house.[34] Also, in other urban areas idiots were maintained in institutions, as for example in Elizabethan Ipswich where two appear in the lists of the inhabitants of Christ's Hospital between 1578 and 1580, together with costs of their clothes and shoes. They were under the charge of the resident 'guider', John Frysell, who was charged with the duty of caring for the aged, the young and the sick, providing 'washinge, nourishinge and other attendance'. Those in this kind of care were clearly distinguished from the 'vagrants and idlers' who had to work in a separate part of the same institution. This kind of provision seems to have been rare at any time, but may have been an occasional resort of hard-pressed officials in the absence of familial alternatives. It was probably impracticable outside well-organised towns. All recent studies agree that the new lunatic asylums of the eighteenth century followed Bethlem in specifically excluding idiots, though this does not mean that they were completely absent. The Norwich Bethel, for example, expelled several inmates because they had become disabled, though presumably only after they had recovered from their lunacy; one of the disablements was described as 'idiotism' or a 'state of idiocy', suggesting a rare diagnosis of an acquired or developmental, rather than an ascribed, deficiency. But nowhere is there any hint of the establishment of 'fool houses' or 'idiot houses', despite occasional half-serious published proposals.[35]

In the framework of the Poor Law, therefore, there was great scope for argument about need and responsibility, and about the balance between private and public provision. The justices had an essential role in enforcing obligations under the Poor Law and, while being dependent on the parish officials and their parishioners, the courts were able to redefine the problem in a way that might conflict with the priorities of the parishes or families. They confined their attentions to the Poor Law problems, responding to requests from carers for 'serious consideration in this their great necessity', as one phrased it. Nowhere is there any sign of a judicial challenge to the definitions of the states of individuals' minds. For example, the panel of justices might appoint one of their number, as the North Riding quarter sessions did in 1655, 'to inquire of the condition of a woman of Helmsley alleadged to be a poor impotent innocent and to give order for her present relief',[36] but there was little debate about her mental disability. This explains why there is little courtroom discussion of the categorisation of people under investigation, since most petitions and reports to the court were made, or vetted, by magistrates who had already made up their minds. Nor does the category of developmental idiocy or lunacy, well established in the textbooks (such as Dalton's above – the condition supposedly arising from injury), have any practical application here: all idiocy cases seem to have been defined either as congenital or, at least, irrevocable. By contrast, justices often regarded physical disabilities with scepticism – too many vagrants had pretended to be 'dumb'. The newspapers reported with great satisfaction the detection of the frauds, when the claimants suddenly rediscovered their powers of speech once they had begun hard labour in the workhouses: there were no hints of this in cases of mental abnormality. It seems that the nature of mental problems was defined by the ordinary people asking for help and was rarely questioned by validating authorities: certainly no parish tried to shirk its responsibilities by debating the nature of the mental disability, questioning only the familial or residential situation of the person in need.[37]

CONCLUSION

The striking feature of early modern discussions, therefore, is that, at the local level at least, little public notice was paid to 'idiots' outside the official structures of the Poor Law and magistrates' courts. No public prurience about idiocy was fostered by the local newspapers, who reported sympathetically on the distressed mental state of suicides or, more dramatically, on wandering madmen, such as a lunatic who in 1749 was rumoured to be living wild in the woods north of Newcastle attracting curious tourists from across the Scottish Border. No one ever seems to have advertised to recover a wandering idiot, as they did for lunatics: one Elizabeth Wilson, aged about 60, had left Wensley, North Yorkshire, seven months earlier and had not been heard of since, reported one Newcastle newspaper seventy miles away. Yet at least one Northumberland idiot was picked up wandering as a 'rogue' (an official term providing probable legal justification for his apprehension) in Durham and incarcerated in the house of correction before being returned home fifteen miles away to his mother and father-in-law (strictly his stepfather – his father in ecclesiastical law).[38] Yet the picture that emerges from the Poor Law evidence is not a simple one of non-institutionalised private care devoid of outside interference, of idiots being unstintingly maintained within their family framework. Such a view was popular much later, when it acquired the sentimental glow of hindsight. William Farr in 1837, for example, supposed that

> In Wales, and remote villages, the idiot lodges in a cottage, and, supported by the parish, is the qualified butt, and of course the favourite, of the neighbourhood: in towns, he would have more difficulty to survive the nursing in a workhouse.

In its portrait of pre-industrial integration, this seems an early version of the sentimentality, also found in Wordsworth's *The Idiot Boy* (and his mother, 'Him whom she loves, her idiot boy'), or Marx's more caustic description of the rural past as 'rustic idiocy'. It also perpetuates a myth that in idiots early modern society found its entertaining fools. Such an image resembles Peter Laslett's 'informal existent dogmatic theory' about the aged, that there was a before and an after in the history of their relationships and social status. In the before, 'ageing was an accepted part of the system of belief, and the aged themselves were both entitled to respect and were usually accorded it'; in the after, 'society tends to proceed as if the aged did not exist, or as if it would be better if they did not exist'.[39]

The elements of an equivalent dogmatic theory of pre-industrial paradise for idiocy could be extracted from their context easily enough: the 'idiot' was a familiar social identity; the person was cared for within an accepted framework of familial or communal obligations, or was left relatively independent within certain bounds; there were no serious misgivings about the costs, personal or financial, of care. Such a view (deliberately exaggerated, admittedly) has its attractions, but misses the key problem of the limitations of our data. The picture that emerges from the cases and the legal framework within which they were handled is that early modern society was clear in its policy towards those it designated 'idiots': they were a familial responsibility, first and foremost, supported or enforced by the local state. As a last resort, substitute families would be found and financed by the parishes or distant relatives; this did not entirely exclude the possibility of institutional care outside the early asylums in places such as workhouses. Such institutions in any case were often modelled on families, to provide the re-training appropriate for the inmates.[40] To later observers this apparently idyllic situation seemed admirable, and may have fed the growth of sentimental nostalgia. But the fact that early modern authorities had both a concept and a welfare strategy to deal with problems of idiocy does not indicate complete social integration. The presence of these court orders enforcing payments suggests that in many instances care and costs were not provided by communities with uninhibited generosity. A bureaucratic device is, therefore, no proof of social acceptance: the family care sanctioned and financed by local authorities might have been an official method of live burial. On the other hand, there is little sign of the wholesale cruel neglect from which nineteenth-century reformers suggested the mentally disabled needed rescuing. Bureaucracy legitimised the family burden by providing the minimum allowed to any poor person, but official compassion hardly ever extended to replacing the family as the primary source of care. In this, the early modern period is not untypical of British welfare traditions: today's carers for the elderly or disabled find that there is little assistance or guidance in doing their family duty, short of their collapse under the burden. Only at that moment is care transferred completely to the state. The family therefore remains, not just at the heart of political sentimental ideology, but at the centre of the state-enforced system of care.[41]

NOTES

1 'Idiot' was perhaps the commonest word used to describe people with learning disabilities in all sources before the nineteenth century, and will be followed here in a non-pejorative sense to refer to those so defined by their contemporaries. We can say little about the reality of their condition, as modern medical or educational theory might define it – there is no acceptable way of 'correcting' history here, to reveal the 'real' problems, as is shown by the unsatisfactory attempt by G. Howells and N.L. Osborn, 'The Incidence of Emotional Disorder in a Seventeenth-Century Medical Practice', *Medical History*, 1970, vol. 14, pp. 19–28.

2 M. Cousins and A. Hussain, *Michel Foucault*, London, 1984, p. 111.

3 Northumberland County Record Office (NCRO) QSB, 34, Midsummer 1771, f.18.

4 D. Thomson, 'The Welfare of the Elderly in the Past: A Family or Community Responsibility?', in M. Pelling and R. M. Smith (eds) *Life, Death and the Elderly: Historical Perspectives*, London, 1991, p. 214.

5 For the traditional history see Sidney and Beatrice Webb, *English Poor Law History*, vol. 1, London, 1963, and E.M. Leonard, *The Early History of English Poor Relief*, Cambridge, 1900. More recent work is that by P. Slack, *Poverty and Policy in Tudor and Stuart England*, London, 1988; W. Newman Brown, 'The Receipt of Poor Relief and Family Situation: Aldenham, Hertfordshire, 1630–90', and T. Wales, 'Poverty, Poor Relief and the Life-Cycle: Some Evidence from Seventeenth-Century Norfolk', both in R.M. Smith (ed.) *Land, Kinship and Life-Cycle*, Cambridge, 1984, pp. 405–22 and pp. 351–404. A critical assessment of historians' myths is D. Thomson, 'Welfare and the Historians', in L. Bonfield, R. M. Smith and K. Wrightson (eds) *The World We Have Gained: Histories of Population and Social Structure*, Oxford, 1986, pp. 355–78. More recent work on the aggregate picture of poverty is by M. Pelling, 'Old Age, Poverty, and Disability in Early Modern Norwich: Work, Remarriage and Other Expedients', in Pelling and Smith, *Life, Death and the Elderly*, pp. 74–101.

6 P. Allderidge, 'Bedlam: Fact or Fantasy?', in W. F. Bynum, R. Porter and M. Shepherd (eds) *The Anatomy of Madness: Essays in the History of Psychiatry*, vol. 2, London, 1985, pp. 17–33; P. Rushton, 'Lunatics and Idiots: Mental Disability, The Community and the Poor Law in North-East England, 1600–1800', *Medical History*, 1988, vol. 32, pp. 34–50; A. Suzuki, 'Lunacy in Seventeenth- and Eighteenth-Century England: Analysis of Quarter Sessions Records', Parts 1 and 2, *History of Psychiatry*, 1991, vol. 2, pp. 437–456, and 1992, vol. 3, pp. 29–44; R. Porter, *Mind-Forg'd Manacles: A History of Madness in England from the Restoration to the Regency*, 1987, London, esp. ch. 3; and Jonathan Andrews in this volume.

7 For the legal framework as it developed with regard to lunacy, see K. Jones, *Lunacy, Law and Conscience, 1744–1845*, London, 1955.

8 J.A. Sharpe, *Early Modern England: A Social History, 1550–1760*, London, 1987, pp. 116–17, and K. Wrightson, 'Two Concepts of Order: Justices, Constables and Jurymen in Seventeenth-Century England', in J. Brewer and J. Styles (eds) *An Ungovernable People: The English and their Law in the Seventeenth and Eighteenth Centuries*, London, 1980, pp. 21–46. Religious attitudes to mental disability have been neglected here, as was kindly pointed out when an earlier version of this chapter was given at the Society for the Social History of Medicine conference in 1992: it remains an area in need of further work.

9 A. Horn, from *The Mirror of Justices*, Selden Society, J. Whittaker (ed.), London, 1895, quoted by D. Pannick, *Judges*, Oxford, 1987, p. 49; N. Walker, *Crime and Insanity in England*, Edinburgh, 1968, vol. 2, pp. 68–9; F. Pollock and F.W. Maitland, *The History of English Law Before the Time of Edward I*, Cambridge, 1968 (originally 1895), vol. 1, p. 481; R. Burn, *The Justice of the Peace and Parish Officer*, 6th edition, London, 1758, vol. 2, p. 224, 'Ideots: see Lunaticks', and pp. 370–2; W. Blackstone, *Commentaries on the Laws of England*, London, 1769, vol. 4, p. 24; *Police and Criminal Evidence Act 1984 (s.66): Codes of Practice*, London, 1991, pp. 37–9, 42, 60.

10 M. MacDonald, *Mystical Bedlam: Madness, Anxiety and Healing in Seventeenth-Century England*, Cambridge, 1981, p. 113; and his 'Popular Beliefs about Mental Disorder in Early Modern England', in W. Eckart and J. Geyer-Kordesch (eds) *Heilberufe und Kranke im 17. und 18. Jahrhundert: die Quellen und*

Forschungssituation, Münster, Münstersche Beiträge zur Geschichte und Theorie der Medizin, 1982, p. 148.

11 See B. Clark, *Mental Disorder in Early Britain: Explanatory Studies*, Cardiff, 1975, p. 58, compared with Dalton below; R.Neugebauer, 'Treatment of the Mentally Ill in Medieval and Early Modern England: a Reappraisal', *Journal of the History of the Behavioural Sciences*, 1978, vol. 14, pp. 161–2.

12 M. Dalton, *The Countrey Justice: containing the Practice of the Justices of the Peace as well as out of their Sessions etc.*, 1666 edition, London, p. 284.

13 H. Swinburne, *A Brief Treatise of Testaments and Last Wills*, London, 1635, originally 1590, pp. 68–9. See Pelling, 'Old Age, Poverty and Disability', in Pelling and Smith, *Life, Death and the Elderly*, p. 74.

14 Blackstone, *Commentaries*, vol. 4, p. 25; vol. 1, pp. 292–3.

15 Swinburne, *Brief Treatise on Testaments*, p. 90; A. Fessler, 'The Management of Lunacy in Seventeenth-Century England. An Investigation of Quarter-Sessions Records', *Proceedings of the Royal Society of Medicine*, 1956, vol. 49, pp. 904–5.

16 J. Locke, *An Essay Concerning Human Understanding*, edited by P. Nidditch, Oxford, 1975, p. 160.

17 K. Thomas, *Man and the Natural World: Changing Attitudes in England, 1500–1800*, Harmondsworth, p. 44; P. Rushton, 'Lunatics and Idiots', p. 44, case from Houghton-le-Spring, County Durham; NCRO, QSB 53, Midsummer 1720, f.57.

18 J. Skinner, *Journal of a Somerset Rector, 1803–34*, edited by Howard and Peter Coombs, Oxford, 1984, p. 125.

19 See Jonathan Andrews' reference to a 'lascivious she-fool' who had to be locked up to avoid her becoming pregnant; for a contrary view, J. Cowell, *A Law Dictionary, or the Interpreter of Words and Terms Used Either in the Common or Statute Laws of Great Britain* ..., London, 1727 (originally 1607), unpaginated, under alphabetical entry for 'ideot'.

20 Walker, *Crime and Insanity*, p. 36, and pp. 26–7, quoting A. Fitzherbert, 1524; Neugebauer, 'Treatment of the Mentally Ill', p. 161; Swinburne, *Brief Treatise of Testaments*, p. 68. For currency, see J. Richardson, *The Local Historian's Encyclopaedia*, New Barnet, 1974, pp. 218–21.

21 Blackstone, *Commentaries*, vol. 3, p. 333 and vol. 4, pp. 24–5; R. Porter, *Mind-Forg'd Manacles*, pp. 112–13, 122–4; Walker, *Crime and Insanity*, pp. 36–7 for Roberts; R. Neugebauer, 'Mental Illness and Government Policy in Sixteenth- and Seventeenth-Century England', unpublished PhD, Columbia University, 1976, p. 292; MacDonald, 'Popular Beliefs about Mental Disorder', p. 148; P. Rushton, 'The Poor Law, the Parish and the Community in North-East England', *Northern History*, vol. 25, for doctors and parishes, p. 146.

22 D.H. Allen, *Essex Quarter Sessions Order Book, 1652–1661*, Colchester, Essex County Council Records Office Publication no. 65, 1974, p. xxvi.

23 The statistics are thirty-three actual or probable cases of idiocy, 1665–1800, in a population approaching 300,000; there seems to have been terrible under-recording, with only one case from Newcastle.

24 A. Suzuki, 'Lunacy in Seventeenth- and Eighteenth-Century England', pt.1, 1991, pp. 442–4; J. Webb, *Poor Relief in Elizabethan Ipswich*, Ipswich, Suffolk Record Society, vol. 9, 1966, p. 138, an innocent 'wants' an

eighteen pence allowance; see Salisbury evidence, P. Slack, *Poverty in Early-Stuart Salisbury*, Devizes, Wiltshire Record Society, vol. 31, 1975, p. 78; for Norwich, see J.F. Pound, *The Norwich Census of the Poor 1570*, Norwich, Norfolk Record Society, vol. 40, 1971, and Pelling, 'Old Age, Poverty and Disability'; Ralph Bell, 1699, NCRO, QSB, 11, Easter 1699, f.53.

25 NCRO, QSB, 17, Midsummer 1702, f.17.

26 See Jonathan Andrews' study in this volume: Londoners used the word 'idiot' more freely. Was this a sign of their greater acceptance of legal categories?

27 Ann Tindall, NCRO, QSB, 59, Midsummer 1723, f.48; QSB, 9, Easter 1697, f.15.

28 The figures are nine parents, two brothers or brothers-in-law, one wife, one probable friend, and one 'tabler' (that is, person who is paid for giving board and lodging).

29 NCRO, QSB, 27, Christmas 1707, f.10, Mauther; QSO, 6, p. 146, George Potts, 1721; QSB, 53, Midsummer 1720, f.57, Batey 1720; EP. 151/1, pp. 42–3, 45–6, 50 and 65, Hedley, parish of Hartburn 1713; QSB, 9, Easter 1697, f.15, QSB, 10, Easter 1698, QSB, 12, Michaelmas 1699, f.28, Twizell.

30 *Quarter Sessions Records*, North Riding Record Society, edited by J.C. Atkinson (NRQS), vol. 6, 1888, pp. 195 and 235, 1673 and 1675: the two brothers had to pay twenty and fifteen shillings, while the probable brother-in-law (Robert Clarke) only five; vol. 7, 1889, p. 2, a son-in-law successfully overthrew an order, 1677; D. Thomson, '"I am not my father's keeper"', note 5 above, p. 269; Allen, *Essex Quarter Sessions*, pp. 151, 155, 167, 174.

31 NCRO, QSO, 5, pp. 72 and 75, Bell; EP./10, unpaginated, annual list 1727, Grieve; Mark Selby, deemed lunatic by the assizes, 1792, Public Records Office (PRO), ASSI 45/37/3/193, and see much earlier example of a friend coming to share a bed with one thought mad, in Rushton, 'Lunatics and Idiots', p. 38, n.15; QSO, 7, p. 255, Mather; CDCRO, Q/S/OB, 3 and 5, p. 249, Jane Carlson.

32 CDCRO, Q/S/OB, 7, pp. 525 and 533, 1678; NCRO, EP. 57/25 unpaginated, Easter accounts of John Cooke's charity, 1714–19; *Account of the Out-poor of the Parish of Gateshead, Taken in March 1815 ...*, printed J. Akenhead, Newcastle. The petitions were: fourteen requests for maintenance or increases; six for enforcement of pre-existing orders; one appeal against a court order; and only one removal request.

33 Care when specified was provided as follows: fifteen by the family, four by the parish, one shared between family and parish; NCRO, EP. 38/57, unpaginated 17 February 1763, Montrose; QSO, 8, p. 140, John Forster.

34 Samuel Starth, 1698, Tyne and Wear Archives Service, 595/49, f.7; in general on this issue, see Rushton, 'Lunatics and Idiots'; Andrews in this volume and A. Suzuki, 'Lunacy in Seventeenth- and Eighteenth-Century England', pt.2, pp. 43–4, in particular the latter's key argument that the relative employability of idiots among others, when contrasted with the intractability of the mad, led to lunatics being the major problem for segregated control in the second half of the eighteenth century. At least one lunatic, when threatened with the house of correction, was confident that he could do the task required, of beating sand, but may have killed himself because of the threat, PRO ASSI 44/115 pt.3, lunacy and post-mortem inquisitions for Northumberland, 1800.

35 Webb, *Poor Relief in Elizabethan Ipswich*, pp. 15–16, 52, 53, 58; M. Winston, 'The Bethel at Norwich: an Eighteenth-Century Hospital for Lunatics', *Medical History*, vol. 38, 1994, p. 48; K. Doerner, *Madmen and the Bourgeoisie: A Social History of Insanity and Psychiatry*, translated by J. Neugroschel and J. Steinberg, Oxford, p. 31; Porter, *Mind-Forg'd Manacles*, p. 121. Whether the Continental private system of incarceration at a family's request also included people with learning disabilities is unclear, though P. Spierenberg suggests the possibility in his discussion of *beterhuizen* in *The Prison Experience. Disciplinary Institutions and their Inmates in Early Modern Europe*, New Brunswick, 1990, p. 226–7.

36 NRQS, vol. 5, 1887, p. 178.

37 See Rushton, 'The Poor Law, the Parish and the Community'; NCRO, QSB, 59, Midsummer 1723, f.48; NRQS, vol. 5, 1887, p. 178; *Newcastle Journal*, no. 677, 28 March 1752.

38 *Newcastle Journal*, no. 541, 19 August 1749; *Newcastle Courant*, no. 107, 13 August 1727; William Turner, 1770, County Durham County Record Office (CDCRO), Q/S/OB, 13, p. 305.

39 Quoted in M. Donnelly, *Managing the Mind: A Study of Medical Psychology in Early Nineteenth-Century Britain*, 1983, London, p. 89; S. Gill (ed.) *William Wordsworth*, Oxford, 1984, pp. 67–80; W. Willeford, *The Fool and his Sceptre: A Study in Clowns and Jesters and their Audience*, London, 1969, p. 133; P. Laslett, 'Societal Development and Aging', in R.H. Binstock and E. Shanas (eds) *A Handbook of Aging and the Social Sciences*, New York, 1976, pp. 89–90.

40 See P. Spierenberg, *The Prison Experience*, ch. 6.

41 C. Ungerson, *Policy is Personal: Sex, Gender and Informal Care*, London, 1987 and J. Lewis and B. Meredith, *Daughters who Care: Daughters Caring for Mothers at Home*, London, 1980.

4

IDENTIFYING AND PROVIDING FOR THE MENTALLY DISABLED IN EARLY MODERN LONDON

Jonathan Andrews

INTRODUCTION

Historians have often emphasised how the mentally ill and disabled[1] must have been a familiar sight in early modern society. Rarely placed under constraints or confined in institutions, the insane and idiotic tended to be maintained in their domiciles, or roamed the highways and byways as vagabonds. Typically, referring to the freedom to be abroad of the 'village idiot' and 'Tom o' Bedlam',[2] or to the importance of the 'fool' in the social and cultural landscape of early modern times,[3] historians have, however, tended to differ as to the meaning and extent of this apparent spatial legitimacy. Did this represent a genuine tolerance extended to the mentally disabled, or was it instead symptomatic of the insignificance and neglect of mental disability as a problem? Furthermore, to what extent were the considerable freedoms and tolerance of former times being gradually eroded during this period? How far were new, or more emphatic, demarcations of deviance placing the mentally disabled – either epistemologically or ontologically – behind bars?[4]

One fundamental problem in addressing such questions has been that the enigma of 'idiocy' has tended to be left out, or removed to the margins, of the analysis. Too often it has been treated as a social and medical issue virtually synonymous with that of lunacy, or dealt with as a subordinate corollary to madness, rather than as a subject in itself.[5] Historians are only just beginning to enquire more deeply as to how far the mentally disabled shared in these putative historical developments. Recently, for example, some historians have seriously questioned the authenticity of the 'village idiot', arguing that this characterisation says more about the stigmatising by the educated, urban élite of the ill-educated and gauche country bumpkin, than it does about the experiential realities of the mentally disabled.[6] Indeed, as the ensuing study will indicate, idiots appear no less conspicuously in the records of early modern metropolitan parishes than in those of rural parishes. On the other hand, the relative freedom enjoyed by the idiotic, or at least the rarity of evidence that they were being placed under restraint, is a striking feature of early modern parish records and a significant contrast to the types of treatment meted out to the insane.

We still know very little about the lives of the mentally disabled and the nature of provision for them in this period, particularly within their local and domiciliary settings. This is partly owing to the fact that scholarship has remained so preoccupied with the literary figure of the 'fool' and the cultural meanings of 'folly', tending to eschew hard analysis of the social problems of the mentally disabled. This chapter will be devoted to redressing these deficiencies in one important respect, that of parochial provision for the pauper mentally disabled. In doing so, I hope it will not underestimate the manifold problems in treating mental disability as a subject separate from that of mental illness in this period, when contemporaries themselves were often so ambiguous in distinguishing one category from the other. My intention is not to advocate even the feasibility, let alone the need, of divorcing an analysis of idiocy from lunacy. My concern is rather to shift the focus of the analysis.

This survey will concentrate pre-eminently on the records of London parishes, and in particular those of: Allhallows the Great, during the periods 1650–90 and 1710–50; St Botolph without Aldersgate, during 1726–40; St Botolph Bishopsgate, during 1625–1721; St Brides during 1634–1755; St Stephen Coleman Street, during 1663–1785; St Dionis Backchurch, during 1639–1769; St Dunstan in the West, during 1700–23; and St Sepulchres Holborn, London, during 1648–86. I will not be greatly concerned with regional variations between parishes, for, given the paucity of existing research, general conclusions on such matters would be premature. Beginning with the question of contemporary definitions, I shall argue for the meaningfulness and coherence in practice of early modern distinctions between types of mental disablement and mental illness – in particular, in so far as the former was recognised as a condition beginning at, or soon after, infancy. I shall proceed to discuss the numbers of mentally disabled being relieved, and the range of provisions and expedients available for, and arrived at in, the care of idiots. This section will suggest just how scanty, if not exceptional, relief was for the mentally disabled, but will emphasise the difficulty of estimating the real proportions being relieved in this period. While examples of long-term parochial aid will be given, overall this chapter will stress how transient were the forms of such provision, often comprising arrangements, for example, to see mentally disabled children through infancy. Some of the rationales underlying decision-making as to appropriate types of relief, as well as to the recipients of relief, will then be explored. This section will look in particular at the precipitators behind idiots falling upon the care of the parish, and at what factors influenced one type of provision over another. I shall also examine the demographic and family profiles of recipients, and emphasise the importance of influences such as the age, household structure, employment, and life-cycle crisis points of mentally disabled individuals and their families, which propelled them to seek aid and provoked the authorities to intervene. Finally, I shall investigate the profiles of those who cared for the mentally disabled, underlining the importance, as well as the rather exigency-led nature of the network of care available through parish nursing. It shall be argued that most of these nurses were temporary operators, and took in a wide range of sick and disabled poor.

Sadly, the early modern idiot is an elusive subject of enquiry. Only in a minority of cases are idiots found within early modern institutions catering for the mentally affected, which tended to exclude them from admission. Idiots are also less conspicuous in parochial records, which were apt to say much more about the characteristically more dangerous and florid cases of lunatics with their heavier implications for domestic management, medical treatment, public order and the parish coffers. There is no escaping the fact that contemporaries spent more time, more money and more energy on providing for and writing about those deemed to be lunatics than on the merely idiotic. While this disparity is a clear reflection of the disproportionate place the two states were accorded as a public concern, it makes the job of the historian of idiocy commensurably more difficult. Furthermore, the historian's problems are multiform when it comes to actually identifying the mentally disabled amongst the ranks of all those described as having some sort of mental defect or affliction.[7]

DEFINING MENTAL DISABILITY

The starting-point when addressing the problem of idiocy, as indeed it was for contemporaries too, must be this very question as to how individuals were identified as idiots and what criteria were utilised for this end. Historians like Foucault and Doerner stressed the fluidity of early modern definitions, arguing that the failure to distinguish the insane and the mentally disabled from each other and from other categories of deviance partly explains the failure to provide separate, specialist institutions for them.[8] Vice versa, recognising the need for, and drawing up, clearer demarcations of deviance has been pointed to as one explanation for the opposite trend, of establishing increasingly exclusive, purpose-built carceral provision. There is much evidence to support this thesis. Recently, however, other historians, better versed in the more mundane records of local medical men, officials and families, have on the contrary drawn attention to the meaningfulness of contemporary language about mental disability in its own context, and the coherence of the distinctions made between various groups amongst the disorderly poor.[9]

My own studies of parochial, institutional and juridical records would tend to lend support to the latter position. Parish records are notable for the precision, rather than the vagueness, with which individuals are referred to as mentally disabled. Descriptions of parishioners as 'idiots' or 'fools' tended to carry a specific meaning, distinguishing their behaviour and appearance from the more serious matter of insanity. Terms such as 'idiot', 'stupid', 'innocent', 'natural', are commonly employed in parish records as distinct from terms such as 'mad', 'lunatic', 'distracted', 'crazie/ey'. Rarely, at least after the mid-seventeenth century, are they merged or interchanged once applied to individual cases, with an 'idiot' parishioner later being referred to by a churchwarden as a 'lunatic'. This must surely suggest some degree of consistency in ascriptions of mental disability by local officials, and by the families and fellow parishioners of the disabled. In general, terms seem to be applied much more definitively in parish records than in literary accounts of the 'witless'. As the period wears on, some more ambiguous terms disappear almost altogether from the language of vestry minutes and churchwardens' and overseers' accounts.

'Innocent' is especially interesting in this connection. Late sixteenth- and early seventeenth-century literature often spoke of the 'brain-sicke bedlam and … innocent' as one and the same.[10] More commonly and increasingly, as time went on, however, it was the fool, or the idiot, who was accorded the stamp of 'innocence', rather than the insane.[11] Parish records seem to have employed the term 'innocent' even more specifically, to identify a mentally disabled child, or someone mentally disabled since birth. But this term vanishes almost completely from metropolitan parochial accounts from the end of the seventeenth century. These trends probably have less to do with any initial appropriation, or subsequent loss, of 'innocence' on behalf of the mentally disabled, than with changing ideas about folly in general and madness in particular, and the virulence of Augustan stigmatising of unreason.[12] The increasing preference for more distinct terms like 'idiot' and 'lunatic' to more metaphorical terms like 'innocent' in parish records may also reflect a generalised trend towards greater uniformity and formalism in administrative documents, and the impact of new standards of literacy and education amongst metropolitan parish officers.

In literary texts throughout the early modern period idiots were often bracketed together with lunatics under the indiscriminate umbrella of folly, or witlessness.[13] The popularity in literature of equivocal terms like 'wit', however, was not extended to the language of officialdom. Indeed, less was to be gained in administrative documents by retaining such ambiguities. The meaning of parochial, legal and governmental records often depended on distinguishing between types of the deserving poor. Richard Neugebauer's examination of the problems of guardianship, and the Court of Wards' dealings with the mentally disabled, has demonstrated how important were legal distinctions between the insane and the idiotic.[14] In the pragmatic terms of local and familial economy too, it made sense to differentiate in some degree between the lunatic and the idiotic.

This is not to assert that the distinctions between the mentally ill and the mentally disabled were tight, or uniformly upheld, even on the legal, institutional and local administrative levels. The mad were not identified according to vagrancy laws as a separate group from the general mass of rootless and masterless poor before the passing of the 1714 Act. Even then, they were not distinguished from idiots. Furthermore, there is only limited evidence that early modern institutions attempted to maintain internal segregation between the mad and the idiotic. Contemporaries clearly distinguished even less between different types of stupidity. It might be argued that medical, legal and philosophical definitions of lunacy and idiocy allowed ample grounds for confusion. Contemporary scrutiny of the mentally abnormal often focused on rather restricted questions of defective faculties or cognition, and, to a lesser degree, on physical symptoms, which could be shared by the mentally ill and the mentally disabled alike. Examinations of idiots characteristically tested subjects' basic arithmetical aptitude, their ability to remember the most elementary aspects of identity, and their powers to reason from simple first principles.[15] Indeed, the available criteria developed little over the course of the period to assist contemporaries in distinguishing one condition from the other.

Yet, there were a number of relatively coherent and precise formulations that seem to have held emphatic sway during this period. Perhaps the most fundamental and workable was the distinction between those disabled since birth, or early childhood (i.e. 'idiots'), and those whose faculties had been lost or impaired subsequently (i.e. 'lunatics'). This was a conception of mental disability that retained currency in legal and medical texts throughout the period,[16] and that is clearly reflected on the parochial level by the frequency with which idiots and fools were identified in parish accounts when young children. Apart from this 'pure'[17] conception of idiocy, idiots might also be recognised by the permanency of their mental defects, the lack of any lucid intervals, as well as by their odd physical appearance, especially the size of their heads, deformities, or enlargement in their features, and vacuousness in their expressions.[18] Most contemporaries also recognised an 'acquired' type of stupidity, embracing individuals 'that by … accident', or 'disease', 'wholly' lose their 'memory and understanding'.[19] It was a well-established orthodoxy of contemporary medical treatises, that lunacy often degenerated into a form of 'idiocy', or 'fatuity' – particularly if long established and indulged, or else neglected or abused by medicine.[20]

Early modern writers made little distinction between idiocy and chronically progressed conditions of mental enfeeblement. Identification of a number of elderly parishioners as 'foolish', or 'idiotic', in metropolitan parish records also suggests the importance of this conflation. In 1662, for example, St Brides paid for the committal of one James Pratt to Bethlem, at that time and subsequent to his discharge referring to him as a 'Madman', or as 'distracted'. The last time his actual condition was specified, however, in 1667 (once Pratt was removed to the country), he was referred to as an 'Ideott'.[21] Cases like Pratt's, where an ascription of lunacy gave way to one of idiocy, were highly comprehensible according to such models of acquired mental disablement. The proximity between perceptions of senile mental disorders and idiocy is further evidenced by the tendency of both states to be compared with that of the child. For example, the elderly Elizabeth Eccles of St Botolph Bishopsgate, was referred to in parish accounts as 'childish', or 'very aged allmost Childish', or 'very aged and helpless'.[22] As in Eccles' case, it seems to have been the weak, vulnerable, dependent state of some elderly and mentally-disabled parishioners that manifested their kinship with children to contemporaries.

Other cases, nevertheless, seem only to be comprehensible in the context of equivocal terminology. For example, Mary or Ann Low/Lole of Bishopsgate was described and relieved initially, during 1699–1706, as 'Lunatissime' and 'Crasie', but once was described as 'fooleish' and seems to have been in the prime of life, being married, with a small child.[23] Clearly, in parish records as in common parlance, 'foolish' had a more ambivalent meaning than the term 'idiot'. While widely employed as a synonym for idiocy,[24] 'foolish' was often employed quite loosely to denote a weakness of intellect, less serious than that of idiocy, or to identify some ridiculous or unreasonable aspect of an individual's behaviour. The influential seventeenth-century physician, Thomas Willis, defined 'foolishness' as emphatically a stage above the more abject mental defect of the idiot. Parochial officials, on the other hand, while evidently using the term more casually than that of 'idiot', more often used both terms interchangeably. Significantly, furthermore, they seem to have used 'foolish' with a degree of gender bias, characterising the intellectual frailties of female parishioners thus more often than those of males.

'Distracted' and 'Lunatike', on the other hand, were terms which seem generally to have been confined by metropolitan parishes to serious cases of mental disturbance, and not infrequently to those cases committed to madhouses. Yet they were terms which were occasionally applied to young children too, possibly suggesting some sort of congenital mental defect (although autism and behavioural problems cannot be discounted). In 1674–5, for example, the Bishopsgate churchwarden recorded a payment of 4s 'to Roberts that dyed in Bedlam [i.e. the residential district surrounding the hospital] leaveing behind him 3 children in want one being distracted'.[25] In the case of another young child, Mary (Magdalen) Browne, relieved by the same parish during 1683–7, who was spoken of variously, as 'a kind of A naturall and sicke', 'allmost A naturall', 'A Lunaticke' and 'Lunaticke sicke', there was clearly an element of doubt in the terminology adopted, although she was most often referred to as 'A naturall'.[26] Very occasionally, the term 'changeling' was applied in parish accounts to mentally disabled children.[27] This term could be synonymous with that of 'idiot', but could also be used to describe the lunatic and the physically disabled.[28] More importantly, it tended to be reserved for children whose abnormal physical or mental characteristics appeared to contradict natural law, and bore little or no resemblance to the characteristics of their parents or relations.[29]

Despite the evident existence and operation of significant criteria distinguishing certain 'idiotic' and 'foolish' types of mental abnormality from other 'lunatic' types, the fact remains that parish records tell us very little about how the distinctions rooted in such terminology were arrived at. More might be hoped for, as Fessler, Rushton and Suzuki have demonstrated,[30] by combining the study of parochial records with an examination of the records of quarter sessions and other courts. Unfortunately, out of twenty-nine lunatic or mentally disabled cases located so far in London Sessions records spread unevenly over the period 1662–1704, the case of Sarah Howard discussed below represents the only 'idiot' to be found.

As Fessler and others have shown, it was common when doubt or argument arose as to the issue of responsibility for the mentally ill or disabled that cases tended to enter the province of Courts of Sessions. Typically, as in Sarah Howard's case, brought before the London Sessions in 1674, witnesses were summoned to establish not only that mentally disabled individuals had no family or friends able (or willing) to provide, but also that they could not sustain, or contribute to, their own maintenance. Sarah was described as 'an Ideott ... soe sottish and void of reason that shee is not able to gett her liveing'.[31] Indeed, this case would tend to support Fessler's evidence that, on the ground level, when decisions needed to be made as to how a mentally disabled individual was to be supported, more pragmatic considerations as to the severity of the disablement were often called into play – considerations such as the individual's ability to work and amenability to being managed within the domestic context.

The overwhelming significance of such purely economic considerations when it came to determining appropriate provision for the mentally disabled, must itself have mitigated the need to distinguish between types of disablement – except in terms of degree, or troublesomeness. On the other hand, the long-term implications for care associated with chronic conditions like mental disability, as against the prospects of remission entertained in cases of lunacy, made distinctions more important. Indeed, these realities must sometimes have rendered the type of burden envisaged and actually experienced by those responsible for idiots a much more onerous and worrying undertaking.

NUMBERS OF IDIOTS AND EXTENT OF PAROCHIAL RELIEF

More often than not the mentally disabled are conspicuous by their absence from London's parish records. Some Poor Law accounts

I have examined do not mention the mentally disabled at all, while others mention only one or two such individuals. For example, all of the seventeen mentally affected parishioners recorded as in receipt of relief in the parish records of Allhallows the Great during 1650–90 and 1710–50, were referred to as 'mad', 'distracted', 'disordere'd in Senses', 'out of their Senses', or 'Lunatick', or else were sent to Bethlem and other madhouses. Similarly, no mentally disabled individuals are identifiable amongst the fifteen 'distracted', 'mad' and 'Lunatick' cases found in the accounts of St Dunstan in the West during 1700–23, while those of St Brides mention only one 'ideott' and one 'Naturall' amongst seventy-three mentally ill or disabled individuals identified during 1634–1755.

It would be unwise, however, to assume, merely on the basis that no, or little, mention is made of 'idiots', that none, or few, were in receipt of poor relief, let alone that none, or few, were resident in a particular parish. Nor, on this basis alone, given the often summary and unrevealing nature of parochial accounts, and the difficulties in identifying the mentally disabled, is it safe simply to presume that provision for this group of the poor was not an important or recognised part of the responsibilities of parochial authorities. As one example of the problems involved: the 'fool' Harry/Henry Southern of Coleman Street is referred to at some length in churchwardens' accounts, but his actual mental state is only identifiable from a single mention of his case in vestry minutes. It is unlikely that any metropolitan parish was completely free of mental disability during this period, or that parish officers distinguished with the same degree of consistency between the mad and the idiotic. It may appear rather futile, then, to hazard any assessment of the numbers, or proportion, of poor mentally disabled parishioners in the metropolitan localities on the basis of parish records – or even to attempt to focus on provision for one group of the mentally affected at all.

The fact that many parochial officials were evidently making some sort of distinction, however, argues otherwise. Furthermore, for a few parishes, like St Botolph Bishopsgate, there is evidence of provision for a substantial number of 'idiots' and 'fools', while, even in those parishes where only an isolated case was mentioned, considerable attention was sometimes accorded it by officials. At least nine Bishopsgate parishioners were described as either 'fooleish' or 'a naturall' during 1625–1721. The existence of such cases, alongside the elliptical nature of parish records and the general tendency towards invisibility of the mentally disabled, warn us that the extent of parochial relief for such individuals was not quite so inadequate as might appear at first glance.

Nevertheless, in many of the same parishes where there is no explicit trace of idiots and fools, the relief of sick, or lunatic parishioners, or of parish children, was spoken of quite explicitly. Even admitting the limitations of the records, there seems scant evidence to challenge the general impression that relief of the poor mentally disabled was extremely scanty. The mentally disabled were and remained the Cinderellas of the deserving poor. Even parish records that do detail provision for idiots more fully suggest that the condition was not regarded as so burdensome and troublesome, financially and socially, to the responsible parties, by comparison with other afflictions. In the majority of cases, and in a notably larger proportion than others identified as 'lunatic', the family was relied upon to provide.

TYPES OF RELIEF AVAILABLE: NURSING AND MATERIAL RELIEF IN THE PARISH

Generally, idiots and fools were lodged in their domiciles with relatives and, as such, remain largely invisible within parish records. Elizabethan Poor Law stipulated that it was the kin who should pay for the poor if able, and idiots were no different in this respect. Likewise, if families without financial means had property which might be sold, leased or mortgaged, to help support a disabled member, the parish was entitled to take steps to enable such action. Thus, after the death of a mentally disabled parishioner's parents, the parish commonly went about selling off their property and goods, in order to defray burial costs and some of the burden of their own, and their family's, care. For example, St Stephen Coleman Street received a sum of £4 by way of the recently deceased 'Mr [Richard] Southern for Goods' in 1719, having taken over the care of his 'foolish' son Harry.[32]

Occasionally, owing to widowhood, hardship, old age, infirmity or sickness, parishioners might receive alms, or a pension, from the parish to help them support a mentally disabled individual. The 'foolish' Martha Stock enters the churchwardens' accounts of St Botolph Bishopsgate when, in 1701, her solitary mother, Alice, begins to receive 6d a fortnight and is described as 'Aged lame & hath A foolish Girle'.[33] Likewise, the young (mentally disabled?) child of Jean/Joan Chees, relieved during 1694–5 as 'A kind of A Lunaticke', enters the same parish's accounts when his 'very poor', widowed mother begins to be paid between 6d and 1s per week.[34] Sometimes, also, the mentally disabled themselves were paid alms or pensions directly, and/or had their rents met by the parish, suggesting some sort of ability to support themselves. The 'foleish' Elizabeth Ratcliffe, passed to Bishopsgate in 1691, 'sicke', unemployed and with three small children, for example, was directly relieved for the next seven years or more by the parish, with occasional payments gradually replaced by a regular pension and payment of her rent.[35] Latterly, Ratcliffe's relief became an occasional item again. The extent of the parish's preparedness to pay pensions and rents for such individuals is difficult to chart, as records were often only irregularly kept. In the case of the 'foelish' Elizabeth Bright of Bishopsgate, her nursing was 'put upon the Penssion Booke' in 1697, and, in the absence of this record, one can only assume that the parish continued to pay as before until her death three years later. Larger-scale and long-term relief for the mentally disabled, including incarceration, was quite a singular phenomenon, unless no family member was forthcoming, or individuals proved especially difficult to manage in a domestic setting.

Apart from occasional alms, or regular pensions, parochial aid for idiots and fools might also take the form of financing nursing and lodging within, or without, the family domicile, either with parish nurses, with landlords and landladies, or some other parishioner. This was the standard form in which parochial relief of the mentally disabled outside of their domiciles was dispensed. It could be provided either short or long term, either inside or outside of the parish. The 'foelish' Mary Browne of St Botolph Bishopsgate was nursed for at least two years in the 1680s, while Dorcas Popkins, 'a Natural' of the same parish, was nursed for a few weeks during 1702.[36] Anne Tweedle, a St Sepulchres' 'ideot', was nursed for a period of about twenty weeks in 1660–61.[37] Often, as apparently in these cases, nursing was provided as a temporary arrangement to help mentally disabled children through their infancy, until some means could be found of getting them removed from the parish charge. In other cases, nursing was more long term. St Sepulchres seem to have paid for 'keeping' the 'innocent', Thomas Walker, for a period of about five years during 1649–53. Over the next twelve years, only one very small payment for 'keeping' was recorded, although substantial amounts were expended intermittently for his clothing.[38] The 'foleish' Elizabeth Bright was nursed at Bishopsgate's charge for over six years until her death in 1700.[39]

That terms such as 'keeping' and 'lodging' were employed as frequently as terms like 'nursing' and 'attendance' to describe the care of mentally disabled persons may reflect a genuine recognition of difference between a basic form of providing accommodation and meeting needs, and a more caring, experienced role. Those referred to as 'nurses', or as 'nursing', were often individuals from within the locale called on quite regularly by the parish to care for the sick and distressed poor. The use of such terminology also seems to have carried a loose gender distinction, in that female parishioners tended more often to be referred to as 'nurses', and male parishioners as providing 'keeping' or 'lodging'. Sometimes, however, such terms were applied to both sexes and, in practice, there may often have been little distinguishing the type of attendance provided by one from the other. Some parishes even employed hybrid terms like 'nursekeeper'. The persistent use of terms like 'keeping' was also some reflection of the pragmatic, containment concerns of parochial provision. While clearly less of an issue when it came to the mentally disabled, literary accounts of vulnerable, lascivious she-fools, needing to be locked away to prevent them being 'pepper'd', imply the existence of genuine concern about containment.[40] Notably, parochial records rarely record nurses and others being paid to house 'idiots' concurrently with parishioners of the opposite sex. Institutions, too, attempted to maintain segregation between the sexes.

Payments for nursing the mentally disabled generally also embraced feeding and cleaning, although less basic necessities, such as 'shaving' or 'snuff', might be itemised as additional luxuries. The rarity as much as the itemising of such provision in parish accounts reflect the rudimentary level at which relief was being furnished. Often, however, parish records are simply not detailed enough to make precise conclusions about what was, or was not, being provided, or for how long. The 'shaving' of Harry Southern while being nursed was mentioned only twice in the accounts of St Stephen Coleman Street during 1719–31, but this does not mean that he was not being shaved at other times. In the event of the death of a poor mentally disabled parishioner, the parish might also pay for the burial and funeral.

Often payments included, or took the exclusive form of, clothing allowances. Clothing might not merely protect poor parishioners from inclement weather and sickness.[41] Clothing was also an important symbol of dignity and humanity for the pauper. The shirt on a pauper's back could also be a last, desperate source of income at the pawn shop. Contrariwise, dishevelment, dirt and nakedness appear to be germane to prevailing perceptions of the poor mentally affected in this period. Parish records reveal that lunatics and idiots were not infrequently 'naked' (a term often connoting poorly clothed, rather than stark naked) at the time clothes were actually provided by the parish.[42] Yet, these records also emphasise that this was not a circumstance peculiar to the insane and the idiotic. The sick and vagrant poor, too, sometimes appeared in the same condition, even as late as the 1740s.[43]

Obtaining any exact calculation as to the extent of parochial clothing allowances to the mentally disabled is rendered virtually impossible by the fact that it was frequently unspecified, recorded in lump sums to a group of parishioners, or obscured for other reasons. Clearly, nevertheless, clothing provision was very basic in this period. Bishopsgate appears to have spent no more than 13s on clothing Mary Browne during 1683–7, including two frocks and some linen, while another four payments totalling 10s 1d were made on behalf of Elizabeth Bright during 1695–6 for 'two Sheifts' and three pairs 'of Stockings'.[44] Clothing allowances for the mentally disabled may seem rather more meagre than they actually were, however. Clothing was less expensive and perhaps less necessary for very young children. Furthermore, in some individual cases parochial provision was plainly more generous. During 1719–31, the Coleman Street 'fool', Harry Southern, received at least 3 strong coats, 6 waistcoats, 14 shirts, 10 aprons, 10 pairs of breeches (or drawers), 15 pairs of stockings, and had his shoes replaced or repaired at least eighteen times, with additional sums spent for unspecified 'goods', 'provision' and 'clothing'.[45] Out of a total of over £32 expended during 1649–65 on the 'innocent', Thomas Walker, St Sepulchres, Holborn, spent over £5 simply on clothing him. The vestry explicitly instructed the churchwarden at times to 'take care to provide Cloathes for Walker the Innocent'.[46]

On the whole, nevertheless, Poor Law accounts suggest an extremely rudimentary form of care being offered to the mentally disabled at this time. The sums of relief involved tended to be very small, and markedly smaller than those afforded to parishioners deemed to be mad. In total, St Botolph Bishopsgate appears to have spent no more than £1 10d during 1687 on parishioners and 'strangers' (i.e. individuals from outside of the parish) described as 'naturals', 'idiots' or 'fools'. During the same year, on parishioners deemed to be 'mad' etc. (six of whom were in Bethlem), it spent more than sixty times this amount.[47]

Often a mentally disabled child was relieved as just one of a number of children in a poor, distressed family. The aforementioned 'naturall', Mary Browne of Bishopsgate, seems to have been the youngest of as many as five children named Browne orphaned and falling to the parish's responsibility during the 1680s. After apprenticing two of the Brownes, in 1688, the Bishopsgate churchwardens paid to 'take' all three remaining Brownes, including Mary, 'of[f] the p[ar]ish Charge', paying £5 to a Henry Harris for Mary and George Browne, and another £5 to a John Bussby for Prudence.[48] Judging by the sums agreed and the fact that Bussby also paid 1s 6d 'for A bond to put forth Prudence Browne', these agreements may only have entailed Prudence's apprenticeship. Most formal apprenticeship terms did not begin until the age of 14.[49] As the work of Pelling and others on early modern child care have stressed, however, informal apprenticeships were regularly arranged between poor families, parishes and employers, throughout the early modern period.[50] As a weaver, Harris probably intended informally to bring the children up in the trade. Pelling has underlined how 'useful and even essential' was the work of young children 'for the survival of the household'.[51] Mentally disabled children were, on the whole, however, a rather inevitable exception to this rule. Indeed (unless one counts Browne's case), I have come across no explicit reference to the apprenticeship of simple-minded parishioners in parish records. Nevertheless, Browne's is one of many cases highlighting the problems in using parish records, both in confidently identifying the mentally disabled and their relations, and in conclusively divining how and why they were being catered for. What emerges clearly from such accounts is that parishes were quite prepared to pay more in the short term so as to remove the burden of a pauper from the rates in the long term. Furthermore, little seems to have distinguished provision for the mentally disabled from that made for ordinary poor, sick or orphaned children, in like social circumstances.

Clearly, not all fools or idiots were, or were regarded as, incapable of work. Within institutions, the tractability of the simple-minded and their ability to work might provide a rationale for preferring them over lunatics. Similar dynamics must have prevailed upon parishioners themselves within the locales. Unemployment might be a significant grounds for the parish actually providing a simple-minded individual with relief. Elizabeth Ratcliffe, for example, was relieved for much of 1692–4 and occasionally thereafter by St Botolph Bishopsgate, not merely because she was 'foolish' and 'very poor', but also because of her having 'little or no worke'.[52] Money earned weekly by the 'foolish' Elizabeth Bright in her 'work', while she was being kept by a parish nurse, amounted to an impressive total of £1 3s 4d when it was received by the parish in 1696.[53] However, parish records are very unrevealing as to exactly what the work and activities performed by fools and idiots within their locales entailed.

In circumstances such as those outlined above, it should be stressed, poor, unemployed idiots were plainly being relieved as much because of their poverty as because of their mental disability. How far provision for individuals as poor should be, or can be, distinguished from provision for individuals as mentally disabled in a study of Poor Law records is open to question, however, when local officials were neither accustomed, nor could have seen much point, in separating these two matters.

UNDERLYING RATIONALES FOR RELIEF

Social and economic pressures were clearly pre-eminent in determining the type of relief available to the poor mentally disabled, as well as whether, when and to what extent the parish intervened in a case. The parish had no obligation to provide for idiots with means of their own, or with families capable of supporting them. Typically, it was some life-cycle crisis, some vital reversal in a family's economic circumstances, or some other circumstance entailing the encumbrance, incapacitation, or elimination of one or other of the family members maintaining an idiot that provoked an application for relief and parochial intercession. Seldom, unless no family members were available, or an idiot proved unruly, or else was apprehended abroad as a vagrant, does the initiative appear to have come from the parish itself. Unfortunately, petitions for relief seldom survive for metropolitan parishes, and the ways in which parishioners actually negotiated for relief almost invariably remain hidden from the historian.

Commonly, parochial aid was sought and granted following the death or illness of a family member. Parochial provision for the 'fool', Harry Southern, of Coleman Street, for instance, commenced only after the death of his elderly father, Richard, in the almshouse. Rarely, furthermore, was the death of just one parent or family member sufficient to warrant the parish taking over the support of an idiot if another was capable of providing. The appearance of the case of Sarah Howard before the London Sessions in 1674 was brought about by the death of her last surviving parent, her mother Martha. Although relieved by Bishopsgate for a brief period around the time of her father's death, the 'naturall', Mary Browne, was only provided with lodging and nursing after the death of her widowed mother, in May 1687.[54] The sickness of simple-minded parishioners, or of their carers, might also be a significant factor in warranting parochial aid. It was not only because Mary Browne was an orphaned 'naturall' that parish nursing was afforded her, but also because she was 'sicke'. Mary Jessup, 'a poor foelish Geirle', also enters the same parish's accounts only when her mother Alice becomes 'sicke' and again after Alice dies.[55] Alternatively (as in Martha Stock's case), the desertion or widowing of married women might provoke them to seek parochial aid for a disabled child. The significance of parental death, sickness and abandonment in provoking the intervention of the parish in the case of the mentally disabled, and the evident absence of support from other relations, also lend weight to the arguments of revisionist historians as to the narrowness of kinship ties when it came to providing for the indigent and sick.[56]

In addition, a new birth in a family, particularly if that family was already large and in receipt of parochial relief, or close to the poverty line, might also precipitate a relief application, or admission to an institution. Emphasis on the size of an afflicted individual's family is a striking feature of lunatic cases discussed at Sessions, and of extant petitions for parochial relief and for admission to Bethlem. This circumstance was likewise often cited in the decisions declared by administrative bodies. On the other hand, as recent work on nineteenth-century idiocy has underlined, large families might actually find it easier to cope, for example through sharing strategies, easing the burdens of the disabled on productive family members. David Wright's work suggests a more significant interface between the age ranks of mentally disabled family members and the point of vulnerability in families' life cycles provoking the decision to cast out that member.[57] It would be surprising if a similar dynamic was not discernible in early modern provision for the mentally disabled. Unfortunately, no sustained research of this nature has yet been attempted.

From only a cursory examination of parochial records, it is clear that the majority of those identified as idiots were very young children. This was obviously encouraged by the bias in contemporary definitions of 'pure' idiocy outlined above. The only two parishioners described as 'naturalls' by the parish officers of St Botolph Bishopsgate during 1627–1721, were both very young children. One, when spoken of for the first time, was just four years old, having been born in 1683. Of course, the mentally disabled were much less likely to survive to adulthood in early modern times than they are today, a grim reality underlined in medical textbooks and literary sources which observed the low life-expectancy of idiots as a truism.[58] Even so, some idiotic parishioners (including Harry Southern) clearly survived into maturity, while other parishioners developed into states resembling 'idiocy' in later life, and became the concern of parish officers.

It was not just the age of mentally disabled members and their positions within the structure of households that might matter, it was also the relative ages of those responsible for them. While young and vigorous parents or relatives might be less likely (as, by definition, members of the 'able poor') to receive a helping hand from the parish, elderly relations, more often infirm, and lacking income from employment, obviously had a better claim. Old age and poverty were not sufficient on their own of course, as is indicated by cases like the 39-year-old 'ideott' Sarah Howard, whose 'poor', elderly parents do not appear to have received any assistance.

That parishes and individuals were prepared to spend time and money going to court to argue a case, and thus avoid the burden entailed by the support of an idiot, is a sign of how expensive such a burden might be, and how seriously and reluctantly it might be regarded. The rarity of those instances when parishes and families went to Sessions to free themselves from an idiot's maintenance, however, may suggest something rather different. First, it must be some reflection of a recognition on the parish's part that they had a responsibility towards idiots. Some disputes as to an individual's place of settlement were clearly resolved without contest, either out of court, or (as in Sarah Howard's case) because no representative from one or other parish turned up to offer a defence, implying a readiness to be pragmatic in recognising lost causes. The exceptional nature of such disputes must also be some reflection of the exceptional nature of parochial provision for idiots *per se*, as against the preparedness to provide for lunacy or physical illness. It may also suggest that parish officials were tending to define idiocy much more narrowly than lunacy.

Some Poor Law historians have sought to place increased stress on evidence in parish records manifesting a 'genuine humanitarian understanding of local needs'.[59] Undoubtedly, 'humane consideration' was an important dimension of parochial provision for the mentally disabled too. Legacies and benefactions, donated to the care of parish poor, were occasionally devoted in some small part to the care of the mentally disabled – as in 1688–99, when 3s 6d of Roger Drakes' £5 legacy to the poor of Bishopsgate was laid out on 'Alice Jessup And [her] fooleish daughter'.[60] In some cases, mentally disabled parishioners are referred to in parish records as 'poor' so and so, possibly reflecting some degree of sympathy for their plight, as well as their poverty.[61] The language in which Elizabeth Bright of Bishopsgate was described, 'a foleish Crature Troubled with sad fitts', seems even more redolent of the sympathetic side of Poor Law provision.[62]

Help afforded to the deserving poor clearly accorded with prevailing notions of 'good neighbourhood', an aspect of local government emphasised by numerous historians from Emmison to Boulton.[63] The

Bishopsgate churchwardens accounts record a number of payments made for, and to secure, 'help' and even 'kindness' for lunatic parishioners.[64] One finds such payments and language more customarily employed on behalf of the insane in parish accounts as a form of expedition, or bribery, with institutions and their servants. While such language was more rarely applied to the poor mentally disabled, a similar ethos presumably prevailed. Nevertheless, quite apart from the sympathetic concerns of 'neighbourliness', the role of parochial officers in disciplining the poor, and upholding the boundaries of neighbourly propriety, has also been underlined by historians.[65]

KEEPERS AND NURSES

The identities of the carers of simple-minded parishioners within the locales is just as difficult and neglected a subject as are the identities of the simple-minded themselves. The stalwart of parochial medical provision in the early modern capital was the female parish nurse. It was these nurses who predominated in caring for the sick in mind and body beyond the home, and who took in mentally disabled children as well as the unweaned, the orphaned, the sick and the distracted. Even when men appear in parish accounts in a proprietorial role, receiving payment and signing receipts for the maintenance of the mentally disabled, this often conceals the fact that it was women who did the caring. Local, as well as rural, nurses were preferred by city parochial authorities, less, no doubt, because they were women, than because they offered the cheapest form of care outside of the family. Rarely, unlike more specialist or large-scale contractors, did they require any more for the manageable mentally disabled than they did for the ordinary sick and infirm. Goody Graunt charged the Bishopsgate churchwardens just 6d per week 'for lookeing to' and 'lodgeing' one 'natural', Mary Browne, in the 1680s, while Mary Dowle was paid between 6d and 1s per week by the same parish during 1702 for the 'naturall', Dorcas Popkins.[66] Dorothy Bayley charged St Sepulchres about 1s per week for attendance on the 'ideot', Ann Tweedle during 1660–61 – apparently the same rate as she charged for attending two other parishioners, one being sick and the other blind.[67] Occasionally, if a mentally disabled parishioner was more trouble, nurses might charge more. Possibly it was the epilepsy suffered by the 'foelish' Elizabeth Bright that justified her nurse, Mrs Gregory, receiving 3s per week for her during the 1690s.[68]

This is not to say that men did not also figure prominently in caring for the mentally disabled. Yet, on the whole, male attendants and proprietors were most conspicuous when it came to more bothersome lunatic cases where security and strong-arm tactics were at a greater premium. Apparently men tended to charge more than women for their trouble. St Sepulchres Holborn, for example, paid a John Shustock of Wapping 2s 6d per week from 1649–53 'for keeping' the 'Innocent', Thomas Walker, with extra amounts for 'clothing' and other 'necessaries'.[69] The 'keeping' of James Pratt (regarded as 'an Ideott' towards the end of his life) by Robert Izard at Walton/Waltham in the 1660s cost St Brides parish 4s per week.[70]

Often parish nurses were elderly women, or widows, seeking to supplement their income, including widow Graunt of Bishopsgate who cared for 'the naturall', Mary Browne in the 1680s – a feature found in other surveys of Poor Law medical provision.[71] Almost as often, however, parish nurses seem to have been women of middle age or in their prime – such as 'goody Hester Rooksby', who briefly took on Mary's care after widow Graunt. Regularly, one mentally disabled parishioner was cared for by a variety of different individuals, implying perhaps problems for the parish in securing long-term arrangements for care, and a reluctance on the part of carers to endure the burden of the mentally disabled for long. Mary Browne seems to have been looked after at parish expense by a total of four persons during the short time-span 1683–8: widow Graunt, a nurse Harris, goody Hester Rooksby and a nurse Hatherell. Elizabeth Bright was 'kept' by 'nurss' or 'Mrs' Elizabeth Gregory at Angell Alley, where a good deal of poor children and parishioners seem to have been relieved and/or lodged at parish expense. For a brief and temporary period in 1695, however, Bright was apparently transferred to the care of 'nurss' Elizabeth Yorke.

Nurses, as was Mrs Gregory, were normally required to supply their mentally disabled charges with 'necessaries'. Often, however, parish accounts fail to specify exactly what was comprised by such 'necessaries'. Carers tended to be paid for supplying clothing restrospectively by the parish. Occasionally, parish nurses seem to have made the clothing themselves, presumably with a mind to increasing their profits. Nurse Harris was paid directly in 1685 so she could buy a coat and linen for Mary Browne, but the following year was given 1s by the Bishopsgate churchwardens 'towards makeing some Cloathes' for her.[72] Often, as in this case, however, one simply cannot be sure exactly when, by whom, or how much clothing was provided.

The role of parish nurses might not only involve clothing, feeding, cleaning and washing, but very occasionally saw them procuring medical treatment for their mentally disabled charges. When medicine was deemed appropriate, nurses were either paid in advance, or billed the parish retrospectively. In the 1690s, for example, nurse Yorke was paid 3d 'to bie something at the Apothecaries for Elizabeth Bright', while nurse Gregory subsequently received 1s to 'get her let blood'.[73] Although it is rarely clear exactly who took the initiative in ordering medical treatment, it is just as likely to have come from carers as from busy parochial officers with hundreds of cases to oversee. Only in the eventuality of an extended and expensive course of treatment does vestry approval of expenditure seem to have been required.

Sometimes, parish nurses seem to have been recognised as possessing a degree of specialist skill, and very occasionally they appear to have specialised in caring for the mentally disabled. Nevertheless, I have failed to find a single instance of a parish nurse evolving into a private madhouse keeper in the way suggested some time ago by Parry-Jones.[74] More often than not, these nurses catered for a whole range of the poor: children, the pregnant, the sick and the physically disabled, as well as the mentally disabled. During 1660–61, for example, Dorothy Bayley of St Sepulchres Holborn was paid 'to attend Anne Gibbs in her sicknesse, Anne Tweedle an Ideot and Elizabeth Kesterson a blind woman five weekes' concurrently, and continued to attend Tweedle and Kesterson for a further sixteen weeks.[75] Likewise, Elizabeth Yorke, the one-time nurse to the 'foelish' Elizabeth Bright, was paid by Bishopsgate throughout the 1690s 'for lookeing to severall Sicke And lame' parishioners, as well as taking in the odd 'Lunatissme'.[76]

A continuity in the arrangements for the care of mentally disabled parishioners, particularly if cheap, was encouraged by the relative constancy of their mental states, as well as the parish's own concerns for expedience and economy. Nurses who had already provided such services to a family and parish were obviously in a good position to continue to do so. Nurse Gregory, for example, who looked after the 'foolish' Elizabeth Bright in the 1690s, was later called upon by the parish to keep the mad Abraham Byard and William Bodley.[77] In Harry Southern's case, Lovett, the same individual whom the parish had paid to nurse his parents before their deaths, continued to nurse the foolish son at parish expense, apparently, for another three years.[78]

CONCLUSION

This chapter began by arguing essentially for the coherence and consistency of early modern definitions of idiocy, as enshrined in the records of parochial and institutional authorities. This was especially the case in so far as idiots were identified (and identifiable) as those whose mental disability dated from birth, or early childhood. It seems to have been this conceptualisation that granted contemporaries their most viable and meaningful resource for identifying the mentally disabled and distinguishing them from the insane. At the local level, I have asserted, this criterion was not only relatively workable, but sustained a broad consensus in its application by parochial officials and families – reflected in the preponderance of mentally disabled parishioners who first appear in parish records when young children. In addition, complementary formulations of idiocy as, for example, an acquired state, if less definitive, also offered contemporaries a way of understanding acquired or progressive mental defects as idiocy.

None the less, I have striven not to underemphasise the vital areas of imprecision and equivocation in contemporary notions of mental disability. This ambiguity, particularly marked in literary discourse, is also evidenced in institutional and parochial records by the occasional liability of distinctions to flux or collapse. Furthermore, the apparent coherence of categories like idiot and natural seems to owe a great deal to the narrowness with which they were often applied in practice – partly as a result of the prejudicial status of the mentally disabled in terms of their claim on social and legal privileges. Despite these manifold problems of identifying idiots, however, parish records testify that, generally, contemporaries were strikingly consistent in distinguishing between the insane and the idiotic, that different labels carried different meanings, and that officials and parishioners knew what they meant. Institutions, furthermore, applied such distinctions from early on in the seventeenth century, and despite some laxity, seem to have evolved relatively stringent and uniformly applied procedures for differentiation.

The second part of this survey has focused almost exclusively on information about the mentally disabled contained in parish records. In a recent article on Elizabethan parochial accounts, J. S. Craig spoke of the current popularity of churchwardens' accounts for social historians. He also stressed, however, historians' 'apparent lack of interest' in such sources 'within the broader context of debates on early modern society'.[79] My own analysis of parish records has highlighted how useful they can be for the study of local solutions to the problems posed by mental disability in early modern England. In addition, however, I have been at pains to point out the problematic nature of these records, owing to their elliptical and summary content, and the fact that they were designed to register expenditure rather than to record the rationales on which expenditure was based.

What emerges quite clearly, as Rushton also concluded in his survey of north-east England parishes, is that metropolitan parish officials 'were experienced, if not enthusiastic, in dealing with cases of mental disability' and 'reacted to the problems in a coherent manner within the structure of limited resources'.[80] Unfortunately, a tendency to relegate idiocy as a medical, legal and social issue of lesser importance, meant a rather woeful lack of provision outside the context of both the parochial community and the family domicile. It was clearly 'the most serious cases [of lunacy and mental disability which] were considered appropriate for the asylum' and other institutions, although not just, as Rushton avers, during the last third of the eighteenth century, but for much of the period.[81] The costs of institutional care were prohibitive, particularly for those adjudged to be merely idiotic or foolish, who might easily and considerably more cheaply be kept at home. The general perception of the mentally disabled as harmless, manageable and irredeemable gave families and parish officers little incentive to make extravagant arrangements for their care. Specialist institutions tended anyway to exclude such cases.

Idiocy was clearly, and not surprisingly, conceived of as less immediate a problem than lunacy, requiring parochial and other authorities to assume lesser responsibilities. As a more positive, if indirect consequence of this, however, enforcement of family responsibility seems to have been less of a difficulty for parishes than in cases of insanity. Nevertheless, it would be 'foolish' to underestimate the considerable responsiveness of local officials and people to the problems posed by idiocy. Indeed, my analysis would support the contention of Rushton and others that the social strategies for dealing with even these more 'minor' problems were quite varied, well worked out and evidently quite broadly accepted. Those identified and relieved as 'idiots' and 'fools' within the locales tended to be children born to very poor families, whose parents had died, or else were sick or otherwise incapacitated – emphasising the limited, exigency-led nature of parochial provision for the mentally disabled. If economic rationales tended to have primacy in parochial relief, then it has also been necessary to acknowledge how inclined parish records are by their very nature to over-stress such influences on decision-making. As this study has demonstrated, furthermore, these records indicate the coexistence and significance of compassionate and responsible attitudes towards idiots. Assistance, occasionally of a relatively substantial nature, was granted and justified within the wider spectrum of neighbourly values.

This survey has also endorsed the striking continuity of responses during this period, a point also highlighted by Rushton's and Suzuki's studies. Nevertheless, given the considerable expansion of institutional provision for mental disability and illness during the latter part of the eighteenth century, and how much more advanced these trends appear to have been in the metropolitan region, more research needs to be done on the inroads being gradually made into traditional local patterns of care for these groups. If customary tolerance for the foolish and idiotic proved more resilient to Augustan stigmatising of the empire of folly and madness than they did in the case of the insane, the reception of idiots into new institutions, like St Patrick's Hospital, and the slow influx of a few mentally disabled cases into workhouses and madhouses, argue that times were changing for the idiot as well.[82]

NOTES

I am grateful to Peter Bartlett, Chris Goodey, Malcolm Nicholson, Roy Porter, Akihito Suzuki and David Wright for helpful comments on earlier drafts of this chapter.

1 I shall be employing the terms 'mentally disabled' and 'idiot' here to differentiate all those individuals categorised by contemporaries as 'idiots', 'fools', 'naturals', etc., from those defined as 'lunatics', the 'mad' etc. I find the use of the term 'mentally disabled' by some social historians to embrace both lunatics and idiots, misleading and insensitive to contemporary semantics. 'Disability' tended to be defined as a more permanent, incurable affliction than mere 'illness'.

2 M. Foucault, *Madness and Civilisation: A History of Insanity in the Age of Reason*, London, 1971, trans. and abr. from *Histoire de la Folie à l'âge classique*, Paris, 1961; N. Hattori, '"The pleasure of your Bedlam": the theatre of madness in the Renaissance', *History of Psychiatry*, 1995, vol. 6, pp. 283–308; A. Suzuki, 'Lunacy in Seventeenth- and Eighteenth-Century England: Analysis of Quarter Sessions records', Pts I and II, *History of Psychiatry*, 1991, vol. 2, pp. 437–56 and 1992, vol. 3, pp. 29–44; M. MacDonald, *Mystical Bedlam: Madness, Anxiety and Healing in Seventeenth-Century England*, Cambridge, 1981, p. 70, pp. 121–2 and pp. 140–41; G. Rosen, *Madness in Society: Chapters in the Historical Sociology of Mental Illness*, London, 1968.

3 For example C. Hill, *The World Turned Upside-Down: Radical Ideas During the English Revolution*, London, 1972; E. Welsford, *The Fool. His Social and Literary History*, London, 1935; P. U. A. Williams (ed.) *The Fool and the Trickster: Studies in Honour of Enid Welsford*, Cambridge, 1979; W. Willeford, *The Fool and his Sceptre: A Study of Clowns and Jesters and their Audience*, London, 1969; B. Swain, *Fools and Folly during the Middle Ages and the Renaissance*, New York, 1976; S. Billington, *The Social History of the Fool*, Brighton, 1984; Foucault, *Madness and Civilisation*.

4 See for example Foucault, *Madness and Civilisation*; Hill, *The World Turned Upside-Down*; MacDonald, *Mystical Bedlam*, p. 70; D. Rothman, *The Discovery of the Asylum: Social Order and Disorder in the New Republic*, Boston, 1971, and Welsford, *The Fool*.

5 For example while MacDonald found a total of over 200 cases who manifested symptoms described by Napier as 'witless', 'sottish' or 'senseless', he was more concerned with the more acute symptomatology of lunacy and barely discussed the issue of mental disability. More recently, Allan Ingram's *The Madhouse of Language: Writing and Reading Madness in the Eighteenth Century*, London and New York, 1991, has treated mad and idiotic language as virtual equivalents. Other early modern historians have likewise tended to discuss all forms of mental illness and disability together. See E.G. Thomas 'The Mentally Defective': 'The Old Poor Law and Medicine', *Medical History*, 1980, vol. 24, pp. 1–19. This issue was explored recently by C. Goodey: 'Why is the History of Idiocy Unsuitable for Historians of Psychiatry?', unpublished paper delivered at European Congress for the History of Psychiatry, London, 1993.

6 For example C. Goodey, 'Intelligence Levels as Criteria of Abnormality: The Pre-history of Intelligence Testing', in B. Mayall (ed.) *Family Life and Social Control: Discourses on Normality*, Social Science Research Unit, London University Institute of Education, 1993.

7 Compare, also, the problems of identifying the elderly in parish records: M. Pelling, 'Old Age, Poverty, and Disability in Early Modern Norwich: Work, Marriage and Other Expedients', in M. Pelling and R. Smith (eds), *Life, Death, and the Elderly*, London, 1991, pp. 74–101, esp. pp. 76–80.

8 Foucault, *Madness and Civilisation*; K. Doerner, *Madmen and the Bourgeoisie: A Social History of Insanity and Psychiatry*, Oxford, 1981, trans. from the original *Bürger und Ire*, Europäische Verlagsanstalt, 1960.

9 MacDonald, *Mystical Bedlam*; A. Fessler, 'The management of lunacy in seventeenth-century England. An investigation of quarter-sessions records', *Proceedings of the Royal Society of Medicine*, 1956, vol. 49, pp. 901–7; P. Rushton, 'Lunatics and Idiots: Mental Disability, the Community and the Poor Law in North-East England', *Medical History*, 1988, vol. 32, pp. 34–50, for example.

10 For example T. Nashe, *Have With You To Saffron-Walden*, London, 1596, in *Works of Thomas Nashe*, London, 1910, vol. 3, pp. 100–1.

11 For the association of madness with 'innocence', see for example M. A. Screech, 'Good Madness in Christendom', in W. F. Bynum, R. Porter and M. Shepherd (eds) *The Anatomy of Madness: Essays in the History of Psychiatry* vol. 1, London and New York, 1985, pp. 25–39; *Erasmus, Ecstasy and the Praise of Folly*, London, 1988.

12 M. Byrd, *Visits to Bedlam*, Columbia, 1974; M. V. Deporte, *Nightmares and Hobbyhorses: Swift, Sterne and Augustan Ideas of Madness*, San Marino, California, 1974; L. Feder, *Madness and Literature*, Princeton, 1980.

13 See for example T. Dekker, *Northwood Ho*, Pt IV, iii, pp. 51–2, 72, 130–31, 175–6, in *The Dramatic Works of Thomas Dekker*, Cambridge, 1955, vol. ii; T. Dekker, *The Honest Whore*, Pt I, IV, iv, pp. 102–3, in *The Dramatic Works*, vol. ii; T. Middleton and W. Rowley, *The Changeling*, N. W. Bawcutt (ed.), London, 1958, Pt I, ii, pp. 79–80.

14 R. Neugebauer, 'Mental Illness and Government Policy in Sixteenth- and Seventeenth-Century England', unpublished PhD, Columbia University, 1976; 'Treatment of the Mentally Ill in Medieval and Early Modern England', *Journal of the History of the Behavioural Sciences*, 1978, vol. 14, pp. 158–69, and 'Medieval and Early Modern Theories of Mental Illness', *Archives of General Psychiatry*, 1979, vol. 36, pp. 477–83.

15 See for example J. Brydall, *Non Compos Mentis* ..., London, 1700, facs. repr. of 1st edition, New York and London, 1979; Fitzherbert, *Natura Brevium*, 1652, p. 583; quoted in J. C. Bucknill and D. H. Tuke, *A Manual of Psychological Medicine*, London, 1858, p. 94.

16 Lord Coke, *Coke's Lyttleton*, p. 247a, quoted in Bucknill and Tuke, *Psychological Medicine*, p. 94; Brydall, *Non Compos Mentis*, p. 6; Sir William Blackstone, *Commentaries on the Laws of England, 1765–9*, Oxford, 1765–9, 4 vols, 1783 edition, i, pp. 292–5; D. H. Tuke, *Chapters in the History of the Insane in the British Isles*, London, 1882, pp. 286–91; T. Willis, *Two Discourses Concerning the Soul of Brutes, which is that of the Vital and Sensitive of Man*, London: 1683, trans. S. Pordage from *De Anima Brutorum*, p. 210.

17 '*Purus idiota*' was a legal term, tending to connote, as it did in Blackstone's *Commentaries*, a congenital absence of understanding.

18 See J. Andrews 'Begging the Question of Idiocy: Definitions and Epistemologies of Idiocy in Early Modern Britain', forthcoming in *History of Psychiatry*.

19 T. Willis, *Concerning the Soul of Brutes*, p. 211; Lord Coke, *Coke's Lyttleton*, p. 247a, quoted in Bucknill and Tuke, *Psychological Medicine*, p. 94.

20 T. Sydenham, *Processus Integri*, in *The Works of Thomas Sydenham M.D.*, trans. R. G. Latham, London, 1850, 2 vols, ii, pp. 290–1; W. Battie, *A Treatise on Madness*, London, 1758, R. Hunter and I. Macalpine (eds), London, 1962, pp. 98–9; P. Pinel, *Traité Medico-philosophique sur l'Aliénation Mentale*, Paris, 1806, translated as *A Treatise on Insanity* ..., D.D. Davis, Sheffield, 1806, pp. 252, 165.

21 Guildhall Library, London (henceforth *Ghall*) *MS 6552/1*, Churchwardens' Accounts 1639–78, 6/5/1662–22/5/1671.

22 *Ghall MSS 4525/21*, fols 84–5, 18/6/1700 and 25/6/1700, *4455/22*, fols 101–2, 25/8/1701, 1/9/1701, for example.

23 For example *Ghall MSS 4525/20*, fols 80–9, 15 May–17 July 1699; *4525/25*, fols 84–108, 125 and 182–8, 20 May 1704–15 January 1705. See, also, case of Elizabeth Ratcliffe, described as 'A Lunatick' when removed to the same parish with her three children, but thereafter was referred to as 'foleish'; *Ghall MSS 4525/13*, fol. 61, cJune and 16 September 1691; *4525/14*, fols 55, 65, 72, 81 and 88–107, 13 April 1692–12 April 1693, etc. until *4525/19*, fols 84, 87, 90 and 102, 28 July, 18 August, 8 September and 1 December 1698.

24 For example S. Johnson, *Dictionary*, London, 1755; J. Walker, *A Critical Pronouncing Dictionary and Expositor of the English Language*, Edinburgh, 1830; 1st edn, 1792.

25 *Ghall MS 4525/5*, 1674–5.

26 *Ghall MSS 4525/7b*, fol. 92, cDecember 1683; *4525/8*, fols 147 and 151–2, 14 May–1 October 1684; *4525/9*, fol. 91, 20 December 1686; *4525/7*, fols

77–89, 136, 175 and 178, 20 June–14 September 1687, and *4525/10*, fols 191 and 236, 4 May 1688.

27 For the only reference I have found in parish accounts so far, see *Ghall MS 4525/15*, fol. 95, 26 February 1694.

28 See for example Walker, *Dictionary*, under 'changling' and 'idiot'.

29 See for example Goodey, 'Intelligence levels', especially pp. 53–4.

30 Fessler, 'The Management of Lunacy'; Rushton, 'Lunatics and Idiots'; Suzuki, 'Quarter Sessions'.

31 *Corporation of London Record Office* (henceforth *CLRO*) *SM44*, 12 October 1674.

32 *Ghall MS 4457/5*, 22 October 1719.

33 *Ghall MS 4525/22*, fols 89, 90 etc., 2 June 1701 onwards.

34 *Ghall MSS 4525/16*, fols 65–76, 5 June–17 August 1694, and *4525/17*, fols 97–119, 4 November 1695–11 April 1696. See also pension granted to James Cole of St Bride's on account of 'his Sonne a Naturall', *Ghall MS 6554/2*, 25 May 1685.

35 *Ghall MSS 4525/13*, fol. 61, cJune and 16 September 1691; *4525/14*, fols 55, 65, 72, 81 and 88–107, 13 April, 23 June, 12 August and 11 October 1692, and 30 November 1692–12 April 1693; *4525/15*, fols 52–101, April 1693–April 1694; *4525/16*, fols 59 and 61, 23 April and 8 May 1694; *4525/17*, fol. 209, 25 June 1695; etc., until *4525/19*, 84, 87, 90 and 102, 28 July, 18 August, 8 September and 1 December 1698.

36 *Ghall MSS 4525/7b*, fol. 92, cDecember 1683; *4525/8*, fols 147 and 151–2, 14 May–1 October 1684; *4525/9*, fol. 91, 20 December 1686; *4525/7*, fols 77–89, 136, 175 and 178, 20 June–14 September 1687; *4525/10*, fols 191 and 236, 4 May 1688, and *4525/23*, fols 74, 76–7, 2, 17, 23 and 30 July, and 6 August 1702.

37 *Ghall MS 3146/1*, 1660–61.

38 *Ghall MS 3146/1*, 1659–65; *3149/2*, fol. 23, 8 April 1663.

39 *Ghall MSS 4525/15*, fols 50–61, 24 April–9 August 1693; *4525/16*, fols 149–51, 23 April, 23 May and 18 June 1694; *4525/17*, fol. 167, 1 May 1695; *4525/18*, fol. 147, 16 April 1697; *4525/19*, fols 73, 16 May 1698 and *4525/20*, fols 152 and 183, 31 January and 2 February 1700.

40 For example F. Beaumont and J. Fletcher's *The Pilgrim* (1621/2), in F. Bowers (ed.) *The Dramatic Works in the Beaumont and Fletcher Canon*, Cambridge, 1966, 7 vols, vi, pp. 111–224 and III, vii, pp. 25–7.

41 In the late seventeenth century, some poor metropolitan parishioners received their allowances seasonally from the parish under the rubric of 'winter clothes' – a clear sign of the inadequate, but significantly need-led nature of parochial relief.

42 For example case of Abraham Byard, *Ghall MS 4525/17*, fol. 137, 9 September 1695, provided with a waistcoat when 'Lunaticke in Bethelem Howse [and] quite naked'. See, also, Andrews, 'Bedlam Revisited: A History of Bethlem Hospital c.1634–c.1770' unpublished PhD, University of London, 1991, ch. 3, pp. 138–53.

43 *Ghall MS 4457/5*, 30 April 1740 and 16 January 1747, cases of Coshaw and Timbrell of St Stephen Coleman Street.

44 *Ghall MSS 4525/7*, fols 77–89, 136, 175 and 178, 20 June–14 September 1687; *4525/17*, fols 139, 156 and 157, 25 September 1695, 9 April and 15 May 1696. The 'foelish' Mary Jessup received just two payments totalling

10/7 in the 1690s and 1700s, including 7/1 for 'A Gowne & Petticoate'; *Ghall MSS 4525/19*, fol. 230, 1698–99 and 4525/25, fol. 146, 22 September 1704.

45 *Ghall MS 4457/5*, 13 May 1719–14 December 1731.

46 *Ghall MS 3146/1*, 1659–65; *3149/2*, fol. 23, 8 April 1663.

47 *Ghall MS 4525/7*.

48 *Ghall MSS 4525/9*, fol. 160, 9 July 1687 and *4525/10*, fol. 236, 3 and 4 May 1688.

49 See for example J. A. Sharpe, *Early Modern England: A Social History 1550–1760*, London, 1987, p. 209.

50 M. Pelling, 'Child Health as a Social Value in Early Modern England', *Social History of Medicine*, 1988, vol. 1, 2, pp. 135–64; L. Schwartz, 'London Apprentices in the Seventeenth Century', *Local Population Studies*, 1987, vol. 38, pp. 18–22; O. Jocelyn Dunlop and R. D. Denman, *English Apprenticeship and Child Labour: A History*, London, 1912; M.G. Davies, *The Enforcement of English Apprenticeship: A Study in Applied Mercantilism*, Cambridge, Mass., 1956.

51 Pelling, 'Child Health'; Pelling, 'Old Age', pp. 85–7.

52 *Ghall MSS 4525/14*, for example fols 65, 72 and 100; 20 June and 12 August 1692 and 22 February 1693; *4525/15*, fols 52–101, 8 May 1693–9 April 1694; *4525/17*, fols 59, 61, 23 April and 8 May 1694, and *4525/17*, fol. 99, 20 November 1695.

53 *Ghall MS 4525/17*, fol. 64, 20 April 1696. Searches through the parish's records have been unable to uncover the nature of this work.

54 See, also, case of the 'foelish' Martha Stock, whose old, lame and solitary mother, Alice, received occasional relief and a pension from 1700. Only following her mother's death was Martha provided with a nurse by the parish. *Ghall MSS 4525/21*, fol. 78, 7 May 1700; *4525/22*, fols 89 and 182, 2 June 1701 and 23 March 1702.

55 *Ghall MS 4525/19*, fol. 230 and *4525/25*, fol. 146. See, also, Elizabeth Bright's case, ref. 58.

56 For example Pelling, 'Old Age', pp. 75, 85–7; R. M. Smith, 'Fertility, Economy, and Household Formation in England Over Three Centuries', *Population and Development Review*, 1981, vol. 7, p. 606; Suzuki, 'Quarter Sessions'.

57 D. Wright, 'The National Asylum for Idiots, Earlswood, 1847–1886', unpublished DPhil thesis, University of Oxford, 1993, ch. 2.

58 For example E. Esquirol, *Mental Maladies*, Philadelphia, 1845, p. 446. See, also, G. White, *Natural History and Antiquities of Selborne*, 1789, pp. 143–4, quoted in R. Porter, *The Faber Book of Madness*, London and Boston, 1991, p. 99.

59 Thomas, 'The Old Poor Law and Medicine', pp. 1, 3, etc.

60 *Ghall MS 4525/19*, fol. 230, 1698–99.

61 The 'foolish' Harry Southern of Coleman Street was referred to in this way only during the last ten months of his life, while Mary Jessup of Bishopsgate was described as 'a poor foelish Geirle her mother Deceased'. *Ghall MSS 4458/1*, 12 May and 10 November 1730 and *4525/25*, fol. 146, 22 September 1704.

62 *Ghall MSS 4525/15*, fols 50–61, 24 April–9 August 1693; *4525/16*, fols 149–51, 23 April 1694–29 March 1695; *4525/17*, fols 139–40 and 157, 25 September and 12 August 1695, 12 May 1696, etc.

63 See F. G. Emmison, *Elizabethan Life: Morals and the Church Courts*, Chelmsford, 1973, and J. Boulton, *Neighbourhood and Society: A London Suburb in the Seventeenth Century*, Cambridge, 1987.

64 For example *Ghall MSS 4525/23*, fol. 25, 25 March 1702; *4525/29*, fol. 8, 10 September 1707.
65 For example A. Tindal-Hart, *The Man in the Pew 1558–1660*, London, 1966.
66 *Ghall MSS 4525/23*, fols 74, 76–77, 2, 17, 23 and 30 July, and 6 August 1702.
67 For Browne's case see previous refs. For Tweedle, see *Ghall MS 3146/1*, 1660–61.
68 *Ghall MSS 4525/17*, fol. 167, 1 May 1695; *4525/18*, fol. 147, 16 April 1697; *4525/19*, fols 73, 16 May 1698 and *4525/20*, fols 152 and 183, 31 January and 2 February 1700.
69 *Ghall MS 3146/1*, 1659–65; *3149/2*, fol. 23, 8 April 1663.
70 *Ghall MS 6552/1*, 6 May 1662–22 May 1671. St Stephen Coleman Street paid a man named Lovett/Lovell 1/ per week (excluding clothing and other necessaries) for keeping the 'fool', Harry Southern, during c1719–26, raised subsequently (during and after Harry's sickness, when his care was taken over by a man named Bucknall), to 2/ per week. *Ghall MSS 4457/5*, 4 December 1718–11 March 1731; *4458/1*, fols 753 and 757, 28 May and 25 September 1719.
71 For example Pelling emphasised the extensive utilisation of elderly women in roles tending to the sick by the Norwich authorities in the late sixteenth century; Pelling, 'Old Age', in Pelling and Smith (eds) *Life, Death and the Elderly*, p. 84.
72 *Ghall MSS 4525/8*, fols 147 and 152, 14 May and 1 October 1684; *4525/9*, fol. 91, 20 December 1686. See, also, *4525/26*, fol. 150, 26 September 1705.
73 *Ghall MS 4525/19*, fol. 73, 16 May 1698.
74 W.Li, Parry-Jones, *The Trade in Lunacy: A Study of Private Madhouses in England in the Eighteenth and Nineteenth Centuries*, London, 1972
75 *Ghall MS 3146/1*, 1660–61.
76 See for example *Ghall MS 4525/15*, fol. 51, 3 May 1693.
77 See for example *Ghall MSS 4525/26*, fol. 224, 10 May 1705 and *4525/27*, fol. 189, 5 November 1706.
78 *Ghall MSS 4458/5*, 4 December 1718–24 October 1726; *4458/1*.
79 J.S. Craig, 'Co-operation and Initiatives: Elizabethan Churchwardens and the Parish Accounts of Mildenhall', *Social History*, 1993, vol. 18, 3, pp. 357–80.
80 Rushton, 'Lunatics and Idiots', p. 34, and chapter in this volume.
81 Rushton, 'Lunatics and Idiots', p. 48.
82 See Elizabeth Malcolm, Swifts Hospital, *A History of St. Patrick's Hospital, Dublin, 1746–1989*, Dublin, 1989, esp. pp. 20, 52–55, 83 and 92–3.

5

THE PSYCHOPOLITICS OF LEARNING AND DISABILITY IN SEVENTEENTH-CENTURY THOUGHT

C.F. Goodey

> Take my advice, when you meet anything that's going to be human and isn't yet, or used to be human once and isn't now, or ought to be human and isn't, you keep your eyes on it and feel for your hatchet.
>
> C.S. Lewis, *The Lion, the Witch and the Wardrobe*

I

The history of idiocy has scarcely been written. While social constructions of madness are common currency among most contemporary historians of psychiatry, I suspect the same historians believe that everyone just knows what an idiot or mentally handicapped person is, and that it is some unfortunate creature with a deficit in something called intelligence and a trans-historical reality. The little history on idiocy that has been done rarely goes back further than the late nineteenth-century statistical concepts of intelligence which subsist in our own period, or else lie in social or legal history. Both of these, by their very nature, can easily sidestep the demands of a critical account of concepts, which I shall attempt to give here for the seventeenth century.

One of the roots of the dyadic formula 'madness or idiocy' lies in John Locke's remark that madness is a mis-match of ideas to the external realities that should correspond to them, whereas idiocy is absence of ideas.[1] The account of madness has long been superseded and contextualised. 'Mental handicap' or 'retardation', to use the clinical terminology, as absence of the mental, remains taken for granted. This historiographical situation reflects exactly Locke's hierarchical classification of madness as human and idiocy as non-human, the background to which forms the topic of this chapter. The philosopher J. L. Austin wrote that any time we find one half of an antithetical pair crumbling beneath our critical gaze, be sure that the other half will have crumbled too, but that this will have escaped our notice. The 'Lockean' psychological dyad is assumed to have influenced a later doctrine in social policy which saw it as the task of progress to distinguish between the mad and the congenitally idiotic. If we nowadays regard this assumption sceptically in relation to the history of madness, then idiocy as absence surely cannot stay unscathed.

Is there a trans-historical idiot? Is there a type from past cultures whom we could recognise as our learning disabled person, congenitally and incurably learning disabled, and with perhaps an organic explanation for this too? If we go back as far as possible, the Hippocratic writers have a clear schema of congenital physical features such as dislocation of the hip.[2] Congenitality here is a major criterion in the classification of physical difference, for even the foetal age at which an injury occurs is said to determine the prognosis. Other Hippocratic texts deal with what may (or may not) be epilepsy, melancholia, depression, or other so-called mental illnesses. We could therefore recognise 'our' physically disabled as a group in ancient history and medicine; the mentally ill would be more contentious, but ultimately there would be some overlap between ours and theirs. However, idiocy in our sense is non-existent. It may be argued that this lacuna does not disprove the trans-historical reality, and is merely due to the legal and property structures of ancient society in which idiots simply did not have a social role. But this is to have your cake and eat it. If madness is mere social invention, then why should we believe that although antithetical idiots did not have an interactive role in ancient society, they did nevertheless positively exist in some other dimension?

The medieval fiscal distinction between congenital fools and those with lucid intervals between bouts of insanity is sometimes referred to as if it were a precursor of Locke's psychological distinction. But proof of incompetence to administer the profits of an estate, and proof of other kinds of unfitness had no generalised basis in common psychological concepts such as would transcend social classes or the disciplines of medicine, theology and law. Even since the late nineteenth-century establishment of a general (lack of) intelligence, the clientele of the interests exploiting this construction has continued to change. Such a rapid turnover has not been achieved in constructions of madness. And yet, I suspect, most of us would assume a continuity between the medieval and Lockean models of idiocy, and that both models can be assimilated to a deficient 'general intelligence', much of which was in fact the product of the later nineteenth century; and this is to read back quite uncritically the assumptions of our own socialisation, in a way which historians have long challenged when the topic has been not idiocy but madness. Lack of generalised intelligence is no such thing, but lack of the specific historical intelligence that gained and became domination.

Neglect of this topic stems from interest. Women address historical texts on hysteria; members of specific ethnic groups tackle the psychological stereotypes of racism. People with severe learning difficulties do not do post-graduate research. As for the mad: the Renaissance melancholics, Locke himself, and later the Romantics, demonstrated that being mad carries status and, similarly, studying it is glamorous. I may not be sane but at least I am clever, since I belong to a social occupation whose status is grounded in putative cleverness. No honour accrues to the academy from natural and incurable idiocy. On the contrary, the confrontational psychosis of the academy and the professions demands both the construction and the personal denial of an inherent deficit in 'intelligence'.

The other reason for neglect is that idiocy, having to do with absence, sits uneasily with the essentially epistemological concerns of madness. These ask us the following questions – where are the grounds of certainty? Who is to dictate to others what is and is not reasonable? To have wrong ideas, you must possess the capability for ideas in the first place. Idiocy as absence of Lockean ideas is not a question of interpreting the world this way as against that way, but of whether someone is competent to interpret the world in any way at all. Interpreting it this way and interpreting it that way share a terrain of discussion; interpreting it any way and not interpreting it any way manifestly do not – they are a mutual exclusion. Inclusion for people with learning difficulties means walking away from the epistemological criterion, as you would walk away from the playground bully. It invites a quite different set of questions: who belongs, and who – permanently – does not? What aspects of humanity, if any, ought we to perfect? What kind of values do we want to rule our social relationships? However seductive the pessimism generated by and after Foucault, I suggest that a history of the uses to which the concept of idiocy has been put should be able to contribute to social policy.

I am not sure that even adventurous historians are yet prepared to meet the consequences of Wittgenstein's dictum that the mind as conceived by Locke, especially of 'ideas' that can be transposed into language, is an occult medium. If Wittgenstein was right, then those humans in whom mental events are allegedly absent keep him company. The real question then is still one of social goals and values: what kind of society might it be (and still a complexly organised society) that had the ability to include people with the severest learning disabilities, to the point of not noticing, or not being anxious about, the difference between Wittgenstein and them? This is the field in which an archaeology of concepts of idiocy would have to begin.

II

Locke's definition of madness by antithesis with idiocy is in fact just one of several allusions in the first edition of the *Essay Concerning Human Understanding*. I have argued elsewhere[3] that his definition of reason is a circularity, maintained by his denomination of 'idiots' and 'changelings'; that these have no basis in any trans-historical type but are simply whatever does not belong within the circle; that certain normative considerations infuse his natural history, in which idiot changelings are a psychologically distinct type and on these grounds different in species. In the *Essay* he draws a distinction, famous for its novelty, between the 'physical' and the 'moral man'. In replacing the Aristotelian definition of a creature whose real essence is 'corporeal rational being' (where the rationality of members of the species as individuals only needs to be intuited) with a definition by nominal essence (where each single member must conform with our idea of man and thus with our idea of what it is to be rational), Locke creates room for a classification of some individuals who in not being rational are at odds with the definition of humans as a species. He calls them 'changelings' – merely physical, non-moral beings. These changelings are used to illustrate the 'principle of plenitude' in the Chain of Being. This states that God does not omit anything from the fullness of creation; idiots, by occupying a niche between genuine humans and other animals, are hierarchically ranked below the madness of genuine humans. They are positively 'excluded out of the species of man' in Locke's natural history. They have no souls, and consequently no after-life; were we able to determine the prognosis at birth, infanticide or at least a refusal to baptise would be justifiable. He emphasises difference in kind: changeling idiocy is not due to inheritance, either parental or Adamite (which could imply at most a difference in degree), but to a difference in 'the Wheels, or Springs (if I may so say) within'. It is assumed therefore that the condition is incurable and the subject ineducable. Finally, the assessment criteria for idiocy are based on the psychological category of 'abstraction', or the ability to sort species and kinds by their most useful characteristics; lack of this capacity is labelled 'idiocy'.[4]

We are not looking at a coherent theory. Several of the themes are contradicted in other texts from before and after the 1680s where Locke is more sceptical, less exclusive. But this only emphasises that his notions are intuitive. What binds them is their location in the mind-set of someone born in 1632, reared a Calvinist, subject to the political events and the theological and scientific–medical disputes of the mid-century, and caught up in the specific conjuncture of 1689. Locke's idiots – and ours – are urgently necessary inventions, squeezed into existence by *ad hoc* demands. The changeable definition of the changeling, however, is facilitated by the relative stability of the concept of absence of 'ability', which emerged from the revolution at the crucial time of Locke's early personal development and has remained central to our culture.

III

Locke grew up in a religious setting still heavily influenced by the Calvinist theory of the elect. According to orthodox Calvinism, all humans are disabled: morally, in that they are impotent to believe, and naturally, in that this moral impotence is congenital, inherited from the fallen Adam. 'Moral' and 'natural' are one unitary disability. Election by grace is God's cure, pre-ordained to only a few. But according to the opposite Protestant doctrine (Arminianism) Christ died to save all humans, not just the elect – on the grounds that 'To beleeuve is of grace' but 'to be able to beleeuve is in nature',[5] in everyone. Everyone can, if they will. To the Calvinist reformed church, this was anathema. Humanists working within it,[6] unhappy about humans being shuffled around by blind forces of predestination, had to try and justify human autonomy without incurring the charge of Arminian heresy. They located it in the 'physicality' of natural ability, of the Understanding as an active power, not passively receiving illumination but permeating body and soul through individual labour. Thus the humanists transformed previous scholastic notions of 'active intellect' into something enshrined in the natural history of individuals. Thus too they speak in new ways about differential rationality. It is no longer simply that some humans are elect, but also that some are more intellectually able than others.

If this contradicts the orthodoxy of pre-ordained election, it also contradicts the Arminian doctrine that everyone can if they will. Rather, everyone will (or should) if they can. This theory was known as 'conditional universalism'. Since the main premise in this formula now rested on intellectual ability, rather than will, it raised the possibility that there might be individuals who 'can' not, and who therefore do not qualify for consideration as universal. The law of nature is, in the biblical phrase, 'written on everyone's heart', but is disapplied where there is idiotic absence of reason; such individuals are morally exempt from the promise we humans make to fulfil our duties in our covenant with God. The absence is explained in terms of a disabled 'nature' that is separate from morals, or morally neutral. Conversely, the moral disability, though it behaves 'as if' it is natural, is something we can improve.

This formulation would have remained vague had it not been for attacks from orthodox Calvinist colleagues. Anyone lacking a whole faculty of Understanding would by definition be a beast: thus the humanists heretically challenge the fixity of species. An all-perfect God could not have created non-human humans; they would have to be considered faulty. One humanist reaction to this *ad hominem* argument is to espouse it, to emphasise species difference. More often it leads them to consider differences of degree, a differential psychology now set in a natural-history framework. For this, a generic classification of impediments already exists in legal notions of competence; and the 'natural' element of the differentiation can be explained by biblical–medical analogies with blindness, amputation and leprosy. From the husk of the old medical and legal discourses, till now embedded in unrelated realms of experience, there will emerge a concept of (absent) reason defined in terms of a purely mental 'nature', sometimes aligned with a species-type difference.

Orthodox Calvinists reject the tendency towards this ultimate differentiation, but only because for them the important boundary is between elect and non-elect. Once others blurred this boundary, it either included its idiots as excused humans, exceptions to the rule (untidy but unthreatening), or was redrawn to exclude a new species existing in the interstice between beasts and humans. This creature is more vulnerable. Is it excusable? Has it a soul? Are we obliged to preserve its life? The exclusion of the non-elect became the exclusion of the idiotic by a process that was occasionally even self-aware. This raises the possibility that the elect, if they did not become the bourgeoisie,[7] became the psychologically human, that eventual 'concept of man' defined by possession of a prerequisite 'human understanding'. If we are not redeemed because we are elect but because we are human and want to be redeemed, then conversely to be human must be to be redeem-*able*, in the sense of having the natural intellectual means to work at it.

IV

Calvinist humanism's distinction between natural and moral disability[8] was taken up in the politically charged English context of the mid-century, by theologians seeking a middle way between the Calvinist orthodoxy of many Presbyterians and Independents and the Arminianism of the bishops and monarch. The most prolific of these was Richard Baxter, who subsequently influenced generations of pastors. It is clear from his observations that the kind of language used to discuss the boundary between elect and non-elect carried over into descriptions of the boundary between psychological humanity and its corresponding idiocy. Calvinist orthodoxy had always warned against prying into God's reasons for calling some and not others; this would be human arrogance, because God pleases himself. Baxter and other champions of the humanists' conditional universalism complained that this is mere evasion; but they transfer exactly the same discourse of evasion to their attempts to answer the question, did God create idiots in nature and if so, why?[9]

In Locke's hands, the widening of the elective boundaries is clearest in his concept of 'moral man'. This assumed innovation in fact followed several earlier moves. Calvin's successors had used this respectably Aristotelian formula (originally signifying the person capable of restraining his desires) to describe their concept of humans in the state in which they are created by God in nature: hence the insistence that 'moral man' and 'natural man' were coterminous. At first this underlined the pessimistic view of man as corrupt: to be moral was to be born a sinner. The moral man was the 'outer' aspect of natural corruption, repentant verbally but still wicked; only inexplicable grace could get you to heaven. But gradually the humanist wedge driven between natural and moral disability forced theologians to clarify how they would define the species on those occasions when they needed to discuss elect and non-elect under one heading. To talk of the Aristotelian 'rational animal' as 'the whole lump of mankind'[10] would be to concede to Arminianism, in which corruption was underplayed and everyone redeemed. It became necessary to clarify the character of the species, however trivial this issue compared with who was or was not elect. The 'moral man' was to become irrevocably a definition premised on ability (albeit, for the orthodox, an ability of the will rather than of the intellect) to discharge one's duty to God.[11] This was a more restricted classification of species than St Paul's 'lump of mankind'. To make a distinction between natural and moral became more acceptable, although in fact the acceptance was still merely verbal among orthodox Calvinists; it is not a distinction they fully understand in practice.

People like Baxter took advantage of this shift. Moral ability, he said, cannot constitute natural ability; it presupposes the existence of a separable natural ability. The humanity of the corresponding idiots is thereby rendered dubious. In the 1650s there were already complaints that the Aristotelian formula 'homo = animal rationale' was circular. 'Homo = animal morale' was a substitution that allegedly cut through the circularity: the species is defined as that which owes a moral duty to God because it has certain natural mental abilities. The point of Locke's *Essay* was to specify what those abilities were and how they worked in detail; they defined for Locke, in contrast to the 'merely physical' changeling, not 'the *moral man*, as I may call him' but 'the moral man, as *I* may call him' – a readjustment of the earlier terminology.[12]

What were those abilities which the new idiots lacked, with such dangerous consequences for the rest of us? Along with the species, the abilities are already envisaged in new ways at the Thermidorean turning-point of the revolution. One can almost specify the day in the calendar when belief ceases to be predominantly a set of principles residing in a place called the Understanding and comes to be determined ultimately by prior intellectual processes, the micro-mechanical 'operations', 'aids and assistances' of ability. These are both necessary and free: necessary in that they exist through nature, proceeding epistemologically (i.e. according to rules of rational evidence and probability), and free in that they involve the will. Such a way of talking about reason and the understanding, and thus of principles as separate from abilities, and sometimes of the mind as *tabula rasa* in this sense, already exists across the political and theological divisions of the late 1650s; the participants themselves are quite aware that they are talking in new ways about a 'new reason'.[13]

The watershed political event is Cromwell's dissolution of the Barebones Parliament, the final phase in the gradual evaporation of hopes for the millennium or at least for a Calvinist political regime in England. If the end itself were not realisable through instant mass regeneration, then the church could at least 'police the means'[14] to conversion. These means are constituted by the epistemological abilities facilitating belief in redemption, and constitute what it is to be human. People lacking abilities are now as crucial and visible as unregenerates who simply lack principles had previously been; they populate a dystopia of active learning disabilities, a fantasy which advances as the utopian vision of a passive receipt of rule by the saints recedes.

V

The theologians were also pastors, and the new way of talking about reason had been accompanied by over a decade of dispute about the practice of excluding would-be communicants. This was perhaps the central ideological battle of the mid-century,[15] involving as it did the unity of the church, the role of the monarch and/or presbytery, and the question of who was to police the congregation: the civil magistrate or the ecclesiastical jurisdiction? The significance of communion, by contrast with the Roman theory of trans-substantiation, lay in self-examination. How could the pastor know what was going on inside the communicant's self? According to those who believed in free admission one could not claim to be able to sort hypocrite chaff from truly regenerate wheat; the attempt of Presbyterian elders or Independent congregations to examine and exclude overstepped the limits of mere human competence, encouraged disunity and usurped the powers of the civil magistrate.

The free admission doctrine made two discrete exceptions to its rule of encouraging all to take communion: one was those who had already been excommunicated for 'scandalous sins', and the other was those naturally disabled from examining themselves such as children and the 'distracted' or mentally disturbed. At the outset, 'fools' are simply subsumed under the latter; if mentioned at all, they are the legal category of 'born fools', the distinction between them and madpeople with lucid intervals being irrelevant. What mattered was that they were all 'excused', in a legal sense, from self-examination. The Presbyterian and Independent counter-attack is initially the orthodox Calvinist rejection of any such separation between will (scandal) and reason (distractedness): the moral man is the inexcusable natural man. But eventually the argument about children and the mad is settled, and psychological (rather than legal) idiocy is the positive exclusion that emerges.

How does this happen? The debate contains an anxious subtext of complicity: surely there is some category of person who, we would all agree, will never be admitted to communion? The argument then would only be a secondary one of how wide this category is. Otherwise, our partisan differences as to who should be admitted, being unresolvable, would lead to a chaos of relativism and church–political disunity, corrupting the natural social order. The rock-like need for all sides to regain unity precedes and actually creates the thing itself, a common absolute exclusion. The excommunicate is still technically a church 'member', albeit 'under care'. The infidel is not a member, but is capable of being baptised and eventually of receiving the eucharist.

Beyond this there must be a level of absolute exclusion. What exactly is it? Opponents of free admission ask its champions whether they should not admit children to communion, since like infidels they have potential to become like us: how on your own criteria can you assess when they will reach the age of discretion? And the distracted or mad: if your rabble can attend in preparation for being 'cured' of their ignorance, the mad can be cured of theirs and so by your rules should be admitted. This still leaves a niche for someone who does not have either potential or curability: but this religious absence is no longer the fiscal disqualification (congenitality) or a strictly medical one (incurability) but absence of the 'inner' man. The supreme aim of the Presbyterians and Independents was to screen out hypocrites; the free admission party thought such exclusions posed a threat to unity. But hypocrites merely have different principles between the 'inner' and the 'outward man'; the argument is simply about whether they can be detected or not (and who does the detecting). There must, however, also be someone who has no principles because they have no inner abilities, and no natural reasoning operations of the new kind I have described above. This new idiot is provoked, initially as a last-resort case, from the partisans of free admission at a precise moment in the 1650s, just as the French humanists had been forced by the *ad hominem* arguments of their opponents to consider the possibility of the intellectually 'naturally disabled' being an interstitial species.

This involved something practical. Pastors have churchwardens. The debate about who was responsible for exclusion necessarily entailed secondary debates about the allocation of administrative duties among lay wardens and clerical deacons, at parish level. Among their administrative duties were, first, the job of ensuring that certain people did not physically get beyond the chancel screen, and second, the application of the Poor Laws. Such officers were expert in methodologies of discrimination. Daniel Defoe's *Essay upon Projects*, drafted at the same time as Locke's proposals on Poor Law reform, is often cited as a precursor to the reforming efforts of the late nineteenth century to establish a clear institutional antithesis between madpeople and idiots, following on Locke's psychological antithesis. However, most of Defoe's 'projects' have since been identified as taken from interregnum pamphlets, and his proposal of separate institutions for the idiotic may well date from the same period as the pastoral debates I have been discussing. One of his arguments was that having more clearly demarcated institutions would reduce the social burden, since it was the existence of a single generalised institution that attracted inappropriate customers from the underclass of 'idle drones'. The psychological justification (with clear theological roots) was that madness could be hypocritically counterfeited, whereas idiocy, being natural, was not. Locke's proposal to shift the job of discriminating between deserving and undeserving from the parish to the state should also be seen against the background of these debates.

VI

The period from the outbreak of hostilities over 'natural disability' within French Calvinism at the beginning of the 1630s, to the general acceptance in England of a new way of describing reason as ability by the time of the Restoration, is of course also that of Locke's upbringing and formal education. He accommodated to it his more immediate intellectual influences, notably through his absorption of Cartesian dualism as a way of discussing the mind and the human understanding, and their pathology. This accommodation, in the period of Locke's maturity, took place against the background of the new political crisis surfacing at the end of the 1660s, occasioned by the attempts of a state church – with temporarily revived political authority of its own – to suppress religious toleration.

Its victims, the dissenters, took up once again the notion of a natural mental disability, not now against waning Calvinist orthodoxies but against the opposite (formerly Arminian) flank, the 'Protestant Papists' of the new church hierarchy. The hierarchy no longer argues theologically against compromise; it simply presents the crude threats of people who believe themselves powerful but realise that their authority is insecure, against those who do not conform. For the archbishop and his chaplains, reason was whatever divine authority (i.e. they) said it was, and faith achievable merely through 'works' and observances. For the dissenters, each human could journey to a redemptive threshold by the labour of reason itself, which was necessarily the effort of an individual and therefore required toleration. It was in political support of this dissenting position that Locke first conceived of the *Essay*.[16]

Locke's epistemological turn was not the result of his asking himself 'How do I really know what I claim to know?' but of church authority interrogating the dissenters, 'How do you really know what you claim to know?' Places on the scale of perfection and the career ladder, and perhaps (who could tell, after thirty years of bloodshed?) continued existence on this earth, hung on the 'ability' to answer this question. If your faith was not a passive acceptance, nor your manner of observing it a decision for the magistrate, if it was the result of your own individual reasoning powers, how could you justify it without being an unthinkable, atomised relativist? Some dissenters realised that one could not simply respond by asserting that it was justified (how could more than one individual belief be justifiable?), but that one would have to look for something universal somewhere. Self-evidently, this universality could not lie in an individual rational weighing of evidence and probability alone. But it might consist in the existence in nature of the micro-processes of mental ability, through which the epistemological justification of individual beliefs emerges; this ability was coming to be the realm of absolute fact, in which a variegation of beliefs might hold together. Locke's *Essay* is simply the most daring attempt to describe it.

The construction which Baxter had intimated – idiocy as lack of the innate ability necessary for weighing evidence – is now politically demanded. The bullies of conformity want to know how the human exceptions to the dissenters' notion of reason can be explained. If they cannot, then it will prove that the dissenters themselves are heretical fools, antinomian individualists – 'changelings' in the sense of having a socially unruly and changeable will (a usage I shall return to). The dissenters too need an absolute exclusion of a 'mental' kind, as a strategy for the defence of unity and against accusations of provoking disunity (it is important to remember that the dissenters saw the right to toleration as the prerequisite for political and church unity). The new reason wants new idiots, and it finds them in conceptualisations which had already helped it into being.

Two dissenters in particular, Joseph Truman and Robert Ferguson,[17] make this conscious revival of the French Protestant humanists, in a new context. Reason as ability was not merely a dissenting aberration. The church authorities themselves accepted the 'new reason' as the determiner of 'doubts of all sorts … by the dictates of nature'.[18] Their job was to recuperate this new concept into a scheme compatible with their own (divine) authority. The concept had been born out of a radical distinction between natural disability and the moral disability of reprobates. However, just like the orthodox Calvinists of the previous generation, they cope with the discourse of a natural (dis)ability only by subsuming it under the 'moral' in its scholastic sense. Here 'the measure of man's natural power of knowing or judging of things is his participating of these things, in some degree, with God', that is, the moral relationship. The authority of reason is a divine, top-down determination, in spite of the separate existence of a specifically human, incorrupt natural ability.

Truman answers by asserting the importance of idiocy. His instincts are inclusive ones. He wants to describe his idiots as different merely in degree, citing the Aristotelian doctrine that degree cannot alter the species, and the forensic category of inculpability: idiots are excused from the effort to make themselves redeemable. His notion of a natural species is not that of Locke, who was an FRS and a medical imitator of Ray's botanical classifications. Nevertheless, at times the force of his own argument, defending mental ability as something belonging to the individual and separate from absolute authority, leads him to concede that (just like the order to work in Locke's conception of the poorhouse) 'the command of loving God … requires the utmost of a mans natural Ability (and no more)'. Therefore the place in nature of the intellectually disabled – in the sense that the threats of hell and promises of heaven are something the earthly intellect is obliged to understand – must be described precisely. He suspects there is a reason for idiocy and its freedom from obligation 'in the nature of things'. Moreover, Truman also reduces the circumference of the species from the 'whole lump of mankind' to 'moral man'. As in earlier debates, it is the defensive posture against authoritarian opponents that forces from the dissenter a sharper definition of the idiot, and this in spite of Truman's inclusive instincts. The naturalism of his 'moral man' is pasted over the chop-logic phrase 'rational animal', as Locke's is: lack of this 'natural power' makes one 'no rational creature'. The new epistemological formula, based on the individual's 'power and knowledge to chuse' on the basis of 'suitable objective evidence', both creates/excludes its corresponding disability and could not exist without it. Comparative psychology is the criterion of species definition.[19]

Truman is indecisive, however, perhaps out of political caution. The church hierarchy wants to say that God wills the conversion of everyone. In opposition to this Romanising or Arminian position, Truman tries to reassert that God's fundamental division is between elect and non-elect. What, then, about the distinction between naturally abled and disabled? He asks us to 'exclude the case of Infants and ideots, as being alien, and of less concernment in Religion, and also difficult'. His opponents seize on this contradiction and deride it: the demarcation line is either one or the other.[20] This discussion is clear evidence that the transition from the boundaries of election to those of intellectual ability could be perceived as such by contemporaries.

It should be noted that in Truman too there is a lurking Calvinist orthodoxy. Just as the church hierarchy claimed to admit natural ability as separate, but simply subsumed it under a passive moral ability to obey, so – in an opposite but equal reaction – the dissenter Truman (and eventually Locke) bestow an assumed moral content upon a secular natural ability. Both approaches override the hesitant subtlety which the natural–moral distinction has in the writings of the Protestant humanists, and both thus restore a version of the original orthodoxy. For the old orthodoxy, the identification of natural with moral disability had spelt 'natural man', Adamite corruption. For the dissenters, the identification of natural with moral ability in the 'moral man' paints a veneer of humanist optimism; but accordingly, its opposite is constructed as the natural intellectual idiot. Did God himself create this contradictory creature? The contradiction can only be resolved by naturalising this idiot, by 'excluding it out of the species', in Locke's phrase.

The self-styled 'politico-theologian' Robert Ferguson, writing in the same year as Truman and the famous discussion which inspired Locke's *Essay*, reconstructs the history of the Calvinist debate about natural and moral disability. He too claims to adhere to the humanist side, but as I have said, this claim is problematical. Ferguson isolates the category 'physical'. In scholastic terms, physical laws are willed by God upon the material universe and upon non-corporeal beings, moral laws upon humans. The French humanists, and their English counterparts such as Baxter, had expressly treated 'physical' and 'natural' as synonymous, and 'moral' and 'ethical' as their joint antithesis. But for Ferguson, to be moral is to be 'connaturalized to the Gospel', and the 'moral ineptitude' of the unregenerate is in this sense[21] a natural deficit. To be an 'ideot', on the other hand, is a 'physical disproportion', as deep between this idiot and ourselves as between ourselves and God. (The soul as well as the body are seen as physical in this sense.) The physical stands in contradistinction to the natural-cum-moral, just as the opposite of Locke's moral man, the changeling, is a man merely 'in a Physical sense'. If you are unregenerate, you are at least 'physically' (i.e. non-idiotically) capable of grasping scriptural truth; you can but won't. Ferguson thinks this moral shortcoming is 'cured' by grace, whereas Locke argues that this is by perfection of the micro-processes of understanding. (In both, the subtlety of Baxter's point about morals only behaving 'as if' natural is glossed over.) But can the natural intellectual idiot be cured? Ferguson says, 'a believing soul … though otherwise simple and ignorant, hath an [already instilled] insight into the things of God': if not exactly a cure, this implies a residue of innate principles. Locke, without this crutch, says that the creature with a human morphology constitutionally incapable of his 'human understanding' is a quasi-species – 'physical' not like Descartes' animal automata (which after all were perfect in their own way, more so than humans) but in an unnatural and contradictory way – a human which is not a human.

He tackles this conundrum with the help of his 'nominalist' argument that we sort species as we find it useful to do rather than by objectively fixed 'real' categories. Changelings as a separate species are explained by, among other things, physiological difference in the 'internal constitution'. Locke has no problem about thus breaching the fixity of species. The problem lies, once he has done so, in saying how his natural history can cope with something which ought to have a mind and doesn't. Can it be just another species, or is it an unnatural one?

The difference between changelings and proper humans is that if to be human is to have reason-as-ability in the realm of pure mind, whether the body attached to it is human or not (it could be a baboon's or a parrot's body), then the changeling is a zero. But this requires a purely mental aetiology. Is such a thing possible? The origins of this dilemma are partly the philosophical ones created by Cartesian mind–body dualism, but partly political. To explain absence by symptoms of absence would be circular. If it can be said, albeit problematically, that bodily events can 'cause' purely mental (non-)events, why does Locke not pursue it? He does not say it cannot or should not be done. Rather, he explicitly passes up the opportunity. Perhaps this can be viewed by contrast to Thomas Willis's version of changeling idiocy as caused by a difference in the anatomical structure of the brain. Medical interest in anatomy was, for various reasons, associated with aristocracy and the church hierarchy. The body, like Willis, was Tory.[22] The mind was Whig, as was Locke's patron, Shaftesbury, who protected the dissenters along with their doctrines of toleration and the individual labouring intellect. The opportunity for a physiological explanation was not so much rejected by Locke as already closed to him. As I will shortly show, this gap in the possibilities for a coherent 'natural history' explanation of idiocy is compensated for by other possibilities which emphasise unnaturalness.

Whatever its explanation, the fact of species difference is explicit. Locke's God calls everyone conditionally, as did Baxter's; what is new is the definition of 'everyone', which is grounded in a definitive exclusion of these changelings. If the displacement of special election to a universal plane seems like an egalitarian move to today's reader (that is, if it seems anything more than pseudo-universal), it can only be because we are ourselves assuming trans-historical criteria in nature for the exclusion of an idiot.

VII

There is a more immediately political context to the discussion of causes; it concerns the role of philosophy as against divinity, and the correct use of language. Against the cultivation of ignorance through obscurity practised by the church hierarchy, Ferguson sees philosophy as a way of asserting the autonomy of the individual's reasoning abilities and thus the public survival of dissent; this is the political importance of using 'civil' or publicly accessible terminology, and it is well known that this was Locke's goal too. In fact the aim of the passage containing his changeling/moral man distinction is to demonstrate precisely that point.

Ferguson makes the same point when he argues for the synonymity between 'natural' and 'moral'. The word 'natural' is more accessible to the lay reader schooled in scriptural accounts of moral disability, which are based on analogies with 'natural' conditions such as blindness. Lack of the physical organs of sight furnishes a descriptive framework for lack of the mental faculty of a labouring, individual understanding. Elision of the analogical character of this mind–body relationship facilitates elision of the difference between natural and moral disability; it helps communicate with a wider public, where 'old terms' (and perhaps old prejudices) 'will serve the turn'. We are confronted with a creature who lacks not only the ability but the specific kind of disability (i.e. the moral one of reprobation) which orthodox Calvinism insists is natural to the human species. It is therefore not a human at all; rather than having some mental operations which are under-active by analogy with Galenism's sluggish 'animal spirits', its defining mental characteristic is an absence. In the patois still informally used by medical practitioners in this field, 'there's nothing there'.

Locke, searching for a word for his extra species, chooses 'changeling' as the existing civil term (one drawn from everyday language) that shapes up as the least square peg in this new round hole. What had been its contemporary connotations? First, extreme difference from the parent, as in Aristotelian and Paracelsian discourses as well as Calvinist debates about the inheritability of election. Second, there is the child who is not a child:

> A virgin became pregnant and said that she was visited every night by a handsome youth. Her parents lay in wait for this lover and the following night found a frightful monster in their daughter's embrace. A priest was called and drove the devil out by reciting St John's Gospel. Thereupon the devil set all the bedding on fire, let off a terrible fart, and made away. The following day the daughter gave birth to a monster or fantastic abortion.[23]

This text appeared in the same year as the *Essay*, and may seem rather different. However, demonology and natural history were not mutually exclusive. Midwives[24] and theologians sought rather to make a correct distinction between fantasised demons and real ones. (Non-belief in their existence was a sign of atheism.) The function of baptism had been to exorcise the devil in the infant, and by this very act to enable divine illumination to enter in. Eventually the passivity of illumination is substituted by the active reason entailed in mental processes, and so the attribution of these latter just is the act of exorcism. Consequently their absence just is devil-possession.[25] There is nothing exotic about the demonological explanation; such idiots, the 'simulacra of hell',[26] are intrinsic to the historical construction of modern psychology.

This mind-set, or at the very least Locke's supposition of it in the reader, is the only possible answer to the question: why did he connect the 'separate species' argument with a justification of infanticide if the difference be detected at birth? One does not kill all animals, just because they are animals. The implicit justification must be utilitarian: it deals with the consequences of the devil's existence in the real world. This method of justification may be compared with the way in which medical science justifies genetic screening for learning disabilities by pointing to the fiscal consequences of allowing certain foetuses to come to term. Likewise the rarity of the seventeenth century's demonological changeling means that it is exposed to the same statistical glare as the trisomic foetus whose abnormality is highlighted by being isolated at one end of the scale of random IQ distribution and is pursued by genetic technology. The statistical abnormality and the demonic paranormality associable with learning difficulties are simply two ways of representing the same thing: the difficulty which a particular society has in coping with the consequences of its own integration.

We can see then why Locke's medical and pedagogical innovations did not extend to the possibility of curing or educating his congenital idiot.[27] He had taken in hand the education of Edward Clarke junior, the son of his close political confidant, who became 'blockheaded' (a medical term in the seventeenth century) following childhood encephalitis; Locke was puzzled, but at least considered education possible.[28] The difference between him and the changelings was not one of degree: it is not that changelings are 'severe' and Clarke merely 'mild'. It all lies in the fact that changelings are congenitally so. Having different internal 'wheels and springs' means one is born different in kind, and if physiology cannot cause mental absence then answers must be sought in the causes of birth itself. For most readers, the devil would be understood here.[29]

VIII

The correct deployment of 'civil' terminology also helps us to understand the *Essay*'s antithesis between madness and idiocy. The formula 'man is a rational animal' was inadequate because it was merely a 'physical' description; it dealt with the body and the soul, but not with that fundamental law of nature which is, in a typical dissenting variant, 'not so much a law which our nature prescribes unto us, as a law prescribed into our nature'.[30] Absence of the Lockean ability to formulate abstract ideas, to think and sort for ourselves, is absence of that law. Magistrates may claim to represent divine authority, but blind obedience to their stipulated observances renders us idiotic. If humans are individually capable of fulfilling their own reasoning abilities, then creatures lacking such abilities do not blend into the lump. They stand out because they do need to obey authority unquestioningly (parents, legal guardians etc.); they are not exceptions to a mere rule of logical classification ('man is a rational animal'), they 'do Unman us',[31] threatening our place in the scheme of natural history and our new-found, individually grounded political maturity, our 'ability' to give rulers our consent or withhold it.

The pathological characteristics of idiocy thus merge with those of idolatry and divine authority, bringing along previous theological, medical and legal discourses. They include mental under-activity, idleness, lethargia, ignorance (enforced by the priesthood), humoral coldness, weakness (impotentia), the 'stupidity' of mere matter, as well as social backwardness and a nostalgia for the Roman religion and the everyday idiocy of the unconverted countryside. On the opposite side, the pathological characteristics of madness merge with those of religious enthusiasm: they are speed, heat, over-activity, and an excessively forward-looking (chiliastic) mentality, associated often with the lower social strata in the towns.

This antithesis between idiotic idolaters and mad enthusiasts exists in various permutated pairings throughout the century, often in medical contexts or analogies. Political and sometimes personal survival depended on finding, in the rapid fluctuation of forces, a fulcrum of 'moderation' between what might be construed by your enemies as nonconforming enthusiasm on the one hand, and Arminian or Roman idolatry on the other. The middle path of political and clinical sanity was a narrow and inscrutable one; you claimed to occupy it because you wanted to keep your head.

The *Essay* contains various subtextual references to this. In the 1690s Locke added both a chapter on the association of ideas and one on enthusiasm.[32] The first of these is almost wholly about mis-association, and is clearly viewed through the same optic as enthusiasm, 'the Conceit[s] of a warmed or over-weening Brain' on the part of 'the untractable Zealots'.[33] The date of the added chapters coincides with the period when, after the exclusion of the idolatrous James II, the main target of the dominant ideology was once again enthusiasm. Locke, under pressure from the victorious doctrines and faced with charges of Socinianism (itself seen as enthusiastic), had to reply. He contrasts the enthusiasts with the Roman Church, in which superstitious belief encourages suspension or absence of reason's operations, whereas enthusiasts let them run amok. Locke's treatment of enthusiasts was somewhat opportunistic. When it did him no harm, he extended his vision of religious toleration to them. His exclusion of Roman idolatry never wavered. At least enthusiasts are mentally able, even if they misuse these abilities. His political rejection of ecclesiastical infallibility and idolatry and his espousal of toleration are inextricably tied up with his psychological rejection of innate ideas and espousal of innate abilities. In terms of pathology, this reflects his lopsided ranking of the antithesis in which the mad are just like us but the idiotic different in kind.

IX

Locke's dissenting contemporaries still talked about needing, on top of the newly optimistic moral/natural abilities, a 'spiritual' entity of saving grace. 'Where there is nothing but a natural Mind, it can act no otherwise than in a Natural way,' says Ferguson.[34] If our minds are no longer naturally corrupt, they are insufficient. But Locke pushes grace aside and uses this kind of formula as his positive starting-point; it is then ready to be born, in the hands of others, as a secular psychology. And the creation of 'idiots' on or beneath a terrain of reason as purely human ability and purely mental labour, is the ploy by which the rest of us are able to present ourselves to authoritarian bullies as intelligent, moderate, autonomous citizens capable of consent and democratic government. The more Locke's leveller credentials[35] extend towards a universalist concept of 'man' – the forty-shilling freeholder, perhaps servants, perhaps (if only hypothetically) women and the slaves of the colonial trading companies – the more sharply are the remaining exclusions etched in, the non-elect detritus of civil society.

This is in theory. But it is important to see that this does not overlap neatly with Locke's perception of the real society around him, and important to understand this perception as a theological rather than a sociological one.[36] A century of Puritan attacks on the notion of honour, and on the aristocracy's disdain for the dishonourably hard mental labour needed to manage their estates, helps explain why Locke stresses that '*Gentlemen* should not be ignorant'.[37] He normally makes a clear distinction between the word idiot as a technical usage and the class idiocy of the village, that general lack of education and metropolitan culture which according to him affects 'the greatist part of mankind' who are mainly concerned to 'still the croaking of their own bellies'. But the two sets of criteria, legal and psychological, are not yet seamlessly one, and the class-restricted sense of the legal criterion is still implied. Locke is worried about the mental shortcomings of members of the social strata for whom the *Essay* was written. At the genesis of strictly psychological 'idiocy' criteria, they operate to some extent with different degrees of strictness according to one's place in the social order. Exclusion only matters where there are grounds for inclusion in the first place. It is gentlemen idiots who are the fly in the ointment of early psychology. The social order is a divinely appointed order of unchanging nature, and the educability of one's social inferiors to an equal level of understanding is, if feasible, mere speculation.

These normative elements in Locke's natural history of idiocy and understanding reveal themselves most clearly when he focuses on ability.[38] Unlike the dissenters, he does not refer to the old humanist debate; but the same pressures of conformity dictate his discussion. He uses 'ability' to try and disconnect the notion of freedom from that of willing. For the champions of ecclesiastical authority, liberty is the opposite of determination and compulsion: it means the social chaos of recent memory, summed up as antinomianism – the freedom to do what one likes, with the excuse that this is divinely sanctioned by the presence of God in oneself. Locke avoids the trap of appearing to defend this by defending 'liberty'. Instead, he denies that liberty and determination are opposites. For this purpose, he brings in the changeling once again:

> To give a right view of this mistaken part of Liberty, let me ask, Would any one be a Changeling, because he is less determined, by wise Considerations, than a wise Man? Is it worth the name of Freedom to be at liberty to play the fool?

It is not clear here whether the changeling is an idiot or a madperson, and this fusion of antithetical characteristics is instructive. In addition to the significances of the term already discussed, there are many Puritan sermons in which the 'changeling' is a unitary self that is always changing its will (rather than being swapped or possessed). This will-changeling can be idiotic in the context of Popery (it allows its opinions to be dictated at a whim by authority), or mad in the context of antinomian enthusiasm (where it changes itself constantly because it takes its own inconstant will to be the will of God). Locke uses this fusion to argue that the pursuit of happiness is itself a constraint; we have an 'ability' to 'suspend the prosecution of this or that desire' which depends upon self-examination, not on obedience to authority. The highest happiness is the afterlife, and the necessity of pursuing it 'is the hinge on which turns the liberty of … finite intellectual Beings'. Changelings, on the other hand, appearing to have complete liberty because anything they do is excusable, are therefore in fact totally determined. 'Agents that have no Thought, no Volition at all, are in every thing necessary [= physical] Agents,' says Locke partly in answer to those who fear liberty of worship and removal of the magistrate's compulsion. Amentia and its spuriously human agents are the concrete examples of total determination.[39]

Changelings in the above context are creatures who either lack the faculty of Will completely, or who have few intellectual abilities to examine it or suspend their action; just as idiot changelings, in the faculty of Understanding, are those who either lack 'abstract ideas' completely or who put ideas together very feebly. The either/or in both cases is significantly fuzzy. The naturalistic and the normative support each other: the separate species construction of the changeling is cultured from the simplicity of the uneducated whose shortage of abilities Locke admits is socially determined. Establishing separate categories in nature in whom humanity is absent is dependent on the notion of differences in (social) degree. Reversing the order in Charles Murray's thought-processes,[40] we could say: without the conception of an underclass there would be no way of positing mental handicap.

We can mix our notions with Locke's because the publication of the *Essay* coincided in some real sense with the birth of the society in which we ourselves seek to participate. The notions of disability and tutelage, and of ability and consent, were pressed into existence through the class and political seizures of the seventeenth century. Though attached to more ancient metaphysical boundaries of absence/presence, under-activity/overactivity/median activity of the mind, curability and educability, what is distinctive about the modern period as a whole is the coexistence of these with certain notions of social control, from chancel screening to genetic screening. The inherently exclusive concept of psychological humanity belongs with exorcisms, farting devils, and the ethics committee of the British Medical Association, whose justification for the termination of foetuses with certain chromosomal dispositions (the alleged cost to the community of servicing them if they were allowed to come to term),[41] is couched in language which Locke, as the author of a far-sighted Poor Law reform proposal with its paranoiac connecting of 'waste' with 'impotence' and its elevation of this 'burden' from the parish to the state, would have understood.

Locke asks us to consider 'the weak and narrow Constitution of our Minds' and that we are apt to waste our abilities, 'not making that use of [our] Understanding [we] should'; but in doing so he also emphasises that our abilities are our own responsibility. This is the unified criterion by which we distinguish those who do not merit species rights (people who have no minds or abilities at all, of the kind we recommend) from those who do (us), and the hierarchical degrees of esteem and honour (read: intelligence) among 'us'. According to Locke's theory of consent, in a volatile society populated by imperfect but fully human people, the liberty he prescribes is a prerequisite for social order. But at the strange birth of liberal England there are some other anomalous offspring emerging. Totally determined inhuman idiots, at the opposite end from liberty, are necessary to the theory of consent.

More recently the line between consenting to be governed and being an idiot has become rather fine. To question the trans-historical nature of idiocy entails disturbingly negative implications for the whole theory of consent.[42] But this questioning might, for us, be as constructive a path through a socio-political impasse, as upholding it was for Locke. He and his contemporaries often use the example of teaching a parrot to speak. If it could speak rationally, it would have to be classified with humans. If there are people of human outward appearance who can be taught to 'speak' only as a parrot actually does, they could not be so classified. But the epistemological criteria in this assessment of personhood have entailed certain social goals: rationality as the weighing of evidence about individual rewards (at first in heaven, but subsequently on earth), or as the classification of species by their public utility. I can think of a different hypothesis, or rather an example from real life. It is easy to teach someone with quite severe learning difficulties the moves in chess, parrot-fashion. What is immeasurably more difficult is to teach them the concept of winning, let alone strategies. It might much more easily occur to them, because it is naturally more pleasant, that the object is to take turns in removing each other's pieces from the board. This would also develop abilities, but of a different ethical cast. I might develop these skills of co-operation and interdependence more quickly and to a greater extent than my 'opponent', but in a society which could admit to itself that such skills were ultimately more fundamental than those of rational choice, would this difference between us have any social significance? How if at all, would we classify these differences among humans psychologically?[43]

NOTES

1 John Locke, *An Essay Concerning Human Understanding*, Oxford, 1975, 2.11.13. References are to book, chapter, and section.

2 Hippocrates, *On Joints* (Withington), 52.60; 53.52; 53.77. I deal with these questions in 'Mental Disabilities and Human Values', in *Archiv für Geschichte der Philosophie* 74/1, 1992.

3 'John Locke's Idiots in the Natural History of Mind', in *History of Psychiatry*, 1994, vol. 5.

4 Locke, *Essay*, 3.11.16; 3.6.26; 4.4.15–16; 3.6.39; 2.11.13.

5 Quoted in Peter Moulin [Pierre du Moulin], *The Anatomy of Arminianisme*, London, 1620. The word 'disability' is commonly used in this sense in contemporary texts; it has a legal origin.

6 Their leaders were John Cameron, Moisis Amyraut and Paul Testard, all based at the academy of Saumur. A detailed history of the conflict between them and the hierarchy of the Reformed Church is in François Laplanche, *Orthodoxie et Predication: l'œuvre d'Amyraut et la querelle de la grace universelle*, Paris, 1965, and B. G. Armstrong, *Calvinism and the Amyraut Heresy: Protestant Scholasticism and Humanism in Seventeenth-Century France*, Madison, 1969. The relevant primary texts are at the Dr Williams Library, London.

7 This suggestion was made by C. B. Macpherson in *The Political Theory of Possessive Individualism*, Oxford, 1962, and challenged by (among others) John Dunn, in *The Political Thought of John Locke*, Cambridge, 1969.

8 The distinction between 'will nots' and 'cannots' survives today, in exactly the same terminology, in education policy for pupils with emotional and behavioural difficulties.

9 R. Baxter, *Universal Redemption of Mankind, by the Lord Jesus Christ*, London, 1694, p. 477. The book was written in about 1656. See also *Observations on*

Some Important Points in Divinity, London, 1672, p. 55, for a discussion of how to define species in both cases.

10 The phrase comes from St Paul, and is typically Arminian. See especially the main Arminian text, S. Hoard, *Gods Love to Mankind Manifested, by Dis-Prooving his Absolute Decree for their Damnation*, n.l, 1633.

11 Baxter, *Apology*, London, 1654, p. 291.

12 My italics.

13 This includes Presbyterians such as Baxter, Independents such as John Owen (Cromwell's chaplain and Locke's Oxford tutor), and even Platonists such as Henry More. Bishop and king went back in the bottle in 1660, but not the active reasoner.

14 W. Lamont, *Godly Rule*, London, 1969, p. 155ff.

15 This point is made by Lamont. The massive pamphlet literature on this topic is in the Thomason Tracts at the British Library.

16 R. Ashcraft, *Revolutionary Politics and Locke's Two Treatises of Government*, Princeton, 1986.

17 J. Truman, *A Discourse of Natural and Moral Impotency*, London, 1671; R. Ferguson, *A Sober Enquiry into the Nature, Measure and Principle of Moral Virtue*, London, 1673. Truman was a close acquaintance of Baxter. Ferguson was imprisoned for his support for the dissenting clergy, and was chaplain to the Monmouth rebellion.

18 H. Hammond, 'Of the Reasonableness of Christian Religion', in *Works*, vol. 2, Oxford, 1847. Hammond was associated with Gilbert Sheldon, head of the Church of England during the Restoration and the enforcement of conformity.

19 Truman, *Discourse of Natural and Moral Impotency*, pp. 39, 43, 50, 80, 87.

20 Ibid., p. 115ff., and G. Bull, *Examen Censurae*, London, 1676, 17.6. Bull was an associate of Hammond and Sheldon.

21 Ferguson, *Sober Enquiry*, pp. 145–8.

22 Thomas Willis, *De Cerebre Anatomi*, London, 1664, p. 51. This point was suggested to me by Rob Martensen. See also his 'Habit of reason: anatomy and Anglicourism in Restoration England', in *Bulletin of the History of Medicine*, 1992, vol. 66.

23 E. Franciscus, *Der Höllische Proteus*, Nuremberg, 1690.

24 I. Rueff, *The Expert Midwife or An Excellent and Most Necessary Treatise of the Generation and Birth of Man*, London, 1637.

25 This is not an exaggeration. See for example Jeremy Taylor's description of what happens at baptism, in *A Discourse of Baptisme, Its Institution, and Efficacy upon All Believers*, London, 1652.

26 The phrase is Baxter's, in *The Unreasonableness of Infidelity*, London, 1655.

27 Willis suggests something of the kind. However, it is not clear whether he would include those changelings who are anatomically different. In *Two Discourses Concerning the Soul of Brutes which is that of the Vital and Sensitive of Man*, London, 1683, section 13.

28 J. L. Gorn, 'The strange "case" of Edward Clarke, Jr.: Attending Physician – John Locke, Gent.', in *Educational Theory*, 1983, vol. 17.

29 Luther's story about the man who drowned his (autistic?) son because it turned out to be the devil was very widely referred to in the 1650s in exactly the circles whose writings I have been discussing.

30 Ferguson, *Sober Enquiry*, p. 81ff.
31 Ibid., p. 112ff.
32 Locke expresses the pathology of 'wrong Judgement' as an antithesis between 'sloth and negligence' on the one hand, and 'heat and passion' on the other: *Essay*, 4.19.1ff.
33 Ibid., 4.19.7.
34 Ferguson, *The Interest of Reason in Religion*, London, 1675, p. 144ff.
35 These are presented, no doubt justifiably, by Ashcraft in op. cit.
36 J. Dunn, 'From Applied Theology to Social Analysis: the Break between John Locke and the Scottish Enlightenment', in I. Hont and M. Ignatieff (eds.), *Wealth and Virtue*, Cambridge, 1983.
37 See also the *Essay*, 4.20.6. My italics.
38 The chapter (2.21) is entitled 'Power'.
39 Ibid.
40 R. Herrnstein and C. Murray, *The Bell Curve*, New York, 1994, in which the two categories are tied together, as so often, by eugenic prescriptions.
41 See, for example, N. Wald *et al.*, 'Maternal Serum Screening for Down's Syndrome in early pregnancy', in *British Medical Journal*, 8 October 1988; Gill *et al.*, in *Social Science of Medicine*, vol. 24, no. 9, 1987, pp. 725–31.
42 See my 'Social History, the Disabled and Consent', in *Bulletin of Medical Ethics*, 1993, vol. 89.
43 A very different first draft of this paper was read by Jonathan Andrews, Javier Moscoso and Roy Porter, whom I would like to thank for their comments.

6

'CHILDLIKE IN HIS INNOCENCE'

Lay attitudes to 'idiots' and 'imbeciles' in Victorian England

David Wright

And tis a blessed charity, The fetters to unbind,
That hold the dull imprisoned soul, The dark and hidden mind.[1]

INTRODUCTION

An investigation of lay attitudes to idiocy in Victorian England cuts against the grain of several areas of historical research: histories of psychiatry which underrate or ignore completely lay attitudes to medicine, sickness or disability;[2] the fixation of historians, and especially sociologists, with the institutional experience of the insane;[3] and an historical interest in lunacy/madness rather than idiocy/mental deficiency.[4] In the few articles which have broached the subject of lay attitudes to insanity, these tend to be derived from the experiences of particularly important individuals – the melancholy of Samuel Johnson or the 'madness' of George III. They thus represent a fourth historical bias: the reliance on the writings or experiences of particularly noteworthy and articulate individuals. Notwithstanding sporadic attempts to write the 'social history' of psychiatry,[5] or survey new research in lay attitudes to medicine in general,[6] it is nevertheless important to remember that we know very little about popular attitudes to insanity and how these changed in response to an emerging coterie of 'experts', or how disability was integrated into more general notions of family, household and kinship in Victorian working-class communities.

With such an undiscovered continent to explore, this chapter will attempt to stake out a small piece of land by centring on lay attitudes towards idiot children in Victorian England. In particular, it will examine the testimony of families to medical practitioners preserved in the admission records of 412 children admitted to the National Asylum for Idiots, Earlswood, in selected years between 1861 and 1886.[7] This chapter will show that parents, aunts and uncles, sisters and brothers, and even grandparents, took an active role in the identification of idiocy and the process of medical certification. Second, the very process of certification and institutional confinement forced these families to formulate and express ideas about idiocy which were distinct and, though not independent of medical discourse on idiocy, were derived from the practical aspects of household life – domestic economy, concerns over household safety, and individual responsibility and duties. This chapter will show how early modern concepts of idiocy persisted into the late nineteenth century, explore how lay ideas were incorporated into medical and educational writing, and reveal how family testimonies anticipated later formal developments in the field of mental classification. Slowly older notions of the pure idiot were supplemented by newer concepts of mental deficiency predicated upon educational failure. The second section of this chapter will investigate the attributed causes of idiocy given in the Reception Orders. This chapter will begin with a survey of the process of certification, discuss indications of idiocy presented by parents of the children, examine the attributed causes of idiocy given to local medical practitioners for inclusion in the admission documents and lastly, discuss developing themes in Victorian definitions of insanity.

THE CERTIFICATION OF IDIOCY IN THE VICTORIAN PERIOD

Under the 1853 Lunatics Amendment Act, each asylum, hospital or private home licensed to receive the insane was required to possess two documents before admitting an inmate: a Certificate of Insanity and an Order for the Reception of a Private/Pauper Patient (Reception Order).[8] Since an 'insane' person, under the definition of the Act, was 'an idiot, lunatic, or person of unsound mind', idiots[9] fell under this legal definition. In the case of county pauper asylums and private 'madhouses', certification usually took place at the union workhouse or at the asylum, respectively.[10] The certification of admissions to the Earlswood Asylum, however, occurred at the residence of a local doctor or, less often, in the home of the prospective inmate. Any doctor licensed under the 1858 Medical Registration Act was permitted to certify a child or adult, provided that the doctor did not have a financial interest in the institution to which the patient was being sent.

The layout of the Certificate remained unchanged for the years under study (1861 to 1886). It asked the medical practitioner to state his reasons for certifying the person as 'an idiot, lunatic or person of unsound mind'.[11] Below he was obliged to add 'indications of insanity communicated to me [the doctor] by others'. These observations, given no less space or prominence in the certificates, were invariably comments from the family of the idiot at the time of presentation to the doctor. These latter 'indications', then, are testimonies of the 'institutionalising' family and can be conceived of as encompassing both precipitating factors which led to institutional confinement as well as general attitudes of what constituted idiocy for poor families.

The Reception Orders were legal certificates transferring, from the guardian to the superintendent of the institution, the care of a person certified as insane. These documents ask for the name of the patients and their respective 'place of abode', 'occupation', 'marital status', 'religious affiliation', 'when and where under previous care or treatment', and whether 'violent', 'dangerous' or 'suicidal'. The Reception Order also asked for the name and place of abode of the guardian, his occupation and 'relationship to the patient'. Since the Reception Orders included the place of abode and occupation of the guardian, one can code the Reception Orders by socio-economic status.[12] This medical and social profile of the patient was transferred by the clerk of the asylum directly into the admission books and the first page of the medical case books.

The core of this chapter derives from a database study of the Earlswood Asylum records, including the complete entries of Certificates of Insanity and Reception Orders for 412 patients admitted in sample years between 1861 and 1886. These documents were 'linked' to admission registers and census enumerators' schedules. Extracts from this database will be supplemented with a few surviving letters from parents to the Matron of the asylum. Most were 'letters of thanks', and thus will tend to represent a rosier picture than otherwise might be painted. Unlike Certificates of Insanity, which were completed outside the control of the asylum authorities and which the institution was required to keep *en masse* for annual inspection, the letters could very well be merely a selection of the best testimonies to the asylum. Given these caveats they contain a less structured and at times extremely revealing insight into the personal reflections of parents and thus serve a useful function as a counterweight to the formal structure of the admission records.

The Earlswood Asylum was the first voluntary (charitable) asylum for idiot children in England and Wales. Having completed its institution on Earlswood Common, Surrey, 1853, the founding charity proceeded to admit children from families who lived throughout England and Wales. Fathers of inmates were occupied as general labourers, tradesmen, clerks, small shopkeepers, merchants, lawyers, and gentlemen. They also showed no predisposition to come from urban or rural environments. Families were typically described as from the 'respectable poor' or the 'middle classes', though there were also some wealthy fee-paying families.[13] The mandate of the charity predetermined the type of children admitted to the asylum. They had to be idiot children between the ages of 8 and 18 at the time of admission, who were likely to benefit from institutional training, but had not ever received Poor Law relief. These families, therefore, represented a remarkable cross-section of Victorian society, allowing for a study not only of middle-class attitudes, but a rare insight also into working-class attitudes to mental disability.

Very little is known about the actual procedure of certification, apart from the date and place where it occurred, and the name and qualifications of the certifying doctor, all of which were required by law to be included in the medical certificate. As stated above, the medical practitioner was required by law to state from whom 'indications communicated by others' were given. Consequently one can make general comments about the 'testifiers'. Fathers tended to sign the Reception Orders, but the facts communicated to the medical practitioners in the Certificates tend to rely heavily on women – hence entries such as 'her grandmother says she cannot be taught', or 'she is at times violent – her sister', show that those primarily responsible for care in the household also took the lead in certification. Indications could be given also by neighbours, continuing a tradition from the early modern period in which friends or neighbours could testify as to the idiocy of a person in civil court proceedings.[14] When testifying, families used a wide range of criteria, telling anecdotes about the child or simply referring to the absence of basic self-help skills. It is therefore useful to illustrate how these issues were intermixed, before a discussion of common themes arising from the certificates is presented.

An example will illustrate the information given in the certificates. In 1871, Robert Campbell was presented by his father and mother to two local medical practitioners. The first medical practitioner, Julius Sankey, listed his only licence as a Member of the Royal College of Surgeons (England) and in practice as a 'surgeon' in London. After inspecting the 10-year-old Robert he certified him as an idiot and stated his reasons, viz.:

> He laughs when spoken to; & does not speak plainly though he seems to understand what is said to him. He has been under the care of Dr Dickinson of St. George's & it is at his request that I [certify] the child.

Below, the mother, Anne Campbell, was quoted as telling Sankey, that Robert was 'mischievous, malicious and spiteful' and that 'he has once broken a child[']s arm when in a fit of passion. At times is very dirty [–] is always restless.' Admission for non-pauper patients in the Victorian period required two medical certificates, so T. R. Hooper, also licensed as a surgeon, wrote that Robert had a 'vacant indifference to objects such as usually attract children and general conduct unlike other children'. Below, the father was attributed as saying what was 'stated above', that is, in the doctor's section. Record linkage with the enumerator's schedule for the Campbell family fills in other missing information. Robert was the oldest boy and second household child of a family headed by Robert Campbell (sen.), a 44-year-old bricklayer living in Rotherhithe, Surrey. The mother, Ann, also 44, was not given an 'occupation' by the census enumerator. The Reception Order alludes to a short stay in the hospital [for sick children] on Great Ormond Street, but does not give any other information about the disability, save for the fact that it was 'from birth'. The limited financial ability of the family to pay for private care qualified them for charitable status and Robert was admitted to the asylum for a five-year period. In 1876 he was discharged and sent back to his family.

The certification of Robert Campbell represents one case of over four hundred which will be studied in the following sections of this chapter, but it does go a long way to underlying some of the possibilities and limitations of these 'admission' records for the study of lay attitudes. They were filled out by (male) medical practitioners rather than the family members themselves, thus adding the problem of what was 'filtered' out, or to what extent formal terms were substituted for the slang or idioms of family members. But one should not automatically assume that family's indications were overridden or 'edited'. Most doctors were more than happy to note the preoccupation or concerns of the family in the certificates, as shall be demonstrated. As seen in the second medical certificate for Robert, sometimes the medical practitioners did not follow the prescriptions laid out by statute and merely quoted the parents in the doctors' own 'medical' sections.

INDICATIONS OF 'INSANITY'

Previous chapters in this edited volume have outlined the notion of the 'pure idiot', the child completely detached from his environment. Similar conceptualisations were related in the Certificates of Insanity. Alice Maidstone's uncle informed the certifying doctor that she sat for hours in the same position. Her grandmother added that she often talked to herself endlessly playing with small rags wrapped around her hands.[15] There were scattered indications that parents found it difficult to comprehend the lack of emotion of the child: '[by the nurse & members of the family] There is an absence of sympathy with the other children of the Family, either in their grief or joy.'[16]

Family members reacted in a variety of ways, some conceiving of an inner and outer child, akin to the idea of the chained lunatic in nineteenth-century discourses. Mrs Mary R., writing about her two sons in the Asylum: 'I quite long to see him! Little darling! … Oh! that they might have the power of speech granted to them to be able to tell out their little wants!'[17] This idea of a perfect mind inside an imperfect shell is repeated throughout the medical literature. As one article in the *Journal of Mental Science* explained:

> It is true that many of those designated idiots are mental starvelings, laggards, undeveloped creatures, to whose cure or quickening or progress the appropriate stimulus is only wanting. But in the mass of whom we speak the imagined potentialities are chained and confined within the impregnable prison of a diseased organisation.[18]

Family members identified the lack of self-help skills in their son, daughter, brother or sister, and principally noted the problems of feeding, dressing, toileting and self-care. Often the cited disability was all-encompassing, such as the case of Miss Harriet Flint, who described her 17-year-old brother, as possessing 'no judgement or capacity of looking after himself'.[19] Mary Burch noted that from his birth, her son, Frederick, had 'been quite incapable of any self help'.[20] More often, however, families identified specific deficits, such as the father of Henry Priestly who stated that his son 'Cannot dress himself, has no memory, unable to do any trifling task set him.'[21] The lack of self-help skills crossed class and gender boundaries: Anne Coates, the home nurse of

James Allan, the son of a banker's clerk, stated that James 'cannot dress or feed himself, that he eats ravenously & bolts his food; that he is inattentive to the calls of nature',[22] and Louisa Deacon, a private patient, was noted as idiotic for her 'unwillingness' to take food and remaining 'in a dull state for hours'.[23] An important indicator to families was also a lack of speech or the production of 'inarticulate noises'. Mrs Alison of Woburn, Bedfordshire, reflected that her son was always 'uttering curious noises such as yelling & crying like a cat'.[24] Similarly, Henry Lee's mother remarked that, besides being almost constantly in motion, her son makes noises 'like an animal'.[25] Talking to oneself and 'incoherent and inexplicable laughter' could all prove unsettling and cause for comment.

Idiocy was identified in childhood, and the disability of the individual evoked strong allusions to the permanency of the childlike dependence. One woman described her 22-year-old sister as, 'almost a woman in appearance [yet] she is quite childish in her ways'.[26] When Harriet Hart wrote to the Matron of the asylum in 1856 she invoked biblical quotations to reinforce her image of her son as a permanent child: 'We may consider him one of those, to whom our Saviour said "Suffer little children, etc.", for he was, as you know childlike in his innocence and truthful simplicity.'[27] Implicit in this conception of childlike idiocy was not just a lack of skills but the relative backwardness of the child *vis-à-vis* other children or adolescents of the same age. Hence Mrs Monk, the wife of a clerk in Dalston, was not alone in informing the certifying doctor that her 8-year-old son, 'hasn't the sense usual to children of his age'.[28] These mirror the early medical conceptualisations of idiocy. 'Idiocy', one eminent alienist wrote, 'may be said to stand in some relation to certain intra-uterine states … It might legitimately be called infantile dementia.' Later the same medical specialist referred to idiocy as 'prolonged infancy'.[29]

The comparison of the child with other children within the same family or in the local neighbourhood reveals that parents used familiar people from which to draw their conclusions as to their child's disability. Continued association with 'very much younger children'[30] might also indicate a retarded social development to a discerning parent. Idiocy, as a condition, therefore, was not identified in isolation, but rather was defined in an interactive context. Parents told certifying practitioners of incidents when their child had wandered out alone at night and got lost, had leapt at the legs of a passing horse, had saluted 'perfect strangers', and had undressed in public. In the language used these acts were often conflated with lunacy as parents described maniacal and 'passionate' behaviour. When one considers the patterns of neighbourhood sharing, which typified working-class communities of a slightly later period,[31] it is unlikely that the retarded development of a child would have been knowledge confined to a single household.

As Akihito Suzuki has shown for early modern London, violence, aggression or dangerous behaviour were common reasons for seeking institutional confinement.[32] Indications of aggression, violence, 'spitefulness' and 'mischievous' behaviour did occur in the Earlswood certificates, especially in the certificates of boys from working-class families. Ernest Ware's father, for instance, told the certifying physician that his son was 'not safe with his mother and sisters', being 'very violent at times'.[33] Parents, it seems, had a particularly difficult time coming to terms with the aggression, violence and destructiveness of problem children. It was common for them to use the term 'passionate' or 'excitable' when attempting to characterise frenzied 'directionless' behaviour, or to describe as 'spiteful' or 'vindictive' the attacks of children on siblings. Sometimes incidences of violence did not need to be relayed to the certifying practitioner: 'I have this day witnessed violent conduct towards me,' wrote one indignant doctor, 'In getting up from my seat to point [to] him where to read in the newspaper, he violently assaulted me.'[34]

So far these 'indications' of insanity will be readily recognisable to those familiar with petitions of idiocy to the Chancery courts or cases of idiocy referred to Quarter Sessions in the early modern period. But the Victorian period also witnessed new developments in attitudes to and conceptions of idiocy. In particular, the rise of informal and formal education in the nineteenth century was beginning to redefine the boundaries of what constituted idiocy in the eyes of family members. Throughout the Victorian period certificates of insanity reveal a growing indication of the inability of the child to learn basic academic skills either in the home or in a local school. Mrs Green, a dressmaker from Birmingham, was only one of many to inform the doctor that her son was unable to read his letters although 'much time has been spent in teaching him'.[35] This had practical household implications, as illiterate and innumerate children could not fulfil tasks vital to the household economies of shopkeepers.

As Gillian Sutherland has noted, compulsory elementary education precipitated a public debate over the problem of 'slow' children in regular classrooms, giving rise to special schools in the 1890s. Sutherland notes that 'no educational authority had made much effort to compel the attendance of children with severe mental defects',[36] and it seems that this process of 'sending' idiot children back home from schools, during the period before special schools were established in the 1890s, had an impact on families' attitudes long before the more formal introduction of mental testing. Many of these sample families noted that they had attempted to send their children to Sunday schools, dame schools or national schools, and had had them sent home, either for disrupting classes, or for their limited capacity for learning. John Ford testified that his son had been going to the 'parish school' for three years, 'but not been able to learn anything but strokes on the slate'.[37] Eliza Mee told her medical practitioner that her son 'has been to school for more than three years but he is unable to give the name of any letter of the Alphabet that is shewn to him'.[38] Being 'sent home' by the local schoolmaster must have had an impact not only on the family's conception of the child's disability, but also that of families of the local neighbourhood.[39]

Finally, it is important to note what was not given as an indication of insanity. Unlike the period after 1890, when considerations of heredity and threats of 'degeneration' focused attention on young 'feeble-minded' women and their sexual activity, indications of this nature are rare in the certificates for Earlswood for this period. One female adolescent was recorded as being 'erotic in her tendencies',[40] and another older girl, aged 18, had recently, 'made an indecent exposure of her person and manifested an unbecoming fondness for the male sex'.[41] However, it must be emphasised that these references are very rare indeed and the prevalence of sex and sexuality as an indicator of mental handicap shows little of the predominance that they acquire amongst the Edwardian intelligentsia outlined in later chapters in this volume.[42]

The certificates varied enormously, combining anecdotal evidence given by family members, answers to basic questions of mental ability and 'expressions' of the child in innumerable permutations. However, the one common feature was that they were all very brief – usually three to four lines. Most doctors, it seems, did not spend a great deal of time during certification. It probably was not a matter of great import to them. This by no means implies that these certificates are unimportant to the evolution of medical ideas about idiocy. Many of these medical practitioners would have been certifying idiots for the very first time.[43] Consequently it would have been an important, if unstructured, introduction to mental disability and its formal identification. The fact that the child was presented by the family, and that the family had an equal role in its identification, would have meant that these ideas would have been shaped as much by the household concerns of self-sufficiency as by 'abstract' medical concepts of mental ability. The importance of 'family indications' of mental ability, need not be inferred, for, contrary to the design and purpose of the certificates, which had one section for practitioners' comments and one for those of the family, many practitioners simply reiterated the anecdotal evidence of the family.[44] For example, in 1861, Richard Weston, a general practitioner licensed in surgery and apothecary, certified George Benbow, an 'imbecile' from Wellington, Salop. He stated that George had 'an absence of all expression, a vague & unmeaning look'. To substantiate his claim he wrote in the section below that 'the Father states the above symptoms have been present ever since birth'.[45] Thus it would be misleading to imply that the labelling of idiocy was being imposed by the medical profession downwards. Instead, one senses a process of negotiating the meaning of disability in which, if anything, the family had the stronger say.

CONSTRUCTING THE ORIGINS OF IDIOCY

The Reception Orders asked for the 'supposed cause' of idiocy in the child, the answers to which were transferred and sometimes amended in the first page of the inmate's section of the asylum medical case book. The fact that the Reception Order itself prefixed the cause with the word 'supposed' implies that discussions about the origins of insanity were still highly problematic. Nevertheless, an analysis of the causes given by the parents might reveal a great deal about their attitudes to mental handicap and popular attitudes to disability in nineteenth-century England. When comparing Reception Orders to the actual Medical Case records what is striking is not the dismissal of parents' suggestions for the 'cause' of insanity, but rather their incorporation into professional writings.

The most common ante-natal cause attributed to idiocy was a fright or anxiety of the mother during her pregnancy. While some simply referred to 'maternal shock', others were more specific. Mrs Cook received a fright from a fire, Mrs Frayling was repeatedly chased by a dog, and the mother of Thomas Spratt was terrorised by a 'flock of geese flying at her' when she was eight months pregnant.[46] Psychological 'shock' could also extend to mild physical trauma. The mother of John Caulton stated that the idiocy of her son was due to cold water being thrown at her when seven months' pregnant.[47] Since every mother could be expected to undergo 'anxiety' of some kind during pregnancy, this was a ready explanation embraced by many parents which exculpated them from blame. Families assigning fright or shock during pregnancy were by no means continuing a 'superstitious' uneducated working-class belief which would eventually succumb to more medical aetiologies: families citing shock spanned class boundaries: fathers of such families were occupied as coachmen, shepherds, carpenters, bakers, schoolmasters, surgeons and clergymen. Nor was this a case of older popular notions of aetiology slowly giving way to more modern, scientific causation: the citation of fright before birth did not decline over the period under study.

Illnesses and 'accidents' of the mother during pregnancy may be taken more seriously. The mother of Anne Hutton suffered from whooping cough during pregnancy,[48] Mrs Sells suffered from a 'fall', and Mrs Dolbe was frightened by being knocked down '2 months advanced in pregnancy'.[49] Surprising by their absence are references to complications during birth, which one would suspect may have been responsible for some idiotic children: only two cases – Joseph Robson and John Monk – were listed in the Reception Orders.[50] Though in an extended report on one inmate, the admitting officer retold the story of the birth and specified that forceps used during the birth had 'lacerated' the head of the child, the child being subsequently paralysed and idiotic.[51]

Since idiocy was defined *vis-à-vis* the development of other children, it is perhaps not surprising that many parents located the commencement of disability at a young age, rather than from birth. Attributions of cause to early childhood far outnumbered those given to ante-natal or natal incidences. Teething, and more specifically 'fits', 'convulsions' or 'paralysis' during teething were very common post-natal explanations for idiocy accounting for fourteen cases in the sample years. Less common were remarks about debilitating childhood diseases. Eliza Anderson's mother stated that her daughter's idiocy was due to an attack of measles in early childhood.[52] Typhus fever, scarlatina and gastric fever were all mentioned as contributing factors in other cases.[53] In one case, diarrhoea during infancy was claimed to be the culprit.[54] The presumed psychological impact of a traumatic event also extended to the youth of the children themselves. Mary Treadgold was idiotic due to 'a fright at young age'.[55]

Accidental injury to the child was the second most common post-natal cause specified. Henry Markley's Reception Order stated that he had been hit by a carriage.[56] Thomas Williams, Robert Gaskell and Ethel Henry all fell down the stairs during childhood, Thomas Williams when he was 9 months old, Ethel Henry when she was 10 years old.[57] The father of Alfred Meaby commented that:

> this child [Alfred] swallowed a bone when about eighteen months old and was nearly choked – never was right since when the bone came up he brought [up] blood and food up altogether and I being the father – I thought it right to mention it, as I have allways [sic] thought that was the cause.[58]

Since the parents were informing the medical practitioners one can be sure that certain contributing factors, like domestic violence, would have been covered up. However, in one certificate there was a startlingly frank admission: Eliza Blackwell's mother, who signed on behalf of her bedridden husband, stated that the cause of idiocy in her daughter was due to 'Ill usage of mother by her husband while pregnant.'[59]

The prevalence of epilepsy amongst these children led many parents to associate the origins of the mental impairment with the onset of the attacks. Ben Russell was liable 'to epileptic fits from his 6th month until 10th years, which will account for his present imbecility of mind'.[60] Fits could be weekly, daily or even, at the worst of times, hourly, and many parents recognised the deleterious effects of repeated attacks: 'His mother informs me', wrote one doctor, 'that since Christmas last, when he had Fits often his memory has failed very much & he has forgotten what he had learnt up to 12 or 13 years of age.'[61]

CONCLUSIONS

In conclusion, there seems little evidence that poor families sought medical treatment for idiocy, distinct from epilepsy,[62] or that a process of medicalisation of lay attitudes occurred in the three decades which followed the Medical Registration Act of 1858. Thus Scull's assertion that, by 1850, insanity was diagnosed as 'uniquely and essentially a medical problem'[63] seems distinctly exaggerated. Furthermore, these results challenge the notion that classification of insanity, be it lunacy or idiocy, widened as professionals attempted to extend their professional territory. It is equally possible that popular and lay attitudes to lunacy and idiocy, encapsulated in the Certificates of Insanity, expanded definitions about insanity which were later incorporated into professional writings by medical superintendents. The medical profession then would have been unwitting recipients of changing popular attitudes rather than self-interested perpetrators of ever-widening definitions of insanity.

Families thus continued to occupy a separate sphere of interpretation. They continued to understand idiocy within the locus of family relations and the child's ability, or rather, inability to perform duties usually expected of his or her status within Victorian households of various classes. If there were any discernible changes over the Victorian period, there was an increasing reference to scholastic attainment due, no doubt, to the impact of elementary education on the world of poorer families. The number of these children sent home from school having learnt little (in comparison to their peers) must have had an impact on the family's conceptualisation of their child's disability. It also represented the first step on the road towards professional and state construction of idiocy as families lost some control over the diagnosis of their own children.

The advent of the certification of idiocy, as a cultural process, must have had an important psychological impact on families and communities. It represented one small aspect of the rise of the identification or 'labelling' of the modern citizen, a process which also encompassed civil registration and census enumeration. The importance of mental disability in the construction of a person's identity was reinforced when the Government Registration Office included 'idiot or imbecile, or lunatic' to the final column of the decennial censuses from 1871 onwards. As a consequence, while families might have recognised dependence or backwardness for centuries before, this disability was in itself not the determining factor in receiving relief from the state, nor did it need to be validated by a recognised professional. The nineteenth century witnessed a new departure in that Certificates of Insanity were a prerequisite for receiving admission into an asylum. In turn, certification itself became an important aspect of the identification of idiocy, as previous certification was used as an indication of idiocy in the new certificates for readmissions to the asylum.

It is tempting to suggest that the effect of standardised medical and legal certificates had an homogenising influence on the language used to describe idiocy. While authors in this volume have identified a variety of terms used in the early modern period – 'changelings', 'innocents', 'solitaires' – the Victorian Certificates of Insanity suggest a more standardised terminology, referring merely to idiots or imbeciles. Whether this represented a new 'modern' terminology or merely reflected a formal language of certification which was not replicated in daily popular discourse is difficult to say.

Fragmentary evidence showing responses to disability suggests that families did not necessarily take a fatalistic view of the potential of their child. Many testified that they had recognised a deficiency, backwardness or idiocy in their child since an early age, but this did not stop them from attempting to impart basic social skills or utilise the child in tasks of running errands or assisting in housework. For many the collective meaning of disability was not in itself a medical one, but rather a familial one – the idiot family member confronted the natural order of progression of the other siblings and presented the family with the difficulty of a permanent child with its attendant impact on household economy and resource allocation. In this sense, the decision to seek asylum care may well have been one predicated less on an acceptance of a medical approach to idiocy than on practical issues of household economy and life-cycle poverty. How this changed in the twentieth century, however, remains to be researched.

NOTES

1 E. Grove, *A Beam for Mental Darkness*, London, 1856, p. 4.

2 See for example F. G. Alexander and S. T. Selesnick, *The History of Psychiatry: An Evaluation of Psychiatric Thought and Practice from Prehistoric Times to the Present*, New York, 1966; G. Zilboorg and G. Henry (eds) *A History of Medical Psychology*, New York, 1941; R. Hunter and I. MacAlpine, *Three Hundred Years of Psychiatry, 1535–1860*, New York, 1983. An exception to this is R. Porter (ed.) *Patients and Practitioners: Lay Perceptions of Medicine in Pre-Industrial Society*, Cambridge, 1987.

3 A. Scull, *Museums of Madness: The Social Organisation of Insanity in Nineteenth-Century England*, London, 1979, and its reprint under the title *The Most Solitary of Afflictions: Madness and Society in Britain, 1700–1900*, London, 1993; D. J. Mellett, *The Prerogative of Asylumdom: Social, Cultural and Administrative Aspects of the Institutional Treatment of the Insane in Nineteenth-Century Britain*, London, 1982.

4 Of the three *Anatomy of Madness* volumes, only one paper was devoted to 'mental deficiency'.

5 A. Scull (ed.) *Mad-houses, Mad-Doctors and Madmen: The Social History of Psychiatry in the Victorian Era*, London, 1981.

6 R. Porter, *Patients and Practitioners.*

7 Those admitted during the calendar years 1861, 1866, 1871, 1876, 1881 and 1886.

8 16 & 17 Vict. c.96 'Lunatics Care and Treatment Amendment Act', 1853.

9 Hereafter I will no longer use quotation marks.

10 Charlotte MacKenzie notes that, in the case of the private Ticehurst asylum, certification usually took place at the institution itself. C. MacKenzie, *Psychiatry for the Rich: A History of the Ticehurst Private Asylum, 1792–1917*, London, 1992, pp. 102–6. My own work on the Buckinghamshire County Pauper Lunatic Asylum suggests that the union workhouse tended to act as a house of certification, before formal admission to county pauper asylums. Records of St John's Hospital, Buckinghamshire Record Office, series AR 100/89.

11 The statutory definition of 'insanity'.

12 A. Armstrong, 'The Use of Information About Occupation', in E. A. Wrigley (ed.) *Nineteenth Century Society: Essays in the Use of Quantitative Methods for the Study of Social Data*, Cambridge, 1972, p. 205.

13 D. Wright, 'The National Asylum for Idiots, Earlswood, 1847–1886', unpublished D.Phil. thesis, University of Oxford, 1993, especially ch. 2.

14 See Rushton in this volume.

15 Certificate for Alice Maidstone, 1871.

16 Certificate for Thomas Williams, 1871.

17 Letter from Mrs Mary Roberts, 13/1/1858.

18 Anon, 'The Psychology of Idiocy', *Journal of Mental Science*, vol. xi, no. 53 [April 1865], p. 14.

19 Certificate for Arthur Flint, 1881, SRO 392/21/29. All certificates and reception orders are listed in the series SRO 392/21 in the Surrey Record Office. Henceforth only the names and years will be given.

20 Certificate for Frederick Burch, 1886.

21 Certificate for Henry Priestly, 1866.

22 Certificate for James Allan, 1881.

23 Certificate for Louisa Deacon, 1876.

24 Certificate for Tom Alison, 1881.

25 Certificate for Henry Lee, 1881.

26 Certificate for Sophia Joseph, 1881.

27 Letter from Harriet Hart to the Secretary of the Asylum for Idiots, 12/12/1856, SRO 392/2/8/2, p. 7. This theme of 'innocence' has obvious resonances to earlier lay uses of the term 'innocent' to refer to an idiot child. See Rushton and Andrews in this volume.

28 Certificate for Henry Monk, 1881.

29 Anon, 'The Psychology of Idiocy', pp. 1–32.

30 Certificate for Joseph Edwards, 1856.

31 E. Roberts, *A Woman's Place: An Oral History of Working Class Women, 1890–1940*, Oxford, 1984, especially ch. 5.

32 A. Suzuki, 'Lunacy in Seventeenth- and Eighteenth-Century England: Analysis of Quarter Sessions Records'. Part I, *History of Psychiatry*, vol. ii (1991), pp. 437–56; Part II, *History of Psychiatry*, vol. iii (1993), pp. 29–44.

33 Certificate for Ernest Ware, 1881.

34 Certificate, 1863.

35 Certificate for William Green, 1871.

36 G. Sutherland, *Ability, Merit and Measurement: Mental Testing and English Education, 1890–1940*, Oxford, 1984, p. 18.

37 Certificate for John Ford, 1866.

38 Certificate for William Mee, 1886.

39 It is interesting to compare the rise in importance of scholastic ability as a familial indication of idiocy to the decline in the use of 'marks' by illiterate guardians in the Reception Orders.

40 Certificate for Charlotte Owen, 1852.

41 Certificate, 1863.

42 During the eugenic 'scare' of the late Edwardian period, there was a concerted effort to prevent the 'feeble-minded' from bearing children. Enshrined in the Mental Deficiency Act of 1913, one of the criteria for

feeble-mindedness was the bearing of illegitimate children. See, among others, G. R. Searle, *The Quest for National Efficiency: A Study in British Politics and Political Thought, 1899–1914*, London, 1990.

43 Idiots admitted to workhouses technically needed certificates, but this was largely ignored and the Commissioners left it unenforced and decided only to require certificates for licensed asylums and hospitals.

44 See for example Reception Order for Helena Barnett, 1861.

45 Certificate for George Benbow, 1861.

46 For 1861 admissions, see certificates for Cordelia Burn, William Kedd, John Wood; for 1871, see certificates for John Cook, Henry Frayling, John Hill; for 1881, see certificates for Arthur Flint, Sarah Godwin, Aleck Ward, Edith Goddard, William Hancock.

47 Reception Order for John Caulton, 1861; [Medical] Case Book, Males, SRO 392/11/4/7, p. 228.

48 Reception Order for Anne Hutton, 1856; [Medical] Case Book, Females, SRO 392/11/4/7, no. 561.

49 Reception Order for Lucy Sells, 1871; [Medical] Case Book, Females, SRO 392/11/4/5, no. 1249; [Medical] Case Book, Males, SRO 392/11/4/7, p. 210.

50 Reception Orders for Joseph Robson, 1861; and John Monk, 1881.

51 [Medical] Case Book, Males, entry for John Peake, 1871. See also remarks on George Frederick Young, Ibid.

52 Reception Order for Eliza Anderson, 1866; [Medical] Case Book, Males, SRO 392/11/4/5, no. 1165.

53 For typhus see, [Medical] Case Book, Females, SRO 392/11/4/5, no. 490 and [Medical] Case Book, Males, SRO 392/11/4/7, p. 221; for scarlatina, see Reception Order for Alfred Chapman, 1866; for Gastric Fever, Louisa Deacon, 1876; see also [Medical] Case Book, Females, SRO 392/11/4/5, no. 490.

54 [Medical] Case Book, Females, SRO 392/11/4/5, no. 489.

55 [Medical] Case Book, Females, SRO 392/11/4/7, no. 1431.

56 Reception Order for Henry Markley, 1871, Ibid.

57 For 1861, see Reception Orders for Thomas Phillips, John Smith, and James Cox; for 1871 admissions, see Reception Orders for Robert Gaskell, Mary Gray, Thomas Stewart, Lucy Sells, and Thomas Williams; for 1881 admissions, see Reception Orders for Ethel Henry, William Wahab and Thomas Ewers.

58 Reception Order for Alfred Meaby, 1881.

59 [Medical] Case Book, Females, SRO 392/11/4/7, p. 241.

60 Reception Order for Ben Russell, 1856.

61 Certificate for Henry Markley, 1871.

62 See D. Wright, 'Familial Care of Idiot Children in Victorian England', in R. Smith and P. Horden (eds) *The Locus of Care*, forthcoming.

63 Scull, *Museums of Madness*, p. 14 or *Most Solitary of Afflictions: Madness and Society in Britain, 1700–1900*, London, 1993, p. 2.

7

THE CHANGING DYNAMIC OF INSTITUTIONAL CARE

The Western Counties Idiot Asylum 1864–1914[1]

David Gladstone

I

There have been at least two consequences of the much publicised closure of the long-stay hospitals for people with mental handicap or learning disability that has taken place over the past decade. The first has been a concern with the effectiveness or adequacy of community care for those discharged from the long-stay institutions: media headlines and more scholarly research have both drawn attention to the 'holes in the net' and the shortcomings of both policy and practice. The second has been to stimulate an interest in the history of institutional care. It is this aspect which this chapter seeks to explore.

This chapter examines the five voluntary institutions for idiots founded in England in the twenty-year period between the late 1840s and the late 1860s. Regionally dispersed, they represented the main institutional provision specifically for people with learning disabilities and were, along with smaller private establishments, Poor Law workhouses and the county lunatic asylums, an important short- or long-term alternative to family care. The second section of this chapter looks at selected aspects of this charitable enterprise; the third and fourth sections more specifically examine the experience of the Western Counties Idiot Asylum at Starcross near Exeter, in the fifty years between its foundation and the outbreak of the First World War. 'The historian may observe the institutions from a distance and note remarkable similarities between them: under the microscope the differences are equally striking.'[2] The Western Counties Asylum was similar in many respects to its counterparts in other parts of the country. But its principal distinguishing feature was its developing reliance on Poor Law-funded patients; a factor which, it is suggested here, owed much to the Institution's continuing search for financial viability and security as well as to the original conception and aims of its founders.

Despite the aura which continues to surround them, public institutions have had a comparatively short history. They have only been part of our welfare history in Britain for the past 150 years. Private madhouses, gaols and parish workhouses, of course, had all existed before the nineteenth century. But it was the nineteenth century itself – with its national system of Poor Law workhouses, the construction of lunatic asylums, the beginning of long-stay hospitals for the mentally handicapped and the development of 'model' prisons – that conceived and implemented the institutional panacea. That fact is reflected in the increase of buildings, their scale and size and the number of inmates they housed. Its legacy has been a persisting negative image of residential establishments which has been reinforced by reported cases of the abuse of inmates, the enforced association and routine of institutional life and the compulsion often associated with entry as well as with subsequent detention.

If that largely negative image of residential establishments has 'embedded itself in popular consciousness',[3] it has also been an important theme in the sociological and historical writing on institutions. This is symbolised especially by Goffman's discussion of the 'total institution',[4] Foucault's writing on the 'structures of confinement'[5] and Scull's analysis of the 'capture of the mad' by the emergent medical profession. Once asylums were established they represented 'a culturally legitimate alternative, for both the community as a whole and the separate families which made it up, to keeping the intolerable individual in the family'.[6] According to this analysis asylums came to represent a dumping ground for deviants where, within a closely regulated and separate community, a controlling environment – be it physical or psychological in nature – was established.

More recent research, focusing on patterns of admission and discharge as well as average length of stay, has called into question the 'total' nature of the nineteenth-century institution.[7] It has also concentrated much more on the dynamics of the institution: the relationship between its component system of management and administration, and in the case of the voluntary asylums, the philanthropic committees, the Superintendents, the staff of attendants and the inmate population; the pattern of admission and discharge; the nature of the inmate experience – in education, training and recreation; the changing legal framework within which the asylums operated and the shifting discourse on mental deficiency in Victorian and Edwardian England which moved from a conscientious commitment to individual improvement to a *fin de`siècle* pessimism redolent with images of degeneration.[8]

Such an agenda necessarily represents an attempt to reconstruct the public and private life of the voluntary asylums. For its sources it depends mainly on printed materials such as relevant Parliamentary Papers and Royal Commissions, Reports of the Commissioners of Lunacy, the Annual Reports, Committee Papers, correspondence and case notes of the institutions themselves (where these have survived) as well as other documentary sources such as local newspapers and, where they still remain, the evidence of the buildings and their physical layout. For more recent times these sources can, of course, be complemented by interview material from residents and their relatives, staff of all grades, managers and administrators and members of the local community. But the questions which such research is especially required to address concern the increasing scale and size of such institutions and the ways in which such growth impacted upon their internal structure and regime.

Those research questions I suggest need to address first of all the inter-relationship of national legislation and local practice. On the one hand the institutions grew and changed because of the changing definitions in the legislation of those who were to be committed to such institutions. On the other hand, these institutions were also affected by local policies about admission and discharge developed and implemented by the Managing Committees of the various institutions themselves. They also need to address the inter-relationship of political and professional factors. This is especially the case at national level, for example, in relation to the Mental Deficiency Act of 1913 and its category of 'moral defective' which brought into the asylums women who had given birth to an illegitimate child while receiving poor relief. In that example, an extension was occurring in the social construction of mental deficiency. But increasingly political decisions about how the socially incompetent could be segregated into institutions came to depend upon professional practice and expertise: compulsory education, age-related pedagogic expectations and increasingly sophisticated methods of testing intellectual ability, with the schoolroom as a laboratory, became the means for differentiating among the population. It was issues such as these that the Defective and Epileptic Children Committee of the Education Department highlighted in its 1898 Report:

> From the normal child down to the lowest idiot there are degrees of deficiency of mental power; and it is only a difference of

> degree which distinguishes the feeble minded children from the backward children who are found in every school … and from the children who are too deficient to receive proper benefit from any teaching which the School Authorities can give … Though the difference of mental power is one of degree only, the difference of treatment is such as to make these children … a distinct class.[9]

The paradigm for understanding change in the voluntary asylums in the years with which this chapter is concerned is thus a complex intermingling between a variety of arenas: national and local, political and professional.

II

The creation of the five voluntary institutions for idiots occurred between the end of the 1840s and the late 1860s. The Western Counties Asylum at Starcross near Exeter was opened in 1864, the same year as the Northern Counties Asylum (subsequently the Royal Albert Institution) at Lancaster. In 1868 the Midland Counties Asylum at Knowle in Staffordshire began in a temporary building and, though six years later it moved to a 12-acre site, its financial difficulties were by no means at an end.

Each of these institutions was based on the initial model created by the Charity for the Asylum for Idiots established in 1847 by the Rev. Dr Andrew Reed, a Nonconformist minister and established charity organiser. Its initial property, Park House at Highgate in London, was soon full and the charity accepted the offer of a lease on Essex Hall, Colchester from Samuel Morton Peto, the wealthy railway magnate, which was used as a branch asylum of the London Charity until 1858. In 1859 Essex Hall became independently established as the Eastern Counties Idiot Asylum electing patients from the counties of Essex, Norfolk, Suffolk and Cambridgeshire. Meanwhile, in the earlier 1850s the Charity for the Asylum for Idiots had acquired a much larger site at Earlswood Common near Redhill in Surrey with space sufficient for a large asylum for 500 patients. Even though the buildings were not complete, it began to move patients there in 1855 from Park House and Essex Hall despite financial insecurity and a potentially damaging confrontation with the Commissioners in Lunacy. The award of its Royal Charter in 1863, however, marked the beginning of a significant period in Earlswood's history:

> Within the next ten years the asylum would expand both its patient numbers and subscribers, revamp its administrative system, create a comprehensive system of case books and admission records and, through its new medical superintendent, receive prominence as a medical institution of some repute.[10]

Not all the institutions founded in its image would be able to claim so much so quickly. The Eastern, Western and Midland Counties operated on a much smaller scale in relation to patient numbers than Earlswood or Lancaster; and financial vulnerability and uncertainty were to be a recurrent experience at the Western and Midland Counties until much later in the century.

What each of these institutions had in common, however, was a commitment to the training of those who, in the language of the time, were defined as educable idiots. The prominence accorded to the twentieth-century 'warehouse' model[11] of institutional care means that it is difficult now to recapture the sense of positive optimism that pervaded the origins of the voluntary asylums in mid-nineteenth-century England. The Western Counties Asylum, for example, had as its principal object to provide opportunities for those 'likely by careful treatment to be capable of mental improvement'.[12] 'Buildings that now fill us with despair were seen as model environments full of promise'[13] in which could occur the creation of economically independent and morally competent individuals by a combination of moral training and task-centred learning in an environment that emphasised health, nutrition, exercise and the creation of habits of discipline.

The notion that 'the idiot may be educated'[14] owed much to the pioneering work of Itard and his pupil Sèguing, in relation to the Wild Boy of Aveyron and the publicity that attended it. The latter's work at the Bicêtre in Paris seeking to prove that idiots were trainable by a combination of experience and association led to the publication in 1846 of *Traitement Moral, Hygiène et Education des Idiots* which 'soon secured him an international reputation'[15] and which was translated into English in 1855. Meanwhile, almost simultaneously the work with cretins of Dr Guggenbühl, who had himself been influenced by the work of Itard, 'became more readily available in English following William Twining's visit to his establishment … near Interlaken which led to the publication of his *Some Account of Cretinism and Institution for its Cure* (1843)'.[16] Periodicals such as the *Edinburgh Journal* and the *Westminster Review* also contributed to the dissemination of information about these schemes by articles published later in the 1840s.[17]

Since, 'tis not decreed the idiot born, Must a poor idiot die',[18] the voluntary institutions were established within a climate of optimistic expectations of improvement. That optimism and the benefits which the institutions thought they could provide:

> are not limited to the advantages which result to the idiots themselves, but they extend in large measure to the poverty stricken homes of their parents, to the relief of many a respectable hard-working family and even to the neighbourhood where the poor lad used to wander a forlorn outcast of society.[19]

If the institutions lifted the burdens of financial vulnerability and constant care from families, they were also concerned to emphasise the benefits accruing to individual inmates themselves. Often this took the form of comparisons of the inmates' behaviour before and after admission published, for example, in Annual Reports or used in fund-raising speeches. Frequently before admission, the medical officer at the Western Counties Asylum pointed out in one such address, the children 'have not been well fed, clothed or cared for'. Once in the Asylum 'they are well clothed, well, judiciously and regularly fed and exercised … (and) from the affection and kindness shewn to them, they are at once much happier'. For the idiot of the lowest class – 'speechless, inexpressibly filthy in his habits, unfit to sit at meals with his family, cramming the food into mouth with his hands, nay choking himself and vomiting it back on his plate' – the institution's training regime held out the prospect of teaching

> him to walk, to eat his food decently with a knife and fork, to leave off his filthy habits, to dress and undress himself instead of tearing his clothes to pieces, perhaps to articulate a few words … make him fit to be kept in the same room with the rest of his family

while for its higher grades reading, writing, acquiring the skills of certain trades and attending in an orderly manner the services of the church were all indicators of improvement.[20]

Sometimes particular instances of individual improvement were cited to illustrate what the Asylum had achieved:

> O.P. a boy of twelve when admitted was very backward in all branches of learning and could not use a pencil … by careful and continuous training … he is now able to write fairly in a copy book and to do sums of long division.

> L.F. This girl came to us from a home for feeble minded girls and

> could neither read nor write. She can now read easy tales and write so well that her friends are delighted with the letters she sends home to them. She has moreover become quite a good housemaid.[21]

Less frequently, letters from former inmates were published extolling the benefits they had received, as in the case of this example, printed as it was received:

> I am trying to be a good girl I often think and talk to mother of what you are doing at Starcross ... thank you for all you have done for me whilst I was with you. Mother says it done me good.[22]

Such stories of individual improvement played an important part in the publicity for institutions, especially for those dependent on subscription income. In the competition for their initial income and continued support, subscribers needed to be constantly reminded that their money was achieving results.

But if such opportunities for improvement existed, they were available to only a small section of the population who might potentially benefit from them. In 1881, for example, only some 3 per cent of the estimated 29,542 idiot inmates of institutions were in special idiot asylums. 'The remainder were still inter-mingled with criminals, lunatics, indigents and others in workhouses, lunatic asylums and prisons.'[23] But Gelband's research has suggested that the number of mentally retarded paupers outside institutions nearly equalled the number of those of that category who were in institutions of all kinds.[24] Progressively, however, during the 1860s the Poor Law Board had sought to abolish outdoor relief where it could, including the small allowances often paid to families looking after a mentally deficient person. At the same time the Commissioners in Lunacy increasingly advocated separate provision for pauper idiots either within, or completely distinct from, the Poor Law workhouse or the county lunatic asylum. In this context the voluntary institutions occupied a small but significant niche. For a considerable section of the population private madhouses were too expensive while the Poor Law workhouses were socially unacceptable.[25] For them the voluntary institutions represented an alternative to the only other available source of help: that of care provided by family or kin.

If individual improvement represented the goal of the voluntary institutions, philanthropic endeavour was to be the means by which it would be attained. In that respect, too, the response to those with the condition of mental deficiency was part of the broader fabric of Victorian society. Notwithstanding the growth of government in social affairs and the development of mutual aid and self-help organisations, philanthropy played a major role in the supply of welfare in Victorian England. 'So many good causes were catered for – stray dogs, stray children, fallen women and drunken men.'[26] If there was no subject which could not arouse the philanthropic urge of the Victorian public, the practice of mental improvement for children would appear to have much to commend it to potential supporters. In fact, as I showed earlier, the financial experience of the various voluntary asylums of nineteenth-century England was by no means comprehensively successful.

What the institutions had in common was a system, already well established in the voluntary hospitals, whereby subscribers were entitled to vote for the election of inmates. It was only the Western Counties which significantly deviated from this practice as it increasingly drew the majority of its inmates from among those publicly funded by the Poor Law Boards of Guardians. At its inception, however, the Western Counties, in common with the other voluntary idiot asylums, looked to subscriptions and donations as its principal source of funding.

The various benefits associated with the philanthropic gift have been discussed in a number of studies.[27] On the one hand it gave subscribers the opportunity of social fraternisation with the aristocratic (and, in some cases, royal) patrons at the frequent social functions which took place both to raise additional funds and to publicise the work of the charity. On the other, in the case of the idiot asylums and the voluntary hospitals on which they were closely modelled, it gave subscribers an entitlement to vote in the election of potential patients or inmates. At Earlswood, for example, in return for the minimum subscription of one half guinea, an individual received the right to vote in the year's two elections of inmates held in April and October, attend its social events and vote on policy at the Annual General Meeting. A life vote was given to each individual who subscribed five guineas which entitled subscribers to one vote at every election until their death. Both general and life votes increased pro rata. This meant that wealthier subscribers had more 'political clout' and potentially disproportionate influence in the competition for inmate selection.[28]

There was general agreement among the superintendents and medical staff of the idiot asylums that children should be admitted at an early age; and the original intention was that they should usually remain for a maximum period of five years and not beyond the age of

15. 'It cannot be too strongly impressed upon persons interested in the education of the feeble minded,' the Superintendent of the Western Counties affirmed, that:

> experience proves childhood and youth to be the best time for developing any latent faculties they may possess ... Better results are obtained when the pupils are between the ages of six and fifteen than at any subsequent period of their lives.[29]

But by the end of the nineteenth century that aspiration was already beginning to be in contrast to the practical reality of the Asylum. In 1898, for example, only a minority (125) of the inmate population (282) at the Western Counties were aged between 5 and 15; the remainder were all older, 64 being aged 20 and upwards.[30] Several factors may, separately or in combination, explain this change: the declining employment opportunities outside the Institution; the need of the Asylum itself to retain trained workers to produce goods themselves and transmit their skills to those who were younger; the shifting discourse on mental deficiency that occurred in late Victorian England. The consequences, however, are less contentious: even before the 1913 Mental Deficiency Act the tendency towards larger-scale, longer-stay institutions with a more adult population was already occurring. In that context it becomes all too easy to attribute their failure to return their inmates to a life outside the institution 'to the hopeless nature of the idiots themselves as well as to the allegedly unrealistic ideas that their educators had about improvement'.[31]

By the beginning of the twentieth century the world of the voluntary asylums looked set for substantial change. There was considerably less emphasis – politically and professionally – on improvement and an increasing discourse on containment which structured the form of the 1913 legislation. Equally, not only in relation to the voluntary institutions for mental defectives but more generally in the debate about social and individual welfare, the boundaries between state activity and philanthropic endeavour were being significantly re-negotiated. And within the institutions themselves, size and scale meant an increasingly segregated and differentiated environment which reinforced the geographical separation of the large purpose-built asylums in their pleasure grounds and agricultural pasturage that had occurred in the second half of the nineteenth century. 'Collecting idiots together as a means of alleviating their solitude and isolation was (evolving) into the mass organisation of their daily life and the denial of their individuality.'[32]

III

The origins of the Western Counties Idiot Asylum lie in a public meeting held at the Castle in Exeter in November 1862 at which it was decided that 'it is desirable to establish an Institution for those idiot children of the poor who shall appear to be likely by careful treatment to be capable of mental improvement'.[33] The first admissions took place exactly two years later in November 1864. Since its sole object was the training of children, the Commissioners in Lunacy decided that it should be exempt from the strict operation of the Lunacy laws, and in March 1865 it was certified by the Poor Law Board as a school to which Boards of Guardians might send their children. Exemption from the Lunacy laws meant that the Institution avoided the annual expense of applying for a licence and the requirement of a resident medical practitioner. The Commissioners in Lunacy did, however, pay occasional visits of inspection. As the Institution became more settled and established, its Management Committee successfully applied in 1875 to the Devon Quarter Sessions and was licensed as an establishment for the reception of idiots. The licence allowed the Institution to accommodate forty inmates and ended the age restriction which had originally been only for children between the ages of 6 and 15.

In 1887 the Institution sought registration under the 1886 Idiots Act for 180 cases. Five years later its official designation, as recorded in the Commissioners in Lunacy returns, changed from being one of the provincial licensed houses devoted entirely to the reception of idiots to that of an 'idiot institution'. By that time there were 200 inmates resident in the Asylum. But, unlike several of the other establishments, there was still no requirement of a resident medical practitioner. The first such appointment was not made until 1937. He became Superintendent in 1945 when the long family tradition of the successors of William Locke, appointed Superintendent seventy years before, came to an end.

Another family with a long-standing influence on the affairs of the Institution was the Courtneys, the Earls of Devon. William Reginald Courtney, eleventh Earl of Devon, chaired both the initial public meeting in 1862 and the provisional committee of Devon nobility and gentry which was established to formalise plans for the Institution. In the process he began a continuing association between the Asylum and the Courtney family which lasted for a long period of its history, even after the Institution became part of the National Health Service in 1948. Successive Earls of Devon served as Presidents of the Institution in unbroken sequence between 1864 and 1935: and, with the exception of the years between 1908 and 1920, members of the Courtney family were also Chairmen of the Managing or General Committee. It was the eleventh Earl of Devon who leased a house and two acres of land adjacent to his own estate at Powderham near Exeter to the fledgling Institution, corresponded with the Commissioners in Lunacy about its legal status, prepared its draft constitution and played an active role in the recruitment of its initial staff. That same Earl of Devon also played a part on the national stage in matters of mental deficiency, as a member of the Charity Organisation Society's 'committee for considering the best means of making a satisfactory provision for Idiots, Imbeciles and Harmless Lunatics'. With its call for a greater recognition of the difference between lunatics and idiots it was one of the influences behind the legislative distinction introduced by the Idiots Act of 1886. Its attempt at clarification, however, was short-lived. The 1890 Lunacy Act 'completely overlooked this distinction, continuing to treat the terms "idiot" and "lunatic" as synonymous'.[34]

In common with many other nineteenth-century residential establishments, the management of the Western Counties Institution was vested in the General or Managing Committee and its House Committee. In addition, specialist sub-committees concerned with buildings and finance were also established. At its monthly meetings, the Managing Committee had general oversight of matters relating to the Institution. These included arrangements for the admission of inmates, appointment of staff, conditions of employment, receiving accounts, stimulating interest in the work of the institution in the Western Counties and contact with statutory bodies such as Boards of Guardians, the Local Government Board and the Commissioners in Lunacy. The remit of the House Committee, which met weekly at the Institution, was to superintend all the domestic arrangements, to inspect the whole establishment and to receive written reports. Initially these were supplied by the Matron – subsequently by the Superintendent – as well as by the Honorary Medical Officer.[35]

Membership of the General Committee was determined by election at the Institution's Annual General Meeting, while the House Committee was chosen from among the members of the General Committee. Both, however, were exclusively male in membership. It was not until the appointment of local authority representatives in the 1920s that women became members of any of the Institution's Committees. While women played no direct role in the management of the Asylum before the First World War, they were involved in its work in 'separate spheres'. Female relatives of the Earl of Devon opened bazaars and helped with other fund-raising activities, while other female supporters provided extra 'treats' for patients including outings, books, magazines and games, and presents at Christmas. Women, of course, were also among those who provided financial support to the Institution by means of their own individual subscriptions and donations. This was of no small importance: for financial viability was one of the major issues in the management of the Institution for at least the first thirty years of its existence.

At its inception there appears little doubt that the officers of the Western Counties Asylum expected that its funds would come mainly from subscriptions and donations, both of which would offer an entitlement to vote for the election of inmates. The first list of subscribers and donors, printed in the 1869 *Annual Report*, indicated a total of 367, drawn overwhelmingly from Devon.[36] The 1904 *Annual Report* listed 219 subscribers and donors who contributed less than 2 per cent of the Asylum's income.[37] Thirty years before, in 1874 almost 30 per cent of the Asylum's income had come from that source. That in itself was a proportion much below what the officers of the Asylum expected. Successive Annual Reports drew attention to the problem. In its first Report the Committee made 'an earnest appeal for increased support'.[38] Two years later only forty-one new subscribers had been added with a total level of subscription of £44 9s 0d, while the contributions of nine subscribers totalling £20 had been lost to the Asylum through death.[39] Establishing local committees in many centres of the Western Counties to provide information about mental deficiency and to raise money for the Asylum met with only limited success. While thirty local secretaries were listed in 1876,[40] ten years later there appeared to be only three local committees in Plymouth, Truro and for the county of Dorset.[41] Writing against the background of a deficit of £350 in 1880, the Committee lamented that 'they can only attribute the want of support to the fact that the Asylum, its objects and its aims are not sufficiently known and understood'.[42] By the 1890s the explanation for low subscription income was 'the growing feeling among the public that institutions of this sort should be supported by the State'.[43] This experience was by no means unique to the Western Counties Asylum. In 1875 the Commissioners in Lunacy regretted that 'sufficient funds have not been obtained in this wealthy district' to aid the construction of an adequate building for the Midland Counties Asylum at Knowle near Birmingham;[44] while David Wright has pointed out that at the more financially successful Earlswood Asylum the level of subscription income depended significantly on the wider economic circumstances of the nation in general.[45]

Income, however, was only one side of the equation. Expenditure was the other element that contributed to financial volatility. Initially at the Western Counties food and salaries consumed a significant proportion of the budget. Interestingly, though the number of attendants and other staff increased as the patient population grew in size, the proportion of total expenditure spent on salaries varied very little, from 27 per cent in 1874 to 28 per cent in 1904 (within a range of from 21 per cent to 31 per cent between the same dates).[46] In 1883 when the patient population had increased by thirteen over the previous year there was no increase in staff, with the Committee anxiously considering ways of reducing its debt on buildings and the recurrent deficit on general expenditure. That represented an exceptional attempt to contain costs, though the Asylum officers were always concerned to emphasise its economic and efficient management especially in relation to average costs per inmate at other voluntary and public institutions.

Writing more generally of the voluntary system of residential care for children in the nineteenth century, Roy Parker points out that while land and buildings were often freely or cheaply available from wealthy patrons (such as the Earl of Devon at the Western Counties) 'homes were expensive to establish and to keep open; charitable donations were rarely sufficient or sufficiently reliable'.[47] Maintaining the buildings in a good state of repair, upgrading them to provide additional facilities and fulfilling requirements such as those ensuring safe exit in case of fire, became increasingly important at the Western Counties once the Asylum had been licensed in 1875 and all aspects of its provision became subject to the scrutiny of visits by the Commissioners in Lunacy. In the case of new buildings the cost was met by special appeals designated specifically for the Building Fund and by events such as the Elizabethan Fancy Fayre, a three-day event held in Exeter in 1882, and a Grand Bazaar under the patronage of the Prince and Princess of Wales. But significant as were such fund-raising events, they were insufficient by themselves to meet the costs involved and borrowing to build became a pattern of the Asylum's financial management.

Building was a response to the growth in size of the Institution (and partly a cause of it) as well as a reflection of its growing diversification. Table 7.1 shows the pattern of growth in the inmate population at the Western Counties over its first fifty years. The particularly large increase between 1885 and 1895 is mainly explained by the completion in the late 1880s of accommodation for seventy-five extra children. Expressing its pleasure that such an expansion had been undertaken at this 'very useful Asylum', the Commissioners in Lunacy pointedly drew

Table 7.1 Growth of the inmate population at the Western Counties Idiot Asylum (1865–1915)

	Males	*Females*	*Total*
1865	65	34	99
1875	96	44	140
1885	154	44	198
1895	158	91	249
1905	183	87	270
1915	231	103	334

Source: Commissioners in Lunacy *Reports*; Western Counties Idiot Asylum *Annual Reports*

attention to 'the great need throughout the country for institutions of this character'.[48] Size seems also to have been a criterion in its change of status from a provincial licensed house to an institution for idiots in the early 1890s.

But its growth, both in absolute and relative terms, had been much slower than that at either Earlswood or the Royal Albert. Built originally for 400 occupants, the asylum at Earlswood became full in 1866 and, after it had expanded its potential size to 600 residents, reached full capacity again in 1878.[49] The growth of the patient population at the Royal Albert was also significantly greater than at the Western Counties. Though they were founded in the same year, by 1874 at Lancaster there were already 196 inmates, with a range of buildings including schoolrooms, workshops, sick rooms, laundry and dormitories already in operation.[50] Different financial experiences would mainly seem to account for the differences between them. At its foundation the Royal Albert was already much more financially secure than its counterpart in Devon. But especially in the twenty years after its formal licensing in 1875 the Western Counties significantly increased in scale and size.

Its commitment to expansion was at least in part an attempt to provide accommodation for those considered eligible who were waiting for admission. During its first forty years 1,023 children had been admitted to the Western Counties Asylum. But, as its Committee of Management report recorded, these figures represented a very small proportion of the numbers who had applied for admission.[51] Unmet demand was only one factor explaining expansion. It came to be more frequently argued by the Superintendent that increased numbers would facilitate a more rigorous classification of the patient population, both in relation to education and its developing programme of industrial training: 'One great benefit attaches to an increase of numbers,' he pointed out in 1877, 'viz. that a better classification of the pupils' training and teaching can be made.'[52] Expansion too could bring the benefits associated with economy of scale.

That applied especially as the Institution began to move in the direction of increased self-sufficiency in relation to foodstuffs and other necessary items from the mid-1870s; and then, in turn, in a second phase towards the end of the nineteenth century, began commercially to sell the products of its expanding training workshops. In 1874 spending on food constituted over 40 per cent of the Asylum's expenditure. The much broader but undifferentiated category of housekeeping and provisions had been reduced to 28 per cent in 1904.[53] Half of the seven acres owned by the Asylum in 1888 were given over to the kitchen garden 'which supplies all the fresh vegetables, potatoes and fruit required for the Asylum'.[54] The acquisition of animals and poultry further consolidated its self-sufficiency and provided training in agricultural pursuits to some of its inmates. In the late 1890s the Commissioners in Lunacy endorsed the Managing Committee's hope that extra land could be acquired especially to provide pasturage for additional cows. 'A good supply of pure milk,' they pointed out, 'is essential in an establishment for idiots.'[55]

Once it was recognised that increased self-sufficiency and the sale of goods could bring the financial security which had eluded the Institution in its early years, the selection of suitable inmates became increasingly important. While the education and training of the improvable idiot had always been part of its *raison d'être*, they increasingly became more central to its economic strategy. This expressed itself in the Managing Committee and Superintendent's opposition to degeneration into a 'mere custodial establishment for helpless and unimprovable idiots',[56] on the one hand and, on the other, to a 'judicious weeding out'[57] of those unlikely to benefit either themselves or the Institution from the training that was offered.

Increasingly, in the later nineteenth century the Institution was able to select its prospective inmates from a geographically wider catchment area. In the years from its foundation to 1877, children from the Western Counties – of Cornwall, Devon and Somerset – accounted for the vast proportion of its inmate population, with children from its local catchment county of Devon accounting for just over two-thirds of the total. In 1914 Devon-born inmates still predominated in relation to those from the four Western Counties: but, by then, patients from South West England (including Dorset) were in a minority compared to those from elsewhere in the country. Of the total of 306 inmates only 103 (34 per cent) were from the Western Counties. This is a reflection of the extent to which the Institution had carved out a distinctive niche for itself not only in relation to the training which it provided (which was not dissimilar to that provided in the other idiot establishments) but also for the specific category of pauper idiots. In contrast to the other establishments with their mainly private, fee-paying inmates elected by subscribers, the Western Counties came increasingly to specialise in the education and training of pauper idiots. It was in fact only the Royal Albert Asylum with 219 pauper patients in 1904 which approached the 261 at the Western Counties at the same date.[58] But as a proportion of the total inmate population its 35 per cent of pauper inmates paled into insignificance compared to the 96 per cent at the Western Counties.

Though the Superintendent was still lamenting in 1901 that 'there are still many Boards of Guardians who endeavour to send us only their helpless and unimprovable cases',[59] the Asylum's own policy of careful and rigorous selection, together with the swift discharge of those unsuited to its regime, transformed it from a purely local and regional institution into one with a national catchment area. In this way the Western Counties Asylum became increasingly dependent on the revenues which flowed in from Boards of Guardians all over the country, in contrast to the static and then declining proportion of subscription and donation income from its more regionally based local supporters. If such a solution had been part of an organised quest for greater financial stability, it had served both to differentiate the Western Counties from other idiot establishments and to fulfil its original purpose as an institution for the idiot children of the poor.

IV

The decision about which prospective candidates should be admitted to the Institution was taken by the General or Managing Committee. The constitution and rules agreed when the Western Counties Asylum was established and confirmed by the Poor Law Board had set the broad parameters. These related to age, likelihood of improvement and financial guarantees. No child was to be admitted before the age of 6 or after they had reached 15, with an expectation that the usual length of stay would be five years. Though there remained a commitment to an early age of admission, by the end of the nineteenth century, as I pointed out above, the upper age limit had been significantly breached.

The child's potential for improvement was another important feature of selection for admission. Children who were blind, deaf or suffered from epilepsy were usually automatically excluded from further consideration. While for the remainder, no case was to be approved 'unless there be a reasonable expectation … that it will derive benefit from the treatment to be adopted in the Institution'.[60] Those who slipped through this net and entered the Asylum, but who showed no sign of improvement there, were discharged back to their families or to the Poor Law workhouse. Financial guarantees were also sought prior to admission. Written arrangements were entered into with Boards of Guardians or parents and friends for the maintenance and support of the children while in the Asylum and the defrayment of all expenses concerned with their removal or burial.

From its earliest years the Management Committee relied heavily on the assessment provided by George Pycroft, a local medical practitioner and long-serving honorary Medical Officer to the Institution. His view was especially important in guiding the Committee to consider the likelihood of improvement. It was based upon his own examination, usually conducted in the Asylum, letters from family and friends and established figures (such as clergymen) in the local communities from which the applicants came. In addition, he had available the answers to specific questions on the application form for admission. In the early 1880s Pycroft described the details of his initial assessment:

> I look him all over, test his mind and the state of his bodily health. I enter his description in a book which is called the Case Book … I put down whether he can speak, count, read, write, walk, dress himself, feed himself, whether he has the use of his hands, is mischievous, what his temper is, what the cause of his idiocy is and so forth.[61]

At the same date, Pycroft also had available the details from the Application Form which asked both about the child's mental condition, sensory abilities and general health as well as the circumstances of the family, the health and intelligence of any other children and whether there was any history of insanity, idiocy or epilepsy in the family.

Pycroft himself became an important advocate for the Asylum. His address to its 1882 Annual General Meeting showed him to be well acquainted with the alternative theories about the causes of idiocy and moving towards an elementary classification in his distinction between low 'little better than an animal'; not quite so low 'where the child can speak a little or make signs'; while those of a higher grade 'can converse tolerably and understand what is said' but have all 'the passions of an ordinary man without the mind of a man to control them'.[62] While he counselled his hearers against unrealistic expectations of what institutions could achieve by way of complete independence, he saw their value in the relief which they offered to parents. An Order of Admission offered them, he suggested, 'joy of happiness, hope of improvement, hope that at last he may possibly be raised out of the gloom of his mental darkness … a response in place of a blank, vacant stare'.[63]

For most of its first fifty years the Western Counties Asylum had more boys in residence than girls. In 1877 there were 34 boys and 19 girls; in 1912, 210 and 94 respectively.[64] There can be little doubt that this distinction by gender was the result of cultural assumptions held by those in charge of selecting from potential applicants, whose numbers always exceeded the available accommodation. While the 1881 Census indicated 'no great disparity between the number of males and females described as Idiots and Imbeciles', the national figures of those admitted to all the voluntary idiot establishments between 1875 and 1884 showed that only one third were female.[65] William Locke, the Superintendent of the Western Counties Asylum, found the preponderance of boys in institutions not at all surprising:

> Weak minded girls with a certain amount of intelligence are more amenable to treatment at home, and in some instances may even be helpful to their mother in small things, while boys soon get beyond maternal control and, being allowed more freedom out of doors, too often become troublesome to their neighbours and the public and their seclusion is then called for.[66]

Seclusion, however, was in a rigorously segregated environment. Supervised meals, church services and organised entertainments were the only occasions on which the sexes were together. Classes, workshops and recreation areas were either for boys or girls and their dormitory accommodation was in separate wings of the large main house, with the accommodation for the Superintendent and his family in between.

Those admitted to the Western Counties Asylum in its early years became part of a training regime which emphasised the three Rs, and lessons in colour and form, singing, speaking, dressing and time, with drill as the means of inculcating habits of discipline and orderliness. In the subsequent phase, in the final quarter of the nineteenth century, the child entered into an Institution which was structured around the acquisition of basic educational skills in the morning and occupational training in the workshops during the afternoon. Once an appropriately qualified schoolmaster and schoolmistress had been appointed in the late 1890s, they took over the preliminary educational assessment which formerly had been undertaken by the Superintendent. In the early years of this century boys were assigned to one of six classes on the basis of age and ability, girls to one of five. In the upper classes the three Rs were taught; in the lower, object lessons were used to awaken an interest and curiosity. Walks and excursions to coast and country were part of the educational programme. So too was character learning. Writing of the teaching staff, the Superintendent pointed out, 'By their precept and example they help to form the tone and character of the more intelligent pupils, whose example, in turn beneficially affects the children of a lower grade.'[67]

Successive reports during the 1890s suggest that as a result of its conscientious commitment to a selective admissions procedure and the education provided in the Institution, a rising proportion of its inmates were by no means ineducable. Thus, of 181 inmates in 1890, 68 could speak well, 31 could read well, 52 could write fairly from dictation, with 36 able to do simple addition and 19 to work sums in either the first four or compound rules. Ten years later in 1900 from a total population of 250, 219 could speak well, 90 could read well, 143 write fairly from dictation, 66 could do simple addition with 80 able to work sums in either the first four or compound rules. By contrast the numbers at the other end of the ability range had significantly decreased over the same decade. Forty-four of the 181 were dumb in 1890 compared to 4 out of 250 in 1900; likewise, 66 knew no letters or words in 1890 compared to only 14 in 1900; 48 could do nothing but scribble in 1890, a figure reduced to 17 in 1900; while 58 could not count at all in 1890, only 8 were unable to do so by 1900. By the same date only 20 were unable to attend service in chapel and 74 were able to recite alone.[68]

But it was its developing programme of industrial training which came increasingly to characterise the regime for the inmates of the institution. The development of an industrial training regime owes much to the appointment of William Locke as Superintendent in 1874 and the licensing of the Institution the following year. It was enthusiastically carried on by his son and successor, Ernest Locke, and by the latter's brother-in-law and sister who continued that family's association with the Institution until succeeded by its first Medical Superintendent in 1945. Before William Locke's appointment, girl inmates assisted the housemaids in making beds and sweeping, boys cleaned knives and shoes, tended the gardens and helped with other outdoor work. In one of its early reports the Committee pointed out that 'very little can be done in the way of education or industrial training'.[69] Locke's appointment brought about change. Initially the limited range of trades were supplied for the institution itself. Thus the children's boots and uniforms and all the window sash cord for its new buildings were made in the Asylum's workshops. But increasingly, as the number of trades increased and diversified, commercial sales began to develop which, in time, contributed to the Asylum's improved and more stable financial position.

By the end of the 1880s boys especially were engaged in a more comprehensive set of occupations: shoemaking, tailoring, sash-cord-making, in addition to gardening, laundry and domestic work and basket-making. At that date the occupation of girls was still severely restricted to sweeping, dusting, bed-making, sewing and knitting and laundry work. By 1904, however, there had been a considerable expansion in the occupations available to both boys and girls. Mat- and brush-making together with carpentry, wood-carving and fretwork as well as work in the bakery had been added for boys; while girls' occupations by that date included dress-making, Honiton lace-making, straw hat-making and embroidery. Much of the occupational training was on an alternate week system which provided a variety of experience for the large proportion of the Asylum's population who participated in such activities. In 1897 only 21 out of 247 residents undertook no work.[70]

Such work not only made the Institution more self-sufficient. The sale of products made in its workshops increasingly added to the Asylum's income. The sale of work brought in £44 5s 11d in the year ended 31 December 1895, by 1904 £234 8s 5d and by 1914 £632 4s 7d.[71] Almost as important was the publicity which the products – such as embroidery and Honiton lace-making – gained for the Institution. No opportunity was missed to exhibit such work in local craft and agricultural shows and to take part in the exhibition of the goods produced by the inmates of all the voluntary institutions such as that held at the Royal Albert in Lancaster in 1897 to mark the Diamond Jubilee of Queen Victoria.

Recreation constituted the third element of the inmate day. Here, too, the trend was one of expansion. In 1880 there was music and dancing on two evenings each week, while swings and gymnastic apparatus were available in the playground. Winter evenings created an especial problem for the attendants. A variety of indoor games –

billiards, draughts, bagatelle, dominoes and house building with bricks – were popular amusements. Many of them were donated by friends of the Institution along with toys, scrapbooks and a rocking horse. Dissolving view entertainments, magic lantern shows, visits by conjurers, pantomime performers and a Welsh male voice choir also helped to pass the winter evenings. At other times athletic games – cricket, football, running and jumping – and drill occurred either outdoors or in the Recreation Hall which was gifted in the early 1880s. Educational visits have already been mentioned, but there were also outings for picnics on the nearby Dawlish Warren, to Powderham Rectory, where one of the Courtney family gave an annual picnic, and, in winter, to the pantomime in Exeter.

Annual events marked the passing of the individual and collective year. Birthdays were celebrated with special tea parties, while Christmas came to be an especially important event. The Recreation Hall 'decorated with flags and evergreens and lighted by 150 electric lamps'[72] was the scene for an annual entertainment provided by the inmates to which the public were invited. Musical drill, action songs by pupils in costume and sometimes a pantomime performance preceded the distribution of presents and toys which had been given by friends of the Institution.

As in its financial affairs, so too the Asylum became increasingly self-reliant in recreation. By the outbreak of the First World War, a Fife and Drum Band had been established as well as a brass band taught by the schoolmaster and one or two members of the staff band; a Rifle Club was also in operation for male attendants. By the same date a separate sitting room had been created where those older inmates who acted as monitors or foremen in the workshops could sit and read, write letters or play draughts.

Events of national importance generated a particular enthusiasm. The fiftieth anniversary of Queen Victoria's accession was celebrated by a Jubilee Fête in the Asylum's grounds; while the coronation of her grandson King George V in 1911 was marked by a day of special events to which the public were invited: a military spectacle resembling Trooping the Colour was held in the morning, organised sports in the afternoon, while in the evening, against the illuminated buildings of the Asylum, a Flag Drill took place accompanied by the Boys Band.

The consequence of this diversification in the Institution's activities was an increase in the number of its buildings. As the Institution sought to house more inmates, extend its facilities and comply with the standards laid down by the Commissioners in Lunacy, its regular routine was frequently interrupted by building work in progress on its expanding site. On more than one occasion the Committee acknowledged the extra strain placed upon its staff of attendants as the adaptation of existing premises as well as new building work prevented outside recreation and confined the children to their schoolrooms and dormitories.[73]

Such a pattern was by no means limited to the Western Counties Asylum. In one of its annual reports the Commissioners in Lunacy referred to recent developments at Earlswood which included the construction of extensive farm buildings, the roofing of the gymnasium and additional staircases to aid escape in case of fire. At the same time it noted that a considerable sum of money was already in hand for building a detached hospital.[74]

If building work was one sign of the developing Institution, another sign of change was the pressure to alter its title. Keen to do away with the 'obnoxious terms of "Asylum" and "Idiot" ', at the beginning of the twentieth century the Superintendent proposed a change of considerable significance: the development by the recently created County Councils of Homes for Helpless and Unimprovable Idiots, but sought for his own Institution a title such as the Western Counties Training Institution for the Feeble-minded to delineate its distinctive character.[75] After some controversy 'Idiot' was deleted, but 'Asylum' remained in its title: though after 1903 the Superintendent and Committee of Management were allowed to amplify its objective as a Training Institution for the Feeble-minded.

V

Ernest Locke's proposals concerned more than simply a change of designation. They were an attempt to respond to broader changes that were taking place in relation to mental deficiency. These broader changes can be considered as the 'reconceptualisation of mental deficiency as a social rather than a private problem'.[76] One facet of this reconceptualisation was the supply of special education. By 1903 special schools had been established in London and fifty other authorities.[77] The origin of such provision in the public sector lay with the establishment in 1880 by the Metropolitan Asylums Board of a school with accommodation for 1,000 pupils at Darenth in Kent. In the event, pressure on space for adults, since its other asylums at Leavesden (Herts.) and Caterham (Surrey) were already full, meant that by 1890 'the fruit of the first attempt by a statutory body to develop the potentialities of subnormal children' housed only 300 boys and 168 girls.[78] The 1890s, however, were a decade which experienced the beginnings of a serious attempt by local School Boards to establish special provision for those who were judged incapable or unsuitable for receiving education in a 'normal' school.

Initially this principally applied to children whose blindness or deafness prevented them from benefiting from such an environment. But in the 'laboratory' presented by the school classroom, 'there were also found to be children who, while apparently fully provided with their complement of senses, appeared unable to learn the lessons of the school'.[79] It was this group who became the focus of the Defective and Epileptic Children Committee of the Education Department, and its proposals embodied in legislation in 1899 gave local authorities permissive powers to create special schools and classes for those who were 'by means of mental defect incapable of receiving proper benefit from the instruction in ordinary schools'.[80] This legislation became compulsory in 1914 but not until after much controversial discussion had taken place in central government concerning the respective interests of the Board of Education and the Home Office.[81]

Such legislation and the growing responsibility of statutory authorities in the education of mentally deficient children posed a significant challenge to institutions like the Western Counties Asylum just at the time when its internal regime was beginning to produce a degree of financial stability in its affairs. It is hardly surprising, therefore, that Locke proposed an alternative scenario which looked to the statutory authorities to make provision for the helpless idiot while proposing that institutions 'outside the state' such as his own should continue to offer education and training to those it deemed capable of benefiting from its regime.

If the voluntary asylum, on the one hand, was increasingly having to come to terms with the implications of universal schooling, on the other was the challenge presented by the changing discourse on mental deficiency. 'Edwardian doctors, psychologists, social workers and social theorists differed widely about the precise causes and symptoms of feeble-mindedness; but … they were virtually unanimous in their belief that the condition was largely incurable.'[82] This was in sharp contrast to the optimism that had attended the foundation of the voluntary asylums in the mid-nineteenth century and the regimes of education and training which they had established. But it reflected the growing prominence of eugenic ideas in the discussion both of mental deficiency and national efficiency in which the idiot came to be perceived less as 'a challenge for scientific and philanthropic pedagogy than as a burden on the nation'.[83]

In the later nineteenth century the public debate on mental deficiency shifted, especially in its gender focus, away 'from the prisons and the habitually criminal imbecile to the workhouses and their transient weak-minded inmates, feeble-minded women in particular'.[84] Whereas the former suggested a discourse predominantly structured around men, the 'faces of degeneration' in the early twentieth-century debate were inescapably female. Not only were mentally deficient women 'seen as the biological source of mental deficiency, they also posed a deep threat to existing middle-class and respectable working-class notions of sexuality and familial morality'. It is this, it has been suggested, which accounts for 'the near hysteria which characterises discussions about the social problem of mentally deficient women'.[85] It also explains the outcome both of the Royal Commission on the Feeble Minded and the 1913 Mental Deficiency Act in the shift towards compulsory segregation and a more custodial system.

The implications of such a shift were clear for institutions like the Western Counties Asylum. Not only were they in danger of losing the educable idiot child to special schools, they would also be less able to select among a more adult population. This too explains Locke's advocacy of different client groups within the general category of the mentally deficient for the statutory sector and the voluntary establishments. It was a defence against change: the compulsory containment of undifferentiated degenerates, as the early twentieth-century debate constructed them, had no place in the regime of his Institution.

This was the background to the emotional outburst by Major Nevil Thomas, Chairman of the Western Counties Management Committee, at its Annual General Meeting in 1914:

> The Committee are most determined to keep this House full of the same class of patients we have always had ... We spent a tremendous lot of money on rooms and appliances for teaching and are not going to have them wasted by having a lot of blithering idiots who cannot learn. We are going to take the very highest class of mental defectives and teach them to the best of our ability.[86]

Such sentiments represented an understandable determination on the part of the Western Counties Asylum to continue its hard-won achievements against the encroachment of change. But, in the event, it would be national policy, especially after the First World War, that would take the Institution into a very different environment from the final vestiges of its nineteenth-century inheritance which Major Thomas so emotionally defended.

NOTES

1 The material in this chapter was collected as part of a longer historical study of the Western Counties Asylum (subsequently the Royal Western Counties Hospital) funded by the Northcott Devon Medical Foundation. I am grateful to the trustees for their support. For access to documents in their possession I wish to thank the Exeter Health Authority and Mr A. B. Rowland.
2 M. A. Crowther, *The Workhouse System 1834–1929*, London, 1981, p. 67.
3 R. A. Parker, 'An Historical Background to Residential Care', in I. Sinclair (ed.) *Residential Care: The Research Reviewed*, London, 1988, p. 14.
4 E. Goffman, *Asylums*, New York, 1961.
5 M. Foucault, *Discipline and Punish*, London, 1977.
6 A. Scull, *Museums of Madness*, London, 1979, p. 240.
7 L. J. Ray, 'Models of Madness in Victorian Asylum Practice', *European Journal of Sociology*, 1981, vol. 22, pp. 229–64; J. K. Walton, 'Lunacy in the Industrial Revolution: A Study of Asylum Admissions in Lancashire 1848–50', *Journal of Social History*, 1979, vol. 13, pp. 1–22; J. K. Walton, 'Casting Out and Bringing Back in Victorian England: Pauper Lunatics, 1840–70', in W. F. Bynum *et al.* (eds) *Anatomy of Madness*, vol. 2, London, 1985.
8 M. A. Barrett, 'From Education to Segregation: An Inquiry into the Changing Character of Special Provision for the Retarded in England c. 1846–1918', unpublished PhD thesis, University of Lancaster, 1987; H.S. Gelband, 'Mental Retardation and Institutional Treatment in Nineteenth Century England', unpublished PhD thesis, University of Maryland, 1979; D. Wright, 'The National Asylum for Idiots, Earlswood, 1847–1886', unpublished DPhil thesis, University of Oxford, 1993.
9 Cited in N. Rose, *The Psychological Complex: Psychology, Politics and Society in England 1869–1939*, London, 1985, p. 99.
10 Wright, 'Earlswood', p. 47.
11 E. J. Miller and G. V. Gwynne, *A Life Apart*, London, 1972.
12 Western Counties Asylum [W.C.A.] Constitution, 1864.
13 J. Ryan with F. Thomas, *The Politics of Mental Handicap*, London, 1980, p. 94.
14 Cited in K. Jones, *A History of the Mental Health Services*, London, 1972, p. 183.
15 J. S. Hurt, *Outside the Mainstream: A History of Special Education*, London, 1988, p. 110.
16 Ibid., p. 111.
17 Wright, 'Earlswood', p. 67.
18 E. Grove, *A Beam for Mental Darkness: for the benefit of the Idiot and his Institution*, London, 1856, p. 4.
19 W.C.A. Annual Report, 1883, p. 13.
20 G. Pycroft, *An Address on Idiocy*, Exeter, 1882, pp. 10–11.
21 W.C.A. Annual Report, 1901, p. 14.
22 W.C.A. Annual Report, 1902, p. 16.
23 Rose, *Psychological Complex*, p. 95.
24 Gelband, 'Mental Retardation and Institutional Treatment', p. 359.
25 Wright, 'Earlswood', p. 24.
26 D. Fraser, *The Evolution of the British Welfare State*, London, 1984, p. 124.
27 R. Porter, 'The Gift Relation: Philanthropy and Provincial Hospitals in Eighteenth-Century England', in L. Granshaw and R. Porter (eds) *The*

Hospital in History, London, 1989; F. Prochaska, *The Voluntary Impulse*, London, 1988; 'Philanthropy', in F. M. L. Thompson (ed.) *The Cambridge Social History of Britain 1750–1950*, Cambridge, 1990.

28 Wright, 'Earlswood', pp. 115, 124.
29 W.C.A. Annual Report, 1899, p. 13.
30 W.C.A. Annual Report, 1898, p. 22.
31 Ryan with Thomas, *The Politics of Mental Handicap*, p. 102.
32 Ibid., p. 99.
33 Cited in J. Radford and A. Tipper, *Starcross: Out of the Mainstream, Toronto*, ,1988, p. 27.
34 Jones, *Mental Health Services*, p. 185.
35 W.C.A. Minute Book, 25 November 1864.
36 W.C.A. Annual Report, 1869, pp. 18–28.
37 W.C.A. Annual Report, 1904, pp. 38–44.
38 W.C.A. Annual Report, 1865, p. 1.
39 W.C.A. Annual Report, 1867, p. 1.
40 W.C.A. Annual Report, 1876, p. 12.
41 W.C.A. Annual Report, 1886, p. 4.
42 W.C.A. Annual Report, 1880, p. 10.
43 W.C.A. Annual Report, 1893, p. 5.
44 'Annual Report of the Commissioners in Lunacy to the Lord Chancellor', P.P. [1875], p. 49.
45 Wright, 'Earlswood', p. 122.
46 W.C.A. Annual Report, 1904, p. 5.
47 Parker, 'An Historical Background', p. 27.
48 'Annual Report of the Commissioners in Lunacy to the Lord Chancellor', [1886], p. 65.
49 Wright, 'Earlswood', p. 76.
50 'Annual Report of the Commissioners in Lunacy to the Lord Chancellor', [1875], p. 243.
51 W.C.A. Annual Report, 1904, p. 5.
52 W.C.A. Annual Report, 1877, p. 19.
53 W.C.A. Annual Report, 1874, p. 11; 1904, p. 37.
54 W.C.A. Annual Report, 1888, p. 6.
55 'Annual Report of the Commissioners in Lunacy to the Lord Chancellor', [1897], p. 381.
56 W.C.A. Annual Report, 1905, p. 14.
57 W.C.A. Annual Report, 1898, p. 14.
58 Radford and Tipper, *Starcross*, p. 48.
59 W.C.A. Annual Report, 1901, p. 12.
60 W.C.A. Rules.
61 Pycroft, *An Address on Idiocy*, p. 10.
62 Ibid., p. 6.
63 Ibid., p. 15.
64 W.C.A. Annual Report, 1877, p. 20; 1912, p. 13.
65 'Annual Report of the Commissioners in Lunacy to the Lord Chancellor', [1884–5], p. 21.
66 W.C.A. Annual Report, 1894, p. 4.
67 W.C.A. Annual Report, 1898, p. 15.

68 W.C.A. Annual Report, 1890, pp. 15–16; 1900, pp. 24–25.
69 W.C.A. Annual Report, 1869, p. 1.
70 W.C.A. Visitor's Book, 19 March, 1897.
71 W.C.A. Annual Report, 1896, p. 18; 1905, p. 34; 1914, p. 36.
72 W.C.A. Annual Report, 1902, p. 33.
73 W.C.A. Annual Report, 1886, p. 8.
74 'Annual Report of the Commissioners in Lunacy to the Lord Chancellor', [1875], p. 254.
75 W.C.A. Annual Report, 1901, pp. 12–13.
76 H. G. Simmons, 'Explaining Social Policy: the English Mental Deficiency Act of 1913', *Journal of Social History*, 1978, vol. 11, p. 389.
77 Rose, *Psychological Complex*, p. 103.
78 Hurt, *Outside the Mainstream*, p. 118.
79 Rose, *Psychological Complex*, p. 99.
80 Ibid., p. 103.
81 G. Sutherland, *Ability, Merit and Measurement*, Oxford, 1984.
82 J. Harris, *Private Lives, Public Spirit*, Oxford, 1993, p. 244.
83 Rose, *Psychological Complex*, p. 95.
84 J. Saunders, 'Quarantining the Weak-minded: Psychiatric Definitions of Degeneracy and the Late Victorian Asylum', in W. F. Bynum *et al.* (eds) *The Anatomy of Madness*, vol. 3, London, 1988, p. 291.
85 Simmons, 'Mental Deficiency Act', p. 394.
86 Radford and Tipper, *Starcross*, p. 52.

8

INSTITUTIONAL PROVISION FOR THE FEEBLE-MINDED IN EDWARDIAN ENGLAND

Sandlebridge and the scientific morality of permanent care

Mark Jackson

I

At the turn of this century, in a pamphlet entitled *The Importance of Permanence in the Care of the Feeble-Minded*, Mary Dendy suggested that the main aim of the newly founded Lancashire and Cheshire Society for the Permanent Care of the Feeble-Minded was 'to force upon the public a great, new principle of right-doing'.[1] This 'great, new principle' comprised the permanent segregation of a section of the population identified as 'feeble-minded'.[2]

In both this pamphlet and in a number of other pamphlets and articles published in the first decade or so of this century,[3] Mary Dendy argued that permanent segregation of the feeble-minded held several benefits both for society at large and for the individuals to be segregated. First, it would prevent a large proportion of crimes supposedly being committed by the feeble-minded. Second, it would relieve the over-crowding of workhouses, gaols, and asylums which were thought to be inappropriately filled with 'mental defectives'[4] of all varieties. Third, it would prevent the feeble-minded from transmitting their condition to future generations. Fourth, and as result of the above benefits, permanent care would be 'ultimately a very great saving of money to the community'.[5] Finally, Mary Dendy argued, permanent segregation would serve to protect the feeble-minded both from themselves and from society.

In Mary Dendy's opinion, the great principle of permanent care constituted a form of 'scientific morality':[6] scientific because it relied upon the results of scientific enquiry and medical expertise in identifying and resolving the perceived problems of mental deficiency; moral because it took into consideration both the good of society and the good of the individual. In the first decade of this century, Mary Dendy and others made considerable efforts to put this principle into practice. In 1902, after several years of campaigning for support, the Lancashire and Cheshire Society opened the Sandlebridge Boarding Schools at Great Warford in Cheshire. As a result of both charitable and state funding, the Schools and the associated Colony rapidly expanded. By 1914, when the Mental Deficiency Act came into force, there were 265 children and young adults resident in the Colony.[7]

Significantly, the belief that the feeble-minded should be permanently segregated was predicated upon a particular, and professedly novel, construction of the nature of feeble-mindedness. For Mary Dendy and other medical and social workers involved in establishing permanent institutional provisions, the feeble-minded constituted a distinct and inherently degenerate subset of society. Life-long segregation was thus legitimated by a belief that mental defectives were categorically different from the normal population, that is, that they were essentially pathological.

In this chapter, I shall explore in detail both the form of the institutional provisions created at Sandlebridge and the rhetoric employed by Mary Dendy and others to legitimate those provisions. The first section sets the scene by charting briefly both the emergence of special provisions for mental defectives in the last half of the nineteenth century and the manner in which those provisions were founded on a perception of mental defectives as educable and improvable variations from the normal population. The second section describes the development of an alternative form of institutional care by focusing on the establishment and maintenance of the Sandlebridge Boarding Schools and Colony between 1899 and 1914. In the third section, I shall examine the manner in which Mary Dendy and other writers legitimated their arguments for permanent institutional care by reference to a particular construction of the feeble-minded as physically and mentally abnormal. The final section critically examines both the extent to which the Sandlebridge Boarding Schools constituted a departure from previous institutional practices and the extent to which Mary Dendy's 'great, new principle' of permanent segregation was endorsed in the first decade of this century.

II

In the last half of the nineteenth century, changing educational policies and the experiences of doctors involved in the management of prisons, asylums and workhouses combined to draw attention to both children and adults with mental deficiency. Specific legislative changes in the field of education initiated and facilitated the process of recognising that a certain proportion of school-age children was defective. The introduction of 'payment by results' in the Revised Code of 1862, the spread of educational opportunities that followed the creation of School Boards by the Elementary Education Act of 1870, and the burdening of parents with a duty to ensure that their children received 'efficient elementary instruction' in 1876 effectively exposed those children who, for a variety of reasons, were either incapable of attending school or unable to benefit from a standard elementary education.[8]

In addition to disclosing the existence of children requiring special instruction, the administration of the Elementary Education Acts afforded a means by which those children could be counted and assessed. The subsequent accumulation of information about the prevalence of mentally deficient children itself generated further and more detailed studies. In the last quarter of the nineteenth century, surveys conducted by the Charity Organisation Society, the British Medical Association, and the Metropolitan Association for Befriending Young Servants, together with reports from the Department of Education further categorised, and exposed the problems thought to be caused by, mentally defective children.[9]

In the last decades of the nineteenth century, adults with mental deficiency were also perceived as problematic in a number of areas. Mentally deficient inmates of workhouses and asylums were regarded as undesirable companions even for the poor and the insane. And as Janet Saunders has pointed out, doctors in the prison medical service also 'saw the mentally handicapped as a problem'.[10] Accordingly, from the 1860s, prison surgeons, such as J.B. Thomson of Perth General Prison and William Guy of Millbank Prison in London (which at that time was being used as an observation centre for assessing prisoners suspected of being of 'weak or unsound mind'), began to collect information about mentally disordered offenders. Guy's conclusion that separate penal institutions should be provided for mentally deficient offenders was reiterated in the report of the Commission on the Penal Servitude Acts published in 1879 which concluded that, as a result of their erratic behaviour and irritating effect on other inmates, mentally deficient prisoners posed special disciplinary problems.[11]

Changing perceptions of the special problems created by mental defectives in schools, workhouses, asylums and prisons, encouraged philanthropists and social reformers to develop institutional provisions designed specifically for mental defectives. Voluntary idiot asylums, established on a charitable basis in the last half of the nineteenth century, demonstrated the plausibility of providing accommodation and training for the mentally deficient in their own institutions.[12] In 1897, convicts thought to be feeble-minded began to be incarcerated at Parkhurst Prison on the Isle of Wight.[13] And, in the 1890s, special schools for educating mentally defective children were established in a number of cities and towns, notably in Leicester, London, and Birmingham.[14]

Significantly, voluntary idiot asylums, special schools and special prisons were established and maintained according to a belief that there was no sharp divide between normal and abnormal mental processes and that the mentally deficient population could therefore be successfully educated and restored to independent social life.[15] Accordingly, voluntary idiot asylums admitted inmates, usually children, for a set number of years only, during which time they were to be trained for some form of productive labour to be continued after their release. At the end of the century, education in special schools was similarly intended to facilitate the development of self-sufficiency in preparation for adult life. In 1898, this belief in the continuity of normal and abnormal mental abilities, and in the educability of feeble-minded children, was expressed in the Report of the Departmental Committee on Defective and Epileptic Children:

> From the normal child down to the lowest idiot, there are all degrees of deficiency of mental power; and it is only a difference of degree which distinguishes the feeble-minded children, referred to in our inquiry, on the one side from the backward children who are found in every ordinary school, and, on the other side, from the children who are too deficient to receive proper benefit from any teaching which the School Authorities can give.[16]

One of the consequences of this report was the passage, a year later, of the Elementary Education (Defective and Epileptic Children) Act. This legislation empowered school authorities to ascertain the number of children in their district who 'by reason of mental or physical defect are incapable of receiving proper benefit' from ordinary elementary education but who would benefit from 'instruction in special schools or classes'. The Act further permitted (but did not oblige) school authorities to 'make provision for the education of such children' by establishing special classes or special schools, or by boarding children out in houses suitably close to a special school or class.[17]

III

In 1898, even before the passage of the 1899 Elementary Education (Defective and Epileptic Children) Act permitted school authorities to establish special schools and classes, Mary Dendy questioned the validity of educating mentally defective children in special schools and classes without providing some form of institutional after-care. Her involvement in the Collyhurst Recreation Rooms in Manchester (founded by her uncle, James Rait Beard) and her experience as a member of the Manchester School Board[18] led her to insist that, even if local authorities did successfully establish special classes, further provision was needed if the problems associated with mental defectives were to be avoided:

> Granted, however, that the special classes are started everywhere, and that they are worked in the most efficient way possible, still, after the children have passed out of them, there remains something to be done. There will always be a considerable number who are quite unable to guide and guard themselves, and these ought to be detained for life. Given a proper place to put them in, this is by no means a difficult thing to do. They are so weakly that if they are caught fresh from school, before they are habituated to a street life, they will be easily managed by anyone who will take the trouble to dominate them. They are generally very affectionate, and readily attach themselves to their teachers and rulers. It is only in this way that the evil can be cured – by preventing it.[19]

The evil to which Mary Dendy referred in this and other pamphlets on the subject encompassed a number of issues. According to Mary Dendy, mental defectives were destined to become paupers, to commit crimes, and to transmit their mental and social ineptitude to their offspring: 'So he grows up through a pitiful and degraded youth to a pitiful and degraded manhood, and dies, leaving behind him offspring to carry on the horrible tradition.'[20] Although such a fate awaited all types of mental defectives, Mary Dendy was particularly concerned about the problems posed by high-grade defectives or the feeble-minded, who by virtue of their physical and mental proximity to the normal population could evade immediate recognition and, therefore, more successfully transmit their feeble-mindedness to future generations. As Mary Dendy explained in a pamphlet published in 1910, in which she spelt out the multiplicity of social problems caused by the feeble-minded, it was

> not the very severe cases which are the most dangerous; it is the mild cases, which are capable of being well veneered, so as to look, for a time at any rate, almost normal, against which there is most need to protect society.[21]

In 1898, having examined nearly 40,000 Manchester school children,[22] Mary Dendy formulated and began to advertise her plans to control the problems associated with the feeble-minded in the Manchester region. Although she recognised that providing special schools was a 'step in the right direction',[23] she insisted that further provisions were urgently required:

> Now it is well known by those who have, in existing homes, undertaken the care of the feeble-minded, that they can be easily detained. But we, in Manchester, have no place in which to detain them. When I finished my work with Dr. Ashby, I consulted him as to a scheme I had been turning over in my own mind for some time, for providing boarding schools for those children who, when they left the special classes, should still be a danger to the community and to themselves, and was glad to find that it met with his approval.[24]

In the absence of state legislation at that time, Mary Dendy was aware that any initiative in this area would 'have to be carried out by private effort'.[25] Accordingly, she set about mobilising both local and national support for a society aimed explicitly at establishing permanent institutional care for the feeble-minded. The success of the campaign depended to a large extent on Mary Dendy's inherited network of wealthy contacts in the Manchester region. Having been brought up and educated in Manchester as part of a socially, educationally, and politically active group of nonconformist Unitarians, Mary Dendy had access to a group of friends and relatives involved in both philanthropic and municipal activities, that is, in local health services, education, in the media and in many branches of local government and charity work.[26] Many of these people donated money, time and effort to the project. The successful mobilisation of interest and financial support was, however, also a product of Mary Dendy's tireless efforts to advertise the work by presenting papers and publishing pamphlets for local, national and international audiences. Mary Dendy's efforts and those of her associates were immediately productive. The Lancashire and Cheshire Society for the Permanent Care of the Feeble-Minded was inaugurated on 26 October 1898.[27] Its constitutional aims, adopted at a meeting held at the School Board Offices in Manchester on 21 March 1899, were to collect funds and establish an institution for the care, education and welfare of 'Feeble-minded Persons', and to promote the welfare of such persons.[28] The campaigning work of the main Lancashire and Cheshire Society was facilitated by the establishment of branch societies in Eccles (1900), in Altrincham, Bowdon and Hale (1901), and in Southport (1904).[29]

The Society's plans to open an institution for the feeble-minded were realised in 1902, when six boys were admitted to the Sandlebridge Boarding Schools (built on a plot of land donated by the David Lewis Trustees near Alderley Edge in Cheshire)[30] in May of that year. The first girls were admitted to a separate house in September of the same year.[31] By virtue of continued donations and subscriptions from individuals, local education authorities and Poor Law unions, both the fabric of, and the facilities available at, the Schools were rapidly expanded. In 1904, a separate school house was built.[32] In 1906, a new building for sixty-five children was constructed and Warford Hall was purchased for adult female residents. In 1913, a new hospital building (referred to as the Ashby Hospital in commemoration of Dr Henry Ashby's services to the Colony from its conception until his death in 1908) was completed.[33] In the first decade of this century, the Lancashire and Cheshire Society also purchased farm land, gardens and livestock both as a means of supplying food for the residents and for occupying and educating young men once they had left the Colony's school.[34] As a result of this expansion, the Sandlebridge Schools and Colony accommodated increasing numbers of children and young adults identified as feeble-minded (see Table 8.1).

Significantly, Mary Dendy's efforts were not limited to dealing with the problems in Manchester. Although the majority of children admitted to Sandlebridge came from Lancashire and Cheshire, the Society was asked to consider admitting children from all over England.[35] Acknowledging the difficulties involved in providing for the whole country, however, Mary Dendy hoped that Sandlebridge would serve as an example of what could be achieved through private effort, as a model for the establishment of similar institutions elsewhere, and as a means of showing 'that it is possible for Government to take in hand a preventive measure which will spare future generations much of the vice and misery and degradation which are amongst us now'.[36]

Table 8.1 Numbers of residents at Sandlebridge, 1905–1914

Year	*Total residents*
1905	57
1906	86
1907	118
1908	160
1909	204
1910	223
1911	232
1912	261
1913	266
1914	265

Sources: Annual Reports of the Lancashire and Cheshire Society for the Permanent Care of the Feeble-Minded, 1905–1929

Mary Dendy's endeavours to promote institutional care for mental defectives at a national level also included pressure to change the law. She was convinced that the 1899 Act was unsatisfactory in at least two ways: first, the Act did not make the provision of special schools and classes compulsory; second, it did not make provisions for mental defectives over the age of 16. Accordingly, in her addresses and published articles, and in her evidence before the Royal Commission on the Care and Control of the Feeble-Minded, she argued, like many others, for state intervention in the matter.[37] Eventually, these arguments proved successful. In 1913, the Mental Deficiency Act obliged local mental deficiency committees either to provide suitable supervision for persons identified as mentally defective or to send them to institutions or place them under guardianship.[38] Significantly, this legislation ensured state support for institutional care previously provided almost exclusively by the voluntary sector. The following year, the Elementary Education (Defective and Epileptic Children) Act extended the 1899 Act by obliging local education authorities to provide educational facilities for mentally defective children between the ages of 7 and 16.[39] Together, these Acts enabled local authorities to segregate mental defectives for life. Mary Dendy's personal contribution to this process was officially recognised in her appointment as one of the commissioners to the newly established Board of Control.

IV

Mary Dendy's campaign to establish permanent institutional care for feeble-minded children and adults depended, to a large extent, on her ability to exploit a variety of contemporary concerns about law and order, public health, poverty, unemployment, declining imperial strength, and racial degeneration.[40] She exploited these fears in two ways. At one level, she insisted that the feeble-minded were not simply part of a wide spectrum of social problems (encompassing crime, unemployment, poverty, inebriety, prostitution, disease and so on) but the root cause of those problems: feeble-mindedness, she argued, was 'an evil which brings all other evils in its train'.[41] At another level, she supported her arguments for permanent segregation by asserting, in contradiction to many earlier commentators and in opposition to the conclusions of the 1898 Departmental Report, that the feeble-minded constituted a distinct, inherently pathological subset of society. This assertion, adopted by a number of commentators in this period, was substantiated in a number of ways.

In the first instance, Mary Dendy (and other writers) argued that feeble-mindedness was an inherited condition. In 1898, for example, she stated that:

> As to the cause of feeble-mindedness, it is, in the main, undoubtedly heredity … It has not been possible for me as yet to get at the family history of all the feeble-minded children I have seen, but very often when the parents put in an appearance their statements bore out the theory of heredity.[42]

In its strongest form, the hereditarian theory of mental deficiency assumed that the defect was transmitted as a simple Mendelian recessive character.[43] While this controversial form of the theory was eventually rejected, the hereditarian approach was reproduced in a number of early twentieth-century texts and reports on mental deficiency.[44] Significantly, it was often employed in a manifestly circular fashion: when a child was diagnosed as possibly feeble-minded, its family was scrutinised for evidence of deficiencies elsewhere; once found, those deficiencies were used to solidify the original diagnosis. Moreover, in the course of constructing genealogies in this way, Mary Dendy and others included not only a family history of feeble-mindedness, but also evidence of ancestral and descendant insanity, inebriety, epilepsy, and syphilis. Thus, feeble-mindedness was regarded as one member of a family of inherited and pathological conditions.

The inherited and permanent taint of feeble-mindedness was thought to be evident not only in family histories but also in the lives of individual defectives. Thus, by virtue of an inherited and predetermined biography of deficiency, a feeble-minded boy or girl was, according to Mary Dendy, destined to become a burden on society on leaving school:

> He knows no skilled work, and cannot keep a situation if he gets one. He comes upon the streets, sells matches, shoe-laces, papers, and generally ends by turning up in gaol. By this time he has become used to a vagrant life, and as he can only move along the path of least resistance, and as it is made so much easier for him to go wrong than to go right, he goes wrong persistently and becomes a confirmed criminal.[45]

The belief that educational disability and social ineptitude were two manifestations of the same hereditary tendency led Mary Dendy to conclude that feeble-mindedness constituted a permanent, and immovable, feature of an individual's life. Significantly, this conclusion was reinforced by the findings of a number of other writers who contended that feeble-minded children and adults were not simply quantitatively removed from the norm, as earlier writers had suggested, but that they were qualitatively different from the rest of the population. Thus, the continuum that had previously stretched from the lowest to the highest intelligence was categorically broken into two distinct and incommensurable groups, the normal and the pathological. In 1910, for example, Dr Alfred Tredgold, renowned for his works on mental deficiency, stated:

> As is well known, normal individuals differ greatly in the degree of their mental capacity, and consequently it might at first sight appear that the feeble-minded were merely the least intellectually gifted – the inferior members – of normal mankind. This is not the case. They belong to a totally distinct and pathological group. They suffer from a deficiency of mind, a failure of mental development, which is of precisely the same kind as, and merely differs in degree from, the states of idiocy and imbecility.[46]

Tredgold and other medical writers substantiated this view of the feeble-minded as belonging to a distinct and pathological group in several ways. First, mental deficiency in general was likened to organic disease. In 1911, at a one-day conference on the care of the feeble-minded held in Manchester, Tredgold insisted that 'feeble-mindedness is not the lowest grade of the normal, but that it is a definite abnormality – that it is, in fact, a disease'.[47] In particular, mental deficiency was likened to infectious diseases. Thus, when giving evidence to the Royal Commission on the Care and Control of the Feeble-Minded in 1904, Mary Dendy alerted the commissioners to the moral and physical degeneration resulting from undetected mental deficiency among the upper, as well as the lower, classes and suggested that medical men should be required by law to report such cases as if they were 'a notifiable disease'. The strength of this metaphorical link between mental deficiency and infectious diseases was reinforced by observations that mental defectives were more susceptible to infectious diseases than the normal population. According to Mary Dendy, the weak-minded were 'peculiarly susceptible to disease, particularly consumption, and succumb more readily than normal persons to epidemics'.[48]

Belief in the distinct and pathological nature of the feeble-minded was also given credence by references to physical stigmata frequently found in mental defectives. The diagnostic significance of physical stigmata was discussed in a number of medical texts published around the turn of this century. In his *Feeblemindedness in Children of School-Age*, published in 1911, for example, Charles Paget Lapage, physician to the Manchester Children's Hospital and a frequent visitor at Sandlebridge, listed a variety of 'stigmata of degeneration', some of which he illustrated with photographs of children from the Sandlebridge Colony itself: defects in the size and shape of the head; deformities of the external ear; deformities of the eyes, palate and jaws; and a defective expression.[49] While medical writers acknowledged that the presence of physical stigmata was not pathognomonic of mental deficiency, they nevertheless noted that stigmata were more marked, more numerous and more often found in mental defectives than in the mentally normal population.[50]

The representation (by Mary Dendy and Alfred Tredgold in particular) of the feeble-minded as a distinct and pathological subset of society was closely linked to the contention that feeble-mindedness was not simply a transient phenomenon amenable to correction and cure but a permanent affliction. In Tredgold's opinion, while 'this defect may be ameliorated it can never be cured, and it is necessary to state most emphatically that by *no* method can the feeble-minded person be converted into a normal individual'.[51] A similar view was forcefully expressed by Mary Dendy throughout the first decade of this century:

> No one can promise to cure the sufferers who are such a curse to themselves and to society. No one can make the faulty brain into a perfect one, change the diseased rickety body for one glowing with health and beauty, strengthen the feeble will so that it has all the power of the highest and strongest of God's creatures. These things are beyond the skill of man.[52]

While she considered human skill incapable of curing the feeble-minded, she insisted that there was nevertheless 'a scientific method of dealing with the feeble-minded',[53] which could prevent the spread of social problems caused by the condition:

> But science has shown us what we can do if we only will. We can develop the faulty brain in those directions in which it has power; we can minimise the bodily weakness and suffering; we can give the feeble will right guidance and support, so that for every sufferer who comes under our care life shall be made as pure and holy and happy as his physical limits will permit. More, far more than this, we can so guard and protect that life, that those terrible physical limits shall not be handed down to a second and third generation. This is the meaning of the word *Permanent*, in the title of the Lancashire and Cheshire Society.[54]

In the first decade or so of this century, then, the representation of the feeble-minded as essentially pathological and distinct from the normal population was closely linked to a belief that the feeble-minded were incurable educationally and socially inept. This construction of feeble-mindedness was in turn used to legitimate claims that the only rational way of coping with the problems supposedly caused by mental defectives, in general, and the feeble-minded, in particular, was to segregate them permanently in institutions built specifically for that purpose.

V

In the last decade or so of the nineteenth century and the first decade of this century, 'the problem of feeble-mindedness' (as it was frequently called) became an increasingly central focus for a number of professional groups. Medical practitioners, in particular, were prominent contributors to debates on the matter. A number of doctors, many of whom worked in institutions for the mentally deficient, published textbooks and articles and presented papers on the subject.[55] In addition, editorials, articles and short notices on feeble-mindedness and on the urgent need for legislation appeared frequently in journals directed at medical practitioners in a variety of situations: for example, in *The British Medical Journal*, *The Lancet*, *The Medical Officer*, and *The Journal of State Medicine*.

A variety of other professional groups also contributed to discussions on the matter. Although most of the witnesses giving evidence to the Royal Commission on the Care and Control of the Feeble-Minded were medically qualified, evidence was also presented by lawyers, teachers and school inspectors, charity workers, and those involved in

Poor Law administration.[56] Similarly, local conferences on the subject, such as the Manchester and Salford Sanitary Association's conference in 1911, were attended by a mix of charity workers, medical practitioners, Poor Law guardians, teachers and local philanthropists.[57]

Mary Dendy made considerable efforts to convince these various audiences that she had devised a new form of institutional care, based on scientific principles, that was guaranteed to solve both the immediate and the long-term problems thought to be caused by feeble-mindedness. To what extent did Mary Dendy's initiative constitute a departure from previous approaches to people labelled as mentally deficient and to what extent did these various professional groups endorse both the principle of permanent care and the practices developed at Sandlebridge?

One of the ways in which Mary Dendy promoted the project at Sandlebridge was to stress that it offered a very different approach to that adopted at the voluntary 'idiot'[58] asylums in the last half of the nineteenth century. On occasions, this amounted to direct criticism of asylum policies. Thus, in a pamphlet entitled *The Problem of the Feeble-Minded*, she made a direct attack on the policies and practices of the Royal Albert Asylum in Lancashire:

> The Royal Albert Asylum keeps its patients for seven years, the longest period devoted to training at any such institution. At a meeting of the supporters of this asylum in 1906 it was reported that since the foundation of the institution 1,502 patients have been discharged from it. It is worse than useless to deal with idiots and other weak-minded persons in this way.[59]

In spite of such explicit criticism of voluntary idiot asylum policy and in spite of her claims to have established a permanent colony for the feeble-minded, it is not clear that the policies and practices adopted at Sandlebridge differed substantially from those of the asylums. Indeed, similarities between the establishments are evident both in the length of stay of residents and in the mix of custodial and educational purposes served by both voluntary idiot asylums and Sandlebridge.

In the first instance, there is evidence to suggest that those involved in running, and subscribing to, voluntary idiot asylums were prepared, from the outset, to consider the possibility of admitting people for life.[60] Conversely, the records of the Sandlebridge Boarding Schools and Colony indicate that many of the children admitted to Sandlebridge did not remain permanently in the institution. Thus, of nearly four hundred children admitted to the institution between 1902 and 1914, only 265 were still at Sandlebridge in 1914.[61] The remainder were removed by Poor Law Guardians to work on Union farms, were discharged to other institutions or to their families, or were forcibly removed by their relatives. Thus, Mary Dendy's claim in 1910 that 'we have lost very few either by death or removals since we opened our first building' is unsupported by evidence from the Colony's records.[62] Even after the 1913 Mental Deficiency Act had facilitated the retention of mental defectives beyond the age of 16, this pattern persisted. Indeed, many residents of Sandlebridge were released when their certificates were not renewed under the terms of the 1913 Act.[63]

Similarities between voluntary asylums, on the one hand, and Sandlebridge, on the other, are also evident in the practical running of these establishments. Although proponents of asylum care publicly emphasised the educational and training aspects of their institutions, it is likely that asylums were also used to exert a discrete custodial power over the disorderly and the socially deviant. Many of the 'motley group' of inmates first admitted to Park House, Highgate in 1848 posed considerable problems to the authorities, not on the basis of their educational deficits but because they were loud, violent and unruly. In 1850, in their annual report, the managers of Park House were as pleased, if not more so, at their success in taming the mob as at their ability to educate them in the classroom:

> Bad habits have been overcome; power has been created for the care of the person; the body has been brought under the control of the will, and both have become subject to mild authority. The power of imitation has been fostered; music and drawing are beginning to find a place in the school: reading, writing, and even figures, which are the severest test to the weak mind, are now claiming general attention. And above all the moral affections have been exercised, and the effects are found in the harmony of the family, and the greater readiness of the mind to recognise and worship an invisible and gracious Presence. There is now order, obedience to authority, classification, improvement and cheerful occupation.[64]

More pertinently, case histories from the Royal Albert Asylum suggest the potential social, rather than purely educational, utility of the institution. Of six children discussed by Michael Barratt in his thesis on the Royal Albert Asylum, four appear to have presented problems of conduct, temperament and disposition, as well as instruction. For example, one boy, admitted in June 1878 at the age of 7, was described as 'a wild, uncouth boy, rushing about and doing mischief'. After a year or so in the asylum, both his educational ability and his behaviour had improved. Significantly, he was 'now gentle, and well-conducted, and very obedient to his teachers'.[65] Such cases challenge Barratt's own claims that voluntary idiot asylums 'were remedial, not palliative, in intent'[66] and that 'they did not have a clear-cut *societal* function'.[67]

Conversely, although Mary Dendy and others involved in Sandlebridge emphasised the social importance of permanently segregating the feeble-minded, they were also aware of the importance of appropriate education and training both as a means of assisting the Colony's financial survival and as a means of occupying the residents in productive and fulfilling work. Accordingly, education in the school rooms at Sandlebridge (which was run by teachers without a resident medical practitioner for nearly forty years) was geared both to the individual abilities of the residents and to the belief that it was through practical work (rather than intellectual endeavour) that the moral reclamation of the feeble-minded would be achieved.[68]

It would appear, then, that in spite of Mary Dendy's claims, the principles and practices adopted at Sandlebridge did not differ substantially from those that had been adopted by the voluntary idiot asylums over the preceding half-century. What appears to have changed, however, around the turn of this century, is the nature of the rhetoric employed to legitimate institutional custody for mental defectives. While the proponents of asylum care in the late nineteenth century had echoed the therapeutic optimism of the period in their slogan 'educate the idiot', the proponents of colonies such as Sandlebridge increasingly exploited contemporary fears about crime, poverty and racial degeneration by publicly advocating the permanent segregation of the feeble-minded on the basis of their pathological and degenerate nature.

In many ways, Mary Dendy, Alfred Tredgold and others advocating permanent segregation of the feeble-minded were successful in promoting their cause. The campaigning efforts of Mary Dendy and her associates in Manchester succeeded in attracting considerable local, national and international interest in developments at Sandlebridge. This interest was evidenced both in the number of visitors to the Colony and in the continued financial support to the Lancashire and Cheshire Society.[69] Her initiative at Sandlebridge also elicited support from witnesses and commissioners participating in the Royal Commission on the Care and Control of the Feeble-Minded between 1904 and 1908. On questioning Henry Ashby about arrangements at Sandlebridge, for example, Henry Burden, a manager of inebriate reformatories, stated that, 'Sandlebridge strikes one as almost an ideal place for these young children'.[70]

In addition, the main tenets of Mary Dendy's arguments were taken up and discussed elsewhere, most notably in medical journals. Thus, in the last decade of the nineteenth century, and the first decade of the twentieth century, *The British Medical Journal*, *The Lancet*, *The Journal of Mental Science*, *The Journal of State Medicine*, and *The Medical Officer* regularly published articles, letters, editorials and conference reports in which Mary Dendy's ideas were sympathetically received and in which arguments both for permanent segregation and for changes in the law were forcibly made.[71] Eventually, such arguments (propagated in particular by members of the Eugenics Education Society, of which both Mary Dendy and Alfred Tredgold were members) proved influential in the framing and passage of the Mental Deficiency Act in 1913.[72]

The passage of the 1913 Act should not, however, be taken as evidence that either Mary Dendy's construction of the feeble-minded or the policy of permanent segregation passed unchallenged in the early years of this century. On the contrary, her arguments were contested at a number of levels. In the first instance, belief in a clear divide between normal and pathological mental processes, which underwrote policies for permanent segregation, was challenged by a growing anthropometric and biometric trend characterised both by the work of Francis Galton and Karl Pearson and by the introduction of intelligence tests into the medical inspection of school children.[73] Based on quantitative, statistical methodologies, biometry not only rejected accounts of mental deficiency that described its transmission as a Mendelian recessive unit character but also stressed the continuous distribution of both physical and mental qualities within the population. Thus, in 1914, after studying the results of intelligence tests applied to groups of supposedly normal and supposedly mentally deficient children, Karl Pearson and Gustav Jaederholm drew the following conclusions:

> In truth there is no such intellectual boundary between the normal and mentally defective. The distribution of intelligence in both normal and mentally defective is *absolutely continuous*, and in purely psychological tests of intelligence there are no rigid and limited categories of normal intelligence and feeble-mindedness. There is a continuous gradation of intelligence, and it appears to us perfectly idle to speak of Mendelian units and lack of determiners in respect of such a character.[74]

Although they acknowledged that there may be 'a pathological type of mental defect' responsible for a small proportion of mental deficiency,

Pearson and Jaederholm insisted that this type could not 'be directly differentiated on the basis of intelligence from the remainder of the tail of the mentally defective population'.[75] They further argued that, since there was 'no sharp division' between mentally defective and normal children, the drafting of children into special classes and schools must be the result of a variety of factors related more to social efficiency, and to the personal opinions of teachers and medical officers, than to intelligence.[76] While accepting the need to segregate the socially inefficient, these authors insisted that segregation should not be determined by intelligence tests and warned that the 'pseudo-scientific dogma which supports an absolute differentiation between the normal and the mentally-defective child is bound to do incalculable social harm'.[77]

Some commentators also questioned whether the feeble-minded were quite as incurable as Mary Dendy and Alfred Tredgold insisted. The Board of Education's persistent ameliorist and environmentalist stance, for example, challenged the assumption that feeble-minded children were beyond redemption and supported the continuing contribution of special day schools to the education and improvement of defectives.[78] And at a conference on child hygiene in 1910, Dr Helen Boyle was reported to have responded to Alfred Tredgold's assertion that feeble-minded children could not be cured, by stating that 'her experience showed that feeble-minded children were more curable than Dr. Tredgold thought'.[79] Nevertheless, even she argued for 'a more prolonged control of these children, such as was obtained in the colonies at Manchester and Tunbridge'.[80]

Although many medical practitioners, social workers and teachers accepted the need for some form of care, Mary Dendy's insistence on permanent care was not unequivocally accepted. For example, the National Association for Promoting the Welfare of the Feeble-Minded refused to include the word 'permanent' in its title.[81] Moreover, even when the need for permanent care was increasingly acknowledged, institutional care was not the sole form of permanency under discussion. 'After-Care Committees' such as that in Birmingham continued to consider the possibility of some form of guardianship or supervision of defectives in the community after discharge from an institution.[82]

Finally, it is clear from reports of debates about the passage of the 1913 Mental Deficiency Act that some commentators, notably the Liberal Member of Parliament Josiah Wedgwood, objected to legislation empowering the detention of mental defectives on the grounds that it constituted 'a monstrous interference with individual liberty'.[83] In spite of such objections, it is evident that by 1913, many politicians, medical practitioners, charity workers and educationalists were convinced that segregation, sanctioned by the state, offered the most effective means of 'putting an end to this terrible evil of our society'.[84]

VI

At the turn of this century, Mary Dendy began to insist that feeble-mindedness was 'a problem which lies at the root of all others, and until we deal with it in a rational manner there is little hope indeed of bettering the general condition of our people'.[85] The rational solution that she had in mind comprised early recognition of feeble-minded children and their subsequent segregation for life in colonies built specifically for the purpose. The magnitude of the problem, she argued, was even sufficient to justify 'over-riding the responsibility of the parent for his child'.[86]

For Mary Dendy, the benefits of permanent segregation were clear. The multiplicity of social problems supposedly attributable to the feeble-minded would be prevented and the feeble-minded themselves would be guaranteed a secure and safe environment in which they could fulfil their limited potential. Significantly, representations of the feeble-minded as essentially pathological and arguments for their permanent segregation served discrete professional and personal interests as well as professedly humanitarian ones. Thus, in claiming that feeble-mindedness was a pathological state analogous to organic disease, medical writers such as Alfred Tredgold were creating and protecting a role for themselves as experts in mental deficiency. In this way, they could ensure that medical practitioners rather than teachers were considered the most appropriate professionals to be given the responsibility of diagnosing feeble-mindedness and of administrating new legislation. Similarly, by acclaiming arrangements at Sandlebridge as the most effective way of dealing with a multiplicity of social problems, Mary Dendy was carving out a niche for herself in a public arena from which women were often excluded. Her success in this endeavour is evidenced not only by her notoriety as the matriarch of a family of feeble-minded children at Sandlebridge but also by her appointment as a paid commissioner to the newly created Board of Control in 1913.

NOTES

1 M. Dendy, *The Importance of Permanence in the Care of the Feeble-Minded*, (n.d), p. 2. This pamphlet was originally published in 1899 in the *Educational Review*.

2 The term 'feeble-minded' was used in the late nineteenth and early twentieth centuries to describe people with a mild degree of what was at that time referred to as 'mental deficiency' but would now be referred to as 'learning disability'. Quotation marks will no longer be used for the terms 'feeble-minded' or 'mental deficiency'.

3 M. Dendy, *Feebleness of Mind, Pauperism and Crime*, Glasgow Provisional Committee for the Permanent Care of the Feeble-Minded, 1901; ibid., *Feeble-Minded Children*, Manchester, 1902; ibid., 'The Feeble-Minded and Crime', *The Lancet*, 1902, vol. 1, pp. 1460–3; ibid., *The Problem of the Feeble-Minded*, Manchester, 1910; ibid., 'The Feeble-Minded', *The Medical Magazine*, 1911, vol. 20, pp. 686–98; ibid., 'Feeble-Minded Children', *The Journal of State Medicine*, 1914, vol. 22, pp. 412–18.

4 On the use of this term, see Note 1 above. Quotation marks will no longer be used.

5 Dendy, *The Importance of Permanence*, p. 6.

6 This phrase appears in Dendy, *Feebleness of Mind, Pauperism and Crime*, p. 8.

7 Figures relating to the number of admissions to, and the number of residents in, the Colony are taken from the *Annual Reports of the Lancashire and Cheshire Society for the Permanent Care of the Feeble-Minded* [hereafter referred to simply as *Annual Reports*], 1900–1929.

8 The legislative provisions were Elementary Education Act, 33 & 34 Vict. c.75, (1870); and Elementary Education Act, 39 & 40 Vict. c.53, (1876). For contemporary comments on the importance of these Acts, see *Annual Report for 1908 of the Chief Medical Officer of the Board of Education*, Cd. 4986, London, 1910, pp. 107, 114; and *Annual Report for 1909 of the Chief Medical Officer of the Board of Education*, Cd. 5426, London, 1910, pp. 157–8.

9 See, for example *Training Schools and Permanent Asylums for Idiots*, London, 1875; *Report of a Special Committee of the Charity Organisation Society on the Education and Care of Idiots, Imbeciles, and Harmless Lunatics*, London, 1877; *The Feeble-minded Child and Adult*, London, 1893; F. Warner, 'Abstract of the Milroy Lectures on an Inquiry as to the Physical and Mental Condition of School Children', *The Lancet*, 1892, vol. 1, pp. 567–8, 623–4, 680–2, 738–9. On investigations into the circumstances of feeble-minded girls and young women, see the discussions in K. Jones, *A History of the Mental Health Services*, London, 1972, p. 186; and J. A. Barclay, 'Langho Epileptic Colony: 1906–1984: A Contextual Study of the Origins, Transformations and Demise of Manchester's "Colony for Sane Pauper Epileptics"' PhD thesis, Manchester, 1988, pp. 37–42.

10 J. Saunders, 'Quarantining the Weak-Minded: Psychiatric Definitions of Degeneracy and the Late Victorian Asylum', in W. F. Bynum, R. Porter, and M. Shepherd (eds), *The Anatomy of Madness: Essays in the History of Psychiatry*, vol. 3, London, 1988, p. 275.

11 Discussed in Saunders, 'Quarantining the Weak-minded'. See also Sidney and Beatrice Webb, *English Prisons Under Local Government* (first published 1922), London, 1963, pp. 201–31.

12 For more details on the voluntary idiot asylums, see Gladstone in this volume.

13 Webb and Webb, *English Prisons*, pp. 225–6, fn.

14 J. S. Hurt, *Outside the Mainstream: A History of Special Education*, London, 1988, p. 127. See also *Annual Report for 1908 of the Chief Medical Officer of the Board of Education*, p. 114.

15 Indeed, the development of self-reliance and self-sufficiency was sometimes acknowledged by asylum administrators on both sides of the Atlantic to be the *raison d'être* of such institutions. See, for example, John Charles Bucknill, *Address on Idiocy*, Lewes, 1873, p. 14. On the importance of educability in selecting inmates, see also the bye laws of the New York State Idiot Asylum reproduced in G. E. Shuttleworth, *Notes of a Visit to American Institutions for Idiots & Imbeciles*, Lancaster, (n.d), p. 5.

16 *Report of the Departmental Committee on Defective and Epileptic Children*, vol. I, Cd. 8746, 1898, p. 3.

17 Elementary Education (Defective and Epileptic Children) Act, 1899, 62 & 63 Vict. c.32.

18 For further details of Mary Dendy's involvement in the Collyhurst Recreation Rooms and the Manchester School Board, see H. McLachlan, *Records of a Family 1800–1933*, Manchester, 1935, pp. 144–8.

19 Dendy, *Feeble-Minded Children*, p. 10.

20 Ibid., p. 8

21 Dendy, *The Problem of the Feeble-Minded*, p. 19.

22 Mary Dendy was assisted by Charles H. Wyatt, clerk to the Manchester School Board, Mr Burke, an attendance officer for the School Board, Dr George Shuttleworth, until 1893 the medical superintendent of the Royal Albert Asylum at Lancaster, and Henry Ashby, physician to the Manchester Children's Hospital.

23 Dendy, *Feeble-Minded Children*, p. 9.

24 Ibid., pp. 18–19.

25 Ibid., p. 19.

26 For an account of Mary Dendy's family and close friends, and of their activities in Manchester, see McLachlan, *Records of a Family*.

27 An account of the events leading to the Society's inauguration can be found in the first *Annual Report*, 1899, pp. 3–4.

28 *Constitution of the Lancashire and Cheshire Society for the Permanent Care of the Feeble-Minded*, (n.d), p. 1.

29 *Annual Report*, 1900, pp. 4–5; ibid., 1902, p. 5; ibid., 1904, p. 4.

30 The David Lewis Trust was founded in 1893 with money left by David Lewis, the founder of the Lewis chain of stores. The Trust originally donated twenty acres of land to the Lancashire and Cheshire Society for the Permanent Care of the Feeble-Minded to be used when they were ready. For further details of the Trust, see 'The David Lewis Story', a fact sheet published by the David Lewis Centre.

31 *Annual Report*, 1902, p. 3.

32 *Annual Report*, 1904, p. 7. This temporary construction was replaced by a more substantial building in 1907.

33 Dr Henry Ashby had served as Honorary Consulting Physician to the Lancashire and Cheshire Society from its inception until his death. For comments on the new hospital building, see *Annual Report*, 1913, p. 14.

34 Comments on the work done in the gardens and farms, and accounts of the farm income and expenditure, appeared regularly in the Society's Annual Reports.

35 *Annual Report*, 1902, p. 5.
36 Dendy, *Feeble-Minded Children*, pp. 19–20.
37 See her comments, for example, to the Royal Commission in the Report of the Royal Commission on the Care and Control of the Feeble-Minded [hereafter simply referred to as the Royal Commission], vol. I, Cd. 4215, 1908, pp. 40–41. See also Dendy, *The Problem of the Feeble-Minded*, pp. 28–9.
38 Mental Deficiency Act, 1913, 3 & 4 Geo.5, c.28.
39 Elementary Education (Defective and Epileptic Children) Act, 1914, 4 & 5 Geo.5, c.45.
40 For general discussions of these concerns, see D. J. Kevles, *In the Name of Eugenics*, Harmondsworth, 1986; G. R. Searle, *Eugenics and Politics in Britain, 1900–1914*, Leyden, 1976; G. Jones, *Social Hygiene in Twentieth Century Britain*, London, 1986.
41 Dendy, *The Importance of Permanence*, p. 2.
42 Dendy, *Feeble-Minded Children*, pp. 5–6.
43 E. Sayer, 'Mentally Defective Children and their Treatment', *The Journal of State Medicine*, 1914, vol. 22, p. 157.
44 See Tredgold's discussion of 'morbid heredity' and 'neuropathic stock' in A. F. Tredgold, *Mental Deficiency (Amentia)*, London, 1908, ch. III. See also C. P. Lapage, *Feeblemindedness in Children of School-Age*, Manchester, 1911, ch. XI; and the evidence presented by Dr Henry Ashby to the Royal Commission, vol. I, Cd. 4215, 1908, p. 580.
45 Dendy, *Feebleness of Mind*, p. 5.
46 A. F. Tredgold, 'The Feeble-Minded', *The Contemporary Review*, 1910, vol. 97, p. 718.
47 *Proceedings at a Conference on the Care of the Feeble-Minded*, Manchester and Salford Sanitary Association, 1911, p. 6. While accepting his assertion that feeble-mindedness was a definite abnormality, Charles Paget Lapage challenged Tredgold's reference to feeble-mindedness as a disease: 'I think to call it a disease is a little misleading. Feeble-mindedness is a definite abnormality. It is a developmental defect. It is a failure of the brain to develop. To many people disease rather implies something that is progressive and something which may be curable. Everything depends upon the fact that feeble-mindedness is not curable.' Ibid., p. 28.
48 Royal Commission, vol. I, Cd. 4125, 1908, p. 45. Dendy, *The Importance of Permanence*, p. 2.
49 Lapage, *Feeblemindedness*, pp. 46–63. This work was a version of Lapage's MD thesis and contained an appendix by Mary Dendy.
50 Ibid., p. 49.
51 Tredgold, 'The Feeble-Minded', p. 718.
52 Dendy, *The Importance of Permanence*, p. 4.
53 Dendy, *Feebleness of Mind, Pauperism and Crime*, p. 1.
54 Dendy, *The Importance of Permanence*, pp. 4–5.
55 See for example G. E. Shuttleworth and W. A. Potts, *Mentally Deficient Children: Their Treatment and Training*, London, 1895; Tredgold, *Mental Deficiency*; Lapage, *Feeblemindedness*.
56 Royal Commission, vol. I, Cd. 4215, 1908, pp. viii–xi.
57 See the contributors to the Manchester and Salford Association's conference in *Proceedings at a Conference on the Care of the Feeble-Minded*, passim.

58 The term 'idiot' was used in the late nineteenth and early twentieth centuries to denote people with severe mental deficiency. Quotation marks will no longer be used.

59 Dendy, *The Problem of the Feeble-Minded*, pp. 25–6.

60 D. Wright, 'The Study of Idiocy: The Professional Middle Class and the Evolution of Social Policy on the Mentally Retarded in England, 1848–1914', unpublished MA thesis, McGill University, 1990, p. 106.

61 Details of the admissions to Sandlebridge are taken from the School's Admissions Register, housed in the Cheshire Record Office (CRO), class-mark NHM 11/3837/42. Details of discharges can be found in the Sandlebridge Special Schools Album, CRO, NHM 11/3837/43. Details of the numbers resident at the Colony are taken from the *Annual Reports*.

62 Dendy, *The Problem of the Feeble-Minded*, p. 30.

63 See comments on individual cases in the Sandlebridge Special Schools Album, CRO, NHM 11/3837/43. After 1914, details of discharges were recorded in a Register of Discharges, CRO, NHM 11/3837/49.

64 Quoted in C. Brady, *The Training of Idiotic and Feeble-Minded Children*, Dublin, 1865, pp. 10–11.

65 M. A. Barratt, 'From Education to Segregation: An Inquiry into the Changing Character of Special Provision for the Retarded in England, c.1846–1918', PhD thesis, Lancaster, 1986, p. 59.

66 Ibid., p. 66.

67 Ibid., pp. 80–1.

68 For Mary Dendy's opinion on the importance of particular types of occupation, see particularly, Dendy, 'On the Training and Management of Feeble-Minded Children', Appendix 1 in Lapage, *Feeblemindedness*.

69 The steady stream of local, national and international visitors to Sandlebridge is recorded in the *Warford Hall Visitors Book*, CRO, NHM 11/3837/19.

70 Royal Commission, vol. I, Cd. 4215, 1908, p. 585.

71 See, for example, Mary Dendy's article and the discussion it received in *The Lancet* in May and June, 1902: Dendy, 'The Feeble-Minded and Crime', *The Lancet*, 24 May 1902, pp. 1460–3; *The Lancet*, 1902, pp. 1477–8; 'The Feeble-Minded and Crime', a letter to the editors of *The Lancet*, 1902, pp. 1643–4.

72 Searle, *Eugenics and Politics*, pp. 106–11.

73 George Newman, Chief Medical Officer for the Board of Education, advocated using the Binet and Simon tests in his *Annual Report for 1911 of the Chief Medical Officer of the Board of Education*, London, 1912, pp. 313–15. For discussions of the work of Galton and Pearson, and of intelligence testing in general, see Kevles, *In the Name of Eugenics*; S. J. Gould, *The Mismeasure of Man*, London, 1984; and N. Rose, *The Psychological Complex: Psychology, Politics and Society in England, 1869–1939*, London, 1985.

74 K. Pearson and G. A. Jaederholm, *Mendelism and the Problem of Mental Defect II: On the Continuity of Mental Defect*, London, 1914, p. 17.

75 Ibid., pp. 29–30.

76 Ibid., p. 18.

77 Ibid., pp. 18–19.

78 See, for example, George Newman's opinion on the importance of education, discussed in R. A. Lowe, 'Eugenicists, Doctors and the Quest for National Efficiency: an Educational Crusade, 1900–1939', *History of Education*, 1979, vol. 8, pp. 293–306; and Hurt, *Outside the Mainstream*, p. 148.
79 *The Medical Officer*, 1910, vol. 4, p. 162.
80 Ibid.
81 See Helen Bosanquet (Mary Dendy's sister), *Social Work in London, 1869–1912*, (originally published 1914) Brighton, 1973, p. 202. The Glasgow Provisional Committee for the Permanent Care of the Feeble-Minded and the Yorkshire Society did, however, include the word 'permanent' in their titles.
82 On the importance of After-Care Committees, see *Annual Report for 1909 of the Chief Medical Officer of the Board of Education*, Cd. 5426, London, 1910, p. 163. See also Lowe, 'Eugenicists, Doctors and the Quest for National Efficiency'.
83 *The Medical Officer*, 1913, vol. 9, p. 132. See also J. Woodhouse, 'Eugenics and the Feeble-minded: The Parliamentary Debates of 1912–14', *History of Education*, vol. 11, 1982, pp. 133–7.
84 Dendy, *Feeble-Minded Children*, p. 9.
85 Dendy, *The Problem of the Feeble-Minded*, p. 6.
86 Ibid.

9

GIRLS, DEFICIENCY AND DELINQUENCY

Pamela Cox

INTRODUCTION

The 1913 Mental Deficiency Act intensified social regulation in England and Wales, widening the existing grounds for state intervention in private life on the basis of mental condition. Observed links between deficiency and crime were used to justify this development. While there are a number of accounts of the legal construction and treatment of the criminally insane, histories of the mental deficiency system have not fully discussed the experiences of those designated 'defective' within the penal realm.[1] This chapter examines the reconfiguration of the relationship between crime and mental status in the context of the certification of girls within the juvenile justice system.

It was widely argued by psychologists, doctors and penal reformers in the 1920s and 1930s that a significant proportion of those appearing before the juvenile courts were mentally defective in some degree, yet these arguments had little impact on the practices of the courts. In the first part of the chapter, I suggest that lack of funding for new initiatives combined with a reluctance to alter traditional court proceedings meant that questions of mental status were effectively ignored. However, beyond the courtroom, concepts of mental disorder, framed above all in terms of mental deficiency, were crucial to the internal regulation of the central corrective institution of the juvenile justice system – the industrial school.[2]

The second part of this chapter focuses on the experiences of 'delinquent' girls who were certified 'defective' during the time they spent in industrial schools. The vast majority of girls left the schools between the ages of 14 and 16 to enter domestic service but a significant minority were discharged into asylums, hostels, workhouses and institutions for the mentally defective. Case studies of girls sent to industrial schools run by the Church of England Incorporated Society for Providing Homes for Waifs and Strays overwhelmingly suggest that certification was used to remove problem cases.[3] The remit and responsibilities of industrial schools were shaped by standards of acceptable, containable behaviour. This had been the case since they were established in England and Wales in the 1850s. This chapter argues that those standards were re-negotiated after the popularisation of notions of mental deficiency in the early part of this century, which produced a new 'unreformable' residuum, and new legislative mechanisms to convey them to new specialised institutions. In this sense, the mental deficiency system soon began to function as a safety valve for the juvenile justice system.

These case studies are valuable in two ways. First, they offer access to the experiences of girls who are very much under-represented within histories of juvenile justice.[4] They also demonstrate that definitions of deficiency and the circumstances of certification were gender-specific. The subject of girls and mental deficiency is generally discussed in terms of sexual degeneracy, waywardness and illegitimacy. However, girls were also certified because they were considered to be violent, disruptive and unemployable. This chapter does not discuss the experience of boys, since direct comparison between the experience of boys and girls in these contexts is extremely problematic. Violent acts, for example, have been historically defined and interpreted in very different ways for males and females. To paraphrase Maureen Cain, using quantitative boy–girl comparison as an investigative strategy invariably leads to the posing of the same question: 'How are girls different?' A strategy which examines girls' experiences only in relation to boys, whose experiences have dominated understandings of the criminal justice system, is ultimately a limited one.[5]

Second, these case studies offer an insight into popular perceptions of mental deficiency. The languages of mental health used in this correspondence are not specialised. This is not an exchange of views between experts, but a search for practical solutions to the management 'problems' faced by staff, who increasingly framed these problems in terms of mental defect. As Mathew Thomson notes, studies of mental deficiency have rarely considered the reception, interpretation and deployment of the legislation at a local level.[6] Yet an understanding of the consumption of new concepts of mentality is just as important as an understanding of the production of those concepts. Tracing the routes by which issues of delinquency and deficiency became objects of knowledge for practitioners can open up new possibilities for histories of mental health and criminal justice.

ADOLESCENCE, DELINQUENCY AND DEFICIENCY

Juvenile crime was perceived as a major social problem in the early twentieth century. In 1910, almost 34,000 young people under the age of 16 appeared before the newly established juvenile courts in England and Wales.[7] This rose to nearer 50,000 during the first world war, then declined in the 1920s and 1930s – in 1930 the figure was just under 25,000. Numbers rose sharply after the 1933 Children Act, which extended the jurisdiction of the juvenile court, and prosecutions peaked during the second world war, reaching over 60,000 by 1946. Girls were called before the court in a minority of cases throughout this period. They accounted for approximately 5 per cent of the total number of appearances in any one year between 1910 and 1940, never exceeding 3,000 cases.[8] Charges in the juvenile court followed a relatively consistent pattern in the first half of this century. Girls committed the same range of offences as boys but in far smaller recorded numbers. Theft was the most common allegation, followed by street and bicycle-related offences, vagrancy, and offences against the Education Acts. Sexually related charges are notably very low for both boys and girls, although girls' treatment in court was very much influenced by their perceived sexual histories. The criminal statistics do not record the high number of children implicated in proceedings against parents for neglect which increased dramatically from the 1890s onwards.[9] Further, these statistics conceal the powerful, informal side of the juvenile justice system. Many girls were sent to industrial schools on a 'voluntary' basis, and thousands more were targeted by religious and charitable groups and sent to private rescue homes, often for many years. Local police and magistrates were aware of these practices, which none the less went unrecorded. The rescue and regulation of girls were therefore widely effected in the informal spaces of the legal system, and are not captured within the criminal statistics.[10]

Industrial and reformatory schools were just two of a number of options available to magistrates. The early juvenile justice system did not depend on institutional correction, with most cases resulting in a fine or probation, or whipping for boys. Between 5 and 10 per cent of cases resulted in committal to an industrial or a reformatory school in the years between 1910 and 1940. Under the 1908 Children Act, industrial schools admitted children up to the age of 14 who were considered to be in need of rescue from parental neglect or who were first-time offenders. Pupil–inmates were usually discharged at 16, though could be allowed out to work on licence before then. Reformatories admitted the more 'hardened' adolescent criminal, between the ages of 12 and 16, and could detain them until the age of 19. Both types of school were registered, inspected and partly funded by the Home Office, but 90 per cent were managed by voluntary groups and remained financially dependent upon their charitable efforts.[11]

One effect of this private ownership was that most industrial schools formulated their own admissions policies, which became increasingly selective in the early twentieth century. The schools had always categorised children by age, gender, religion and ethnic group, and in the wake of the Mental Deficiency Act, many of them refused to accept children with obvious mental, moral or physical problems. The small number of schools that would admit these excluded cases were separately registered by the Home Office from 1913 as 'special' and divided into two groups; one group of schools was set up for girls only, dealing with 'immoral girls' and girls 'with moral contamination and knowledge of evil', and a second group for the mentally defective of both sexes.[12] A third set developed in the 1920s for those with physical disabilities. The separate registration of these schools signified a change in Home Office policy. Before 1913, there was an emphasis on the integration of children with 'special needs' within the industrial school sector, which gave way to a later emphasis on more exacting classification and the segregation of the delinquent from the physically and mentally disabled.

Mental defect was framed by the 1913 Act as a generalised moral debilitation – the cause of pauperism, alcoholism, promiscuity and criminality. Justifying its call for segregation, the 1908 Royal Commission on the Care and Control of the Feebleminded had warned of the 'very large numbers of mentally defective persons … over whom no sufficient control is exercised, and whose wayward and irresponsible lives are productive *of crime and misery*'.[13] In the period between 1900 and 1930, the eugenic and psychological debates connecting defect and crime centred on children and adolescents. Healthy children built a healthy race, and the monitoring of their mental and physical development presented the ideal opportunity to reduce the incidence of both deficiency and crime. Children represented the possibilities of social reform, and much was written in Western Europe and the United States on the subject of delinquency and mental status in this period. Leading writers included William Healy, L. Grimberg, August Aichhorn and Cyril Burt.[14] They posited quite different causal relationships between mental disorder and crime – Aichhorn prioritised disordered psychic forces, Grimberg the defective endocrine system, Burt the defective family relationship. Most were agreed, however, that crime was a mental symptom with a mental origin, complicated in the case of girls by puberty, sexual over-development and emotional excess.

After the first Binet-Simon intelligence tests were published in 1905, a number of quantitative psychological and social research projects were carried out which aimed to calculate more exactly the proportion of young offenders who were also defective. Findings varied widely, as did definitions of defect, intelligence and educational ability. Cyril Burt found nine out of ten of his London delinquents to be educationally below average, whereas 40 per cent of those appearing before Manchester juvenile courts in 1936 were said to show 'poor attainment' and 80 per cent of those charged at Southend juvenile court in 1937 were described as 'retarded'.[15]

It has been argued, notably by Nikolas Rose, that this type of research transformed the juvenile courts into 'a new site for social enquiry' which established a 'new psychological jurisdiction'.[16] The juvenile courts occupy a central role in Rose's account of the expansion of psychological practice as a tool of social management from the late nineteenth century onwards, an expansion which he characterises as the growth of 'the psychological complex'. He argues that legal adjudication was increasingly based upon behavioural disorders and that children were increasingly dealt with on the basis of the 'origins of their pathological conduct' rather than on the basis of their illegal acts.[17] Contrary to Rose, this chapter argues that expert writings and academic research stressing the high incidence of mental defect among young offenders had very limited impact upon the daily functioning of the English and Welsh juvenile justice system. It is more fruitful to turn Rose's hypothesis on its head, and to ask why the juvenile courts did not incorporate psychological or mental considerations into their proceedings, despite the fact that they were a central point of contact for neglected and delinquent children, that they had an obligation to consider the welfare as well as the punishment of the child, and that they had clear responsibilities for civic and criminal mental certification under the 1913 Act.

Rose's argument 'that juvenile offences were no longer seen as acts to be punished but as disorders to be treated' must therefore be questioned.[18] Little use was made of the new powers given to the courts by the 1913 Act to deal with defective offenders. Sections 8 and 9 of the Act stated that a person found guilty of an offence and also found upon examination to be mentally defective could be sent to a certified institution or be placed under guardianship instead of being detained in prison. Children under 14 coming within this category were supposed to be sent to 'special' industrial schools, while those over 14 were to be referred mainly to mental deficiency institutions, as few reformatory schools could accept defective cases.[19] Yet, between 1914 and 1922, Sections 8 and 9 were invoked in just 1,312 cases – a fraction of the thousands of juveniles and adults appearing in court over the same period and a matter of concern for the Board of Control.[20] A breakdown of the number of those found guilty and dealt with as mentally defective in the 1930s does show, however, that children and young persons were proportionally more likely than adults to be dealt with in this way. In 1936, 21 per cent of the 367 cases involved children under 15. A further 44 per cent were aged between 16 and 20.[21] These figures are not broken down by gender, but Mathew Thomson's chapter suggests that boys were more commonly diagnosed defective at this stage. Gendered definitions of defect are difficult to determine, but it could be that the circumstances and behaviours which brought girls before the courts were less likely to be taken as evidence of mental defect. A Liverpool University study of delinquency and deficiency in the 1930s concluded that more girls than boys who were sent to approved schools displayed above average mental ability, leading the researchers to suggest that 'the problems which beset girls and cause their delinquencies bear more strongly on the intelligent than is the case with boys'.[22] If it is the case that girls were less likely to be diagnosed defective at this stage, their later certification in industrial schools is all the more significant.

That defect went largely undetected was blamed on perfunctory medical examinations, and the fact that only the relatively small proportion of children ordered to be birched or committed to an industrial or reformatory school were required to be examined at all. The Juvenile Organisations Committee, appointed by the Home Secretary in December 1916 to investigate the war-time increase in juvenile delinquency, reported in 1920 that 'without doubt, many children who appear before the magistrate would, if examined by an expert, show some degree of mental retardation'.[23] In the 1920s there were only three areas in England where an offender of any age could be referred by a court for detailed mental examination, despite repeated recommendations by reform groups and the Home Office. In Birmingham, prison psychiatrists Drs Hamblin Smith and Potts set up a scheme in 1919, which was copied on a smaller scale in Bradford. Neither of these were particularly geared towards children – the two main groups referred by the courts to the Birmingham scheme were women who had attempted suicide and male sex offenders.[24] In London, Cyril Burt set up a clinic for juveniles referred from education officers and magistrates. The East London Child Guidance Clinic established by Emmanuel Miller had a reasonably close relationship with the Old Street juvenile court after 1927, though this was largely due to the 'progressive' personal views of William Clarke-Hall, the presiding magistrate. During the 1930s, more children were seen at other child guidance clinics. These numbered twenty-five in 1934, though they received at most 4,000 children per year, and had no formal connection to the juvenile courts.[25] By the mid-1930s, then, provision for the mental examination and treatment of young offenders consisted of a handful of specialist but disparate clinics. Home Office plans to set up new state observation centres for young offenders were dropped from the 1933 Children Bill after pressure from the Treasury, despite the fact that youth crime was a stated government priority.

Where magistrates were aware of a child's mental status, lack of institutional space for children may explain their reluctance to apply Sections 8 and 9 of the Act. In 1915 for example, only a handful of the 107 institutions registered under the Act to accommodate the mentally defective specified that they would accept children – the minimum age of admission was commonly 14 or 16.[26] Magistrates wishing to send children to special industrial schools faced similar constraints. While these absorbed a certain number of cases referred by the courts, they often had fewer beds than ordinary industrial schools, and more long-stay pupil–inmates. 'Special' accommodation was therefore at a premium, and also cost local authorities and the Treasury more money to maintain.[27] Children waiting for vacancies in special institutions had to be housed in remand homes where beds were even more limited. London magistrates were aware of these problems and suggested that it would be 'helpful' if the doctors 'would bear these in mind' when making their assessments for the courts.[28] In short, identifying children as mentally defective or disturbed and providing for them within the juvenile justice system was expensive, time-consuming and confounded by a shortage of appropriate accommodation.

In addition to these practical problems, a key reason why juvenile courts did not confront mental problems and why psychological work remained under-funded was that the philosophical traditions of the English court room proved to be incompatible with the psychological reconfiguration of delinquency. August Aichhorn broadly summarised the position of English psychologists when he said that, 'truancy, vagrancy, stealing and the like [are] symptoms of delinquency, just as fever, inflammation, and pain are symptoms of disease'.[29] Following the logic of this biomedical metaphor, he argued:

> If the physician limits himself to clearing up symptoms, he does not necessarily cure the disease … In the re-education of the delinquent, we have an analogous situation. Our task is to remove the cause rather than to eliminate the overt behaviour.[30]

On this point the English legal system proved intractable, since it was concerned to adjudicate on the basis of overt offending behaviour. As Winifred Elkin wrote, 'the court has not got to solve the problem [of the cause of crime] as a preliminary to any rational solution of the question of treatment'.[31] The courts' first priority was to establish the facts of the case and secure legal redress. It was only reluctantly concerned with the personal problems or diminished responsibility of the offender, because these were seen to compromise the notional principles of fair trial and equality before the law. As far as the judiciary, the police and the majority of the public were concerned, the court was primarily a site for the resolution of communal differences, of public problems. The cause of individual delinquency was not, therefore, central to the legal process. This was not the case in parts of northern Europe, the United States and Australia, where links between delinquency and deficiency did find judicial expression. But in England and Wales, legal tradition certainly slowed the advance of the psychological complex.

THE WAIFS AND STRAYS SOCIETY

If the question of mental deficiency was suppressed within legal proceedings, it re-emerged within industrial schools. Evidence from the Waifs and Strays Society shows that new concepts of mental deficiency were used to manage old behavioural problems and to limit institutional disruption. The Waifs and Strays Society was founded by the Church of England in 1881 to provide homes for destitute children. The Society was dominated for nearly forty years by its founder, Edward Rudolf, who acted as secretary until his retirement in 1919.[32]

By 1913, it managed over one hundred homes, seven of which were certified by the Home Office as industrial schools for girls.[33] Industrial schools in general were informally ranked and organised around the principle of a child's corruptibility. As far as possible, innocent 'victims' were to be protected from the 'dangerous' influence of criminal and corrupted children. Even though this protection was supposed to be effected through the separation of industrial and reformatory schools, distinct hierarchies emerged within the industrial school system, with certain schools being recognised to admit the 'worst' cases referred by the courts. Two of the schools run by the Waifs and Strays Society came into this category: St Ursula's in Teddington and St Michael's in Shipton-under-Wychwood, Oxfordshire. The existence of this hierarchy is central to this discussion, because it means that, where possible, disruptive girls were dealt with by being transferred to another industrial school. However, transfer was not an option for those schools, such as Shipton and St Ursula's, which were already expected to accept girls expelled from elsewhere. The girls that reached these two schools, from which my case studies are drawn, had, by definition, reached the end of the industrial school line.

The language of deficiency was by no means the only discourse available to ascribe and assess concepts of mental 'abnormality' in children. Psychological, psychiatric and psychoanalytical studies also sought to explain delinquency and maladjustment. It is significant then, that the correspondence of the Waifs and Strays Society, drawn from the staff of its homes, outreach workers, parents, education and local government officers, and sometimes the young people themselves, indicates that the language of mental deficiency was the most prevalent in shaping popular notions of mental abnormality and policy responses. The message of mental deficiency was generally much more accessible to the general public, drawing on familiar concepts of poverty and degeneracy, whereas other discourses of mentality were not public discourses, but tended to be addressed and debated within small professional and academic circles. More importantly, psychiatric and psychological conditions were not incorporated into legislative discourses and categories. Transfers out of industrial schools on the basis of mental defect were, however, perfectly legal. The Mental Deficiency Act authorised transfer by order of the Home Secretary to a certified institution or to the guardianship of a suitable person. The 1908 Children Act authorised the transfer of cases found to be defective from an ordinary to a special certified school. But definitions of deficiency varied greatly according to gender and social background as well as the attitude and experience of individual doctors. The cases featured here suggest that social factors outweighed physiological factors in certification decisions.

The Waifs and Strays Society explicitly stated, from at least 1907, that it would not accept any feeble-minded children in either its children's homes or its industrial schools. Satisfactory medical and educational reports had to accompany each child admitted. The fact that all the girls admitted to the schools had been through this process suggests that few of them displayed any obvious mental defect at the time. Further, most children exhibiting clear symptoms of defect 'recognisable from birth or an early age', such as microcephaly, idiocy or epilepsy, would have been picked up during school medical inspections, introduced in 1907 and routinised by 1920. Further, the 1907 Probation Act specifically recommended that probation should be used in all cases where the offender, regardless of age, displayed mental defect. It would seem, therefore, that those who were certified defective in the months and years after their court appearances were certified on the basis of 'challenging behaviour' of some kind.

Clara was sent to Shipton at the age of 12 in 1915 after her 'respectable' parents successfully petitioned a magistrate that she was beyond their control. Their petition, compiled by a school attendance officer, described Clara as 'a source of constant worry and anxiety to her parents and to her Teachers by reason of her Lying and Pilfering habits' and her tendency to 'wander away and sleep out'. She had been examined by 'a London specialist' – the only case I have found where independent expert opinion was consulted – but he did not think she required a special school. Eighteen months later, aged 13, she had been certified by a doctor and a magistrate under the Lunacy Acts as being of unsound mind and sent to the Oxford County Asylum. What had happened during that year and a half? The answers to this question begin to unravel the complex issue of girls' transgressive behaviour. Clara's disruption of the school began to be seen as evidence of mental defect very soon after her arrival – with the matron complaining that,

> Conduct of several of the girls has been very unsatisfactory. I attribute this to the bad influence of Clara. She is having a harmful effect on other weak girls. She is a very bad girl and seems to have no moral sense. I am inclined to think she is defective.[34]

Shortly afterwards Clara was certified as a moral imbecile,[35] even though her local education authority stated that they could 'find no record of imbecility in [her] history'.[36] Despite her increasingly 'ugly temper', she was not removed from the home at this point.[37] However, after further medical certificates described her as 'unsafe to be left with younger children', as suffering from the eating disorder *pica*, as being 'very destructive', 'spiteful and cruel to animals' and as having the 'habits of an animal', she was certified under the Lunacy Acts.[38]

This was certainly extreme behaviour, but it seems that Clara's designation, first as defective and then as insane, was directly defined in terms of her violent temper, her hostility to young children and animals, her eating disorders, her bad effect on others and thus because of the general management problem she presented. Her perceived transgression of multiple 'norms' of rationality and gender make her case a prime example of gender deviance. This is in no sense a reference to essentialism, but a suggestion that this behaviour in a boy would not have attracted the same response at the same stage.[39] Persistently disruptive boys were certainly punished and also transferred out of industrial schools, but their behaviour did not raise questions about their stability as boys, or by extension, about their general mental stability. It is difficult to make any direct, meaningful comparison of violent expression in boys and girls, or of institutional responses to that expression. However, there is no question that rough physical behaviour was tolerated and encouraged in boys generally and in boys' industrial schools in particular, where aggression was channelled through physical exercise, scouting, and cadet training. Most boys were placed in the army after they left industrial school, a culture predicated upon the channelling and disciplining of violence, whereas almost all industrial schools' girls were required to enter domestic service, where they were expected to be quiet and biddable.

Another group of girls who were likely to be removed from ordinary industrial schools were those who were thought to be prematurely sexually aware. Described as 'morally contaminated' or as possessing 'knowledge of evil', and most commonly the victims of sexual abuse, or the children of prostitutes or 'morally unfit' parents, their mere presence was seen to threaten the 'innocence' of the others. After 1913, such girls were mostly sent to one of the special industrial schools set up for 'immoral cases', where they were rarely subject to certification as feeble-minded or morally defective. Although their own agency in the matter of their 'moral contamination' was often presented as ambiguous and confused, they were most commonly pitied as victims of 'vicious' family circumstances and were not generally seen to lack moral sense.[40] However, some of the girls sent to schools for 'immoral cases' were eventually certified mentally defective. In 1913, Emily was transferred to St Ursula's, opened in 1912 for girls 'rescued from immoral surroundings', from one of the Society's ordinary girls' homes, St Jude's in Selhurst. She had initially been committed to the care of the Society by the Guildford Guardians who had adopted her following her parents' imprisonment for neglect, alcoholism and for keeping a disorderly house. Soon after her arrival, the matron of St Jude's reported that she was 'found to be given to self abuse and immoral tendencies' and requested that she be removed 'to prevent her from contaminating the other children' who 'although orphan and destitute are practically innocent'.[41] Emily's mental condition was said to have worsened after her admission to St Ursula's, prompting an application to the National Association for the Welfare of the Feebleminded, who accepted her case and put her on the waiting list for the Princess Christian Farm Colony at Hildenborough. In this case, persistent though unspecified sexual deviance seems to have been the only 'signification' of mental deficiency.

It is important to note that insubordinate behaviour was only taken as evidence of defect in certain contexts. Where it was possible for girls to be transferred within the industrial school sector, certification was not considered in the first instance. Maggie's case exemplifies this. The long-suffering matron of Mumbles, one of the Society's industrial schools in Wales, complained in 1900 that,

> I am quite at my wits end about Maggie. Her temper is vile! She kicks, bites, yells and screams if the other girls offend her in the least. They have had to fetch a Policeman on two occasions to her, I want to avoid anything like that. She tries to run away for the silliest little quarrel; she took a knife to them and in her blind passion would have killed one if she had not been overpowered.[42]

The matron suggested that Maggie be transferred to another school. Certification was not mentioned. In a second example, Gwen, a pupil–inmate at the same school at the same time and another suspect defective, was said to 'tear every stitch of her clothes into little bits and [do] the most extraordinary things! [But] at least she has no temper.'[43] Although her case prompted much further correspondence, she was not certified, and eventually entered domestic service, which indicates that 'destructive' behaviour was also seen as evidence of mental defect, but was tolerated if it was not expressed violently or in a way that was very disruptive to the group. The date of these two cases is significant here. They suggest that disruptive behaviour was not necessarily seen as evidence of defect in girls prior to the 1913 Act, and points to a rewriting of girls' resistance in pathological terms after that time.

Other evidence indicates that before 1913, troublesome industrial school girls were more likely to be sent to a reformatory. Traffic between the two types of Home Office schools was sanctioned by the 1908 Children Act though such cases were relatively rare. Justifications for the removal of a girl to a reformatory broadly resemble those later used in certification processes; charges of insolence and insubordination were especially common. Sarah, described as 'rude, coarse in conduct and disobedient', was transferred to the Devon and Exeter Reformatory for Girls in 1909, having kept Shipton 'in a ferment' since her arrival.[44] Girls were still transferred to reformatories after 1913, although this option seems to have been reserved for those who were thought to have 'criminal natures'. This set them apart from the girls who were considered to be defective. Very often, girls transferred to reformatories had repeatedly tried to abscond or steal. In 1916, the staff of Cold Ash, another industrial school managed by the Waifs and Strays Society, took steps to remove Ada, described as a liar, a thief and persistent escapee.[45] Two years earlier, the matron of Cold Ash had written to Rudolf about 13-year-old Winifred;

> [She] is such a desperately bad character we seem to able to do nothing with her. As she develops she becomes more desperately criminal in her ways and nothing is safe from her hands. She steals keys, breaks into rooms, through windows or doors – whichever is convenient – and wherever there is anything to lay her hands on. Even the chapel is not sacred to her ... She is a Criminal and at present untrainable and a danger and an evil influence to all sent in.[46]

While it is difficult clearly to identify the factors which distinguished a reformatory case from a mental deficiency case, 'criminal' behaviour was not observed in cases which resulted in certification. Mental defect was in this sense defined by its positioning in relation to the concept of criminality.

By 1915, some special industrial schools and mental deficiency institutions certainly believed that legal transfer mechanisms were being misused. Jane was admitted to Shipton in 1909 aged 7, at which point she was described by the matron as 'intelligent and affectionate', even though she had been found by the juvenile court to be beyond the control of the Poor Law Guardians. Yet six years later, the Shipton medical officer wrote that she had 'a highly neurotic temperament' and 'violent fits of uncontrolled temper', that she was 'backward in her school work, not being able to answer simple questions' and that 'her mental capacity is deteriorating'.[47] However, Jane was turned down by at least two mental defective institutions in 1915. A spokesman for one of them – Stoke Park – reported, very tellingly, 'that when [her] case was submitted to the School Committee they felt some doubt whether the girl was not rather insubordinate than mentally defective'.[48] These transfers were also a matter of concern to the London County Council (LCC) by 1918. In that year, an LCC industrial school inspector criticised the fact that the 'majority of the girls' at Dovecot, a special industrial school for defectives, were the 'difficult cases in the schools or homes from which they have been sent'.[49] Thus, the practice of using certification to remove 'difficult' cases allowed the industrial school system to distil the reformable from the unreformable and thereby to redefine its own remit.

Educational performance was rarely a factor in these cases of certification. One reason for this is that industrial school children in general were not expected to perform well academically. As few schools employed trained teachers, girls usually attended local elementary schools, although they often left before the formal leaving age in order to undertake domestic work in the industrial school. When intelligence was used as a measure of a girl's mental state, it was assessed informally, by casual reference to old school reports, rather than on the basis of any systematic psychometric test. Edith's assessment is typical. Before being sent to the Stoke Park Mental Colony in 1917, descriptions of her intelligence referred obliquely to her inability 'to read or do simple calculations' or to 'remember lessons ... or even stories'.[50] These assessments seemed to carry little weight, even if they turned out to be positive. Emily was certified despite the intervention of her local education authority, who reported that she had been top of her elementary school class before being committed to Shipton because of parental neglect.[51]

More important than intellectual ability was the girls' employability. Violent, disruptive and disrespectful girls were unlikely to adjust to the role of demure domestic servant as soon as they were discharged. A recurring pattern in these studies is that girls were much more likely to be seen as defective if it was thought that they would be difficult to place in service. The Society was quite explicit about this, and used its admission policy to avoid future work placement problems. Noting that a Norwich education officer had described a 7-year-old candidate as 'not very bright', the Society was quick to advise the officer that 'you will understand that the Society can only accept her provided that she is suitable for training for service ... Perhaps you can ascertain whether she is really mentally defective and therefore more suitable for a special school?'[52]

A number of things were at stake here. Domestic service jobs guaranteed, at least in the short term, a girl's housing and financial independence within a carefully chosen middle-class Christian home. It was hoped that this environment would keep the girls from the streets, and from seeking to return to their 'unfit' families – although very often the 'unfit' families were not in the least interested in taking their teenage daughters back. Another key consideration was the reputation of the school as both a local source of reliable girl labour and as a worthy charitable cause – a reputation which could be, and, indeed, was on occasion, easily jeopardised by a 'bad' or unreliable girl.

Mary, aged 6, was charged by a London court in 1902 with being found wandering and having no proper guardianship, and was sent to Shipton soon afterwards. Her mother, an alleged prostitute, was awaiting trial for stabbing the man she lived with. Mary attracted little attention in the school until her case was referred to Rudolf by the matron who warned that there was 'likely to be great difficulty in providing for this girl when she should be old enough to earn her own livelihood', as she was 'below the average intelligence for her age, rather deaf and stammered badly'. The Society requested the LCC education department to find 'a suitable institution for such defective children, to which she can be transferred with the official sanction of HM Government'.[53] Their case was strengthened by the school medical officer's report on Mary, which described her as 'given to violent fits of temper and loss of higher control' and with 'defects of hearing, speech and sight'. The doctor concluded,

> In my opinion she is a degenerate and there is very small possibility of her ever being able to earn her own livelihood in service or in any other honest way. I therefore strongly recommend her removal to a special Home.[54]

Within the month Mary was admitted to Stoke Park Industrial Colony.

Again, in Mabel's case, sent to Shipton with two of her sisters in 1912 after her parents had been imprisoned by a Suffolk court for neglect, certification was only mentioned when she was due to be discharged in 1915. The Society had hesitated to admit her in the first instance, as she had been described by a Suffolk doctor as 'rather dull'. They agreed to do so having received 'a definite assurance' from the Shipton medical officer that she was not feeble-minded. Although her 'mental growth had been somewhat stunted' by her 'home circumstances', it was hoped she would improve with 'proper care and training'. Apparently Mabel had not 'improved' sufficiently by 1915, and the matron feared 'it will not be possible to send her to service'. In this case, institutionalisation was used as a last resort. It was generally agreed that Mary was 'dull' rather than defective, but it was also agreed that her family remained 'unfit' and that she should not be allowed to return home. Another option was foreclosed when Suffolk local authority claimed that the mother would not agree to her daughter entering the workhouse. On Home Office advice, Mabel was eventually certified defective and transferred to the Royal Eastern Counties Institution in 1918.[55]

I am not arguing – in any reductive, functionalist sense – that the certification of 'unemployable' girls was driven by the needs of market capitalism. As David Garland points out, the expression of social regulation is not determined by economic processes, but negotiated within them.[56] Mental deficiency institutions could be extraordinarily productive economic communities. Many were not only self-sufficient but produced a surplus of goods which were sold locally to raise income.[57] Deficiency institutions did not represent, as Andrew Scull has argued, 'repositories for the refuse of the capitalist system'.[58] Nor were these girls necessarily unemployable *per se* – they were simply considered unsuitable for domestic service. Alternative employment options available to other young women at the time, such as shops and factories, were not explored in their case, both because of the freedom of association which they offered and because, unlike domestic service, they did not offer accommodation. Rented rooms and 'common' lodging houses were considered equally unsuitable for this group of 'vulnerable' young women in the minds of the matrons and patrons of industrial schools.

Girls who were not suited to service could face severe problems. Once the term of legal committal had expired, little or no money was available to assist those who did not settle immediately into a job, as Rose's case exemplifies. As a 10-year-old she was committed to the care of the Waifs and Strays Society in 1914, after her parents 'absconded'. She had been 'frequently criminally assaulted' and was therefore sent to St Ursula's. The business of providing for Rose became very difficult when, having reached the age of 16, she was discharged on licence from the Home, with a history of violence, unable and unwilling to hold down a domestic service job, and with little family support. Her uncle had initially agreed to take her in, but was soon writing to the Society exhorting them to 'remove Rose at [their] earliest convenience as we can't stand to keeping her a minute longer'.[59] In the three years after her discharge from the industrial school in 1920, Rose experienced life in eight different institutions, including Waifs and Strays auxiliary homes, two Church Army hostels, a Salvation Army home, a detention home, a workhouse, and two infirmaries, where she received unspecified mental treatment, having been admitted after her more 'violent turns'. She was passed from one institution to another when she became too violent, or when money to maintain her ran out. Rose's case exposes the fragile network of charitable 'community care' which took over when statutory responsibility ended.

Her story also shows how young women could drift in and out of the emerging mental health system, which was not as organised and draconian as it is sometimes said to have been.[60] Not all the girls who were certified during their time in the schools were sent to institutions for the defective or the insane. The few from 'respectable' families could be returned to their parents. For others, there were often no vacancies in suitable institutions. Frequently, there was no agency willing to accept responsibility for maintenance payments. Local authorities were often reluctant to agree to the certification of children under their immediate care because this utterly transformed the nature of their commitment to pay for the maintenance of the child – from a period of detention limited by a magistrate to an indefinite period of institutional care. This was especially the case where a child was resident in a different authority area at the time of the certification or where a child, usually as the result of parental neglect prosecution, had been adopted by the Poor Law Guardians. Many girls who were the legal responsibility of the Guardians were simply returned to the workhouse on their discharge from industrial school. This happened in three of the eleven cases here.[61] To give one example, Ellen was certified defective in 1916 by the Shipton medical officer. Her mother had been committed to an asylum as a pauper lunatic in 1907, and, when Ellen's behaviour 'altered sadly for the worse in 1916', her family's 'history of insanity' was looked to as an explanation.[62] The Home Office could not find a vacancy in a special industrial school, and more surprisingly, reported that the Board of Control would not accept responsibility for her. They concluded that there 'was no alternative' but to return the girl to the care of the Brackley Guardians, the authority which had committed her to Shipton in 1907.[63] This case shows that the certification process and the prescription of institutional treatment were both highly contingent on the resources made available for individual maintenance. In this sense, it was possible to be too poor to be diagnosed and treated as a mental defective. The fact that a number of people were allowed to fall through the institutional net introduces a new dimension to the study of the emerging mental health system in Britain, a system which aimed to control the activities of the very poorest, 'degenerate' members of society.

Life became very different for the girls that were sent to mental deficiency institutions. They lost many of their rights and personal freedoms – limited as these may have been. Under Section 9 of the 1913 Act, the Board of Control had the power to extend the period of detention beyond the expiration of the industrial school sentence set by the court. At least two of the young women discussed here who were sent to a mental deficiency institution remained there until their seventies. Family contact could also be restricted as a result of the transfer. Often parents were not told that their child had been transferred from industrial school. Home Office recommendations stated that parents ought to be informed of this and that they should be made aware of their right to apply to the Board of Control to have the child returned to them. However, the recommendations also advised industrial school managers to request that the Home Secretary waived these requirements if they thought 'it desirable in any case', either because of 'the vicious or immoral character of the parents' or 'for some other good reason'.[64] Although family interest in and support for these girls can by no means be assumed, the limitation of the opportunity for personal communication represents another instance where their rights were undermined within the mental deficiency system.

The journey undertaken by these girls from the industrial school to the mental institution was an extremely symbolic one. This was no simple substitution of one state institution for another. The act of transfer out of the juvenile justice system into the mental deficiency system represented a transfer of judicial and adjudicating power and had profound implications for the juvenile justice system. For these girls, the transformation from delinquent to defective meant crossing a line of reformability, becoming 'unreformable' and 'unimprovable'. Even a progressive like Aichhorn saw no therapeutic potential in the mentally defective delinquent. Since their dissocial behaviour was seen as constitutionally rather than socially determined, he argued that in 'these cases … we can accomplish nothing because educational means do not help us'. He concluded that, 'We must classify these cases as incapable of social adaptation and thereby excluded from the possibilities of social retraining.'[65] Their certification as defective dramatically extended their 'need' for 'care and control' as defined by the juvenile court and stretched the concept of penality beyond a simple crime–punishment trajectory.

CONCLUSIONS

Reconfigurations of delinquency which emphasised individual mental status had very little impact on the procedures of the English courts at least into the 1950s, and even beyond. The hanging of Derek Bentley in 1953 and the trial of Robert Thompson and John Venables following the murder of James Bulger in 1993 may be extreme examples, but they nevertheless testify to the enduring reluctance of English legal practice to take the mental capabilities of an offender into account. Beyond the court room, however, ideas of mental disorder, conceptualised most commonly in terms of mental deficiency during the first half of this century, were central to the internal organisation of the juvenile justice system.

As communal institutions, industrial schools operated according to certain rules and standards. A priority for matrons and staff was to manage a large number of girls with as little disruption as possible, and to place them successfully in domestic service. A second priority, as a private institution, was to maintain the reputation of the school. Girls who absolutely confounded these priorities by being violent, disruptive and resistant were likely to be removed. Where transfer within the industrial school system was possible, a girl would be removed to another school or removed to a reformatory. When such transfer possibilities had been exhausted, a further set of disciplinary options opened – the infirmary, the workhouse, the asylum, the mental deficiency institution. It was through this circumscription of the possibilities of individual reform that the juvenile justice system defined itself and its agenda. Institutional 'failures' were required in order to define institutional 'successes'. Industrial schools were concerned to deal primarily with those who exhibited the potential to become an institutional 'success', those for whom social retraining remained a possibility.

For girls, 'difficult' behaviour in industrial schools was defined in terms of violence, disobedience and unsuitability for domestic service work. These represented multiple gender transgressions which were by no means confined to sexual deviance and had less to do with mental capacity than with the standard institutional management problem of maintaining order. Industrial school management problems were thereby disguised by the medicalising and pathologising of individual institutional 'failure'. These girls do represent a minority of the hundreds passing through the industrial schools in this period. They are a marginal group, but I hope to have shown here that the overall remit of the juvenile justice system was crucially defined by its margins, and by those who crossed them.

NOTES

1 See R. Smith, *Trial by Medicine: Insanity and Responsibility in Victorian Trials*, Edinburgh, 1981; N. Walker, *Crime and Insanity in England, vol. 1: The Historical Perspective*, Edinburgh, 1968; J. Eigen, 'Delusion in the Courtroom: The Role of Partial Insanity in Early Forensic Testimony', *Medical History*, 1991, vol. 35, pp. 25–49.

2 Industrial and reformatory schools, based on Scottish and European models, were founded in England and Wales in the 1850s and extended to Ireland in 1868. They were intended to keep children out of the adult prison system. Industrial schools were originally established for destitute and vagrant children, and reformatories for young offenders. The two schools were amalgamated by the 1933 Children and Young Persons Act, and were renamed approved schools, later becoming known as community homes with education. See the following for accounts of the early development of these schools: M. Cale, 'Working for God? Staffing the Victorian Reformatory and Industrial School System', *History of Education*, 1992, vol. 21, no. 2, pp. 113–27; J. Martin, '"Hard-Headed and Large Hearted": Women and the Industrial Schools 1870–1885', *History of Education*, 1991, vol. 20, no. 3, pp. 187–201; J. Stack, 'Reformatory and Industrial Schools and the Decline of Child Imprisonment in Mid-Victorian England and Wales', *History of Education*, 1994, vol. 23, no. 1, pp. 59–73; J. Barnes, *Irish Industrial Schools 1868–1908*, Dublin, 1989.

3 Popularly known as the Waifs and Strays Society, this organisation operates today as The Children's Society. I am very grateful to Ian Wakeling, archivist at The Children's Society, for allowing me access to these records. All names and case numbers have been changed to protect the identity of the girls and their families.

4 See V. Bailey, *Delinquency and Citizenship: Reclaiming the Young Offender 1914–1948*, Oxford, 1987.

5 M. Cain, 'Towards Transgression: New Directions in Feminist Criminology', *International Journal of the Sociology of Law*, 1990, vol. 18, pp. 1–18.

6 M. Thomson, in this volume; K. Jones, *A History of the Mental Health Services*, London, 1972; G. Jones, *Social Hygiene in Twentieth Century Britain*, London, 1986; H. G. Simmons, 'Explaining Social Policy: The Mental Deficiency Act 1913', *Journal of Social History*, 1978; D. Barker, 'How to Curb the Fertility of the Unfit', *Oxford Review of Education*, 1983, vol. 9; E. Larson, 'The Rhetoric of Eugenics: Expert Authority and the Mental Deficiency Bill', *British Journal for the History of Science*, 1991, vol. 24, no. 80, pp. 45–60.

7 The juvenile courts were established by the 1908 Children and Young Persons Act.

8 Criminal Statistics 1910–1946.

9 See H. Ferguson, 'Cleveland in History: The Abused Child and Child Protection 1880–1914', in R. Cooter (ed.) *In the Name of the Child: Health and Welfare 1880–1940*, London, 1992, for discussion of NSPCC activity. See R. Dingwall, J. M. Eekelaar and T. Murray, 'Childhood as a Social Problem: A Survey of the History of Legal Regulation', *Journal of Law and Society*, 1984, vol. 11, no. 2, pp. 207–32 for discussion of the decline of prosecutions for neglect in the 1930s.

10 This chapter is concerned with the formal social regulation of girls in official institutions and processes, but the disciplining of girls has never been contained within this narrow arena. Much contemporary criminology argues that discipline and censure must be seen as institutionally unbound as well as institutionally bound. See A. Howe, *Punish and Critique: Towards a Feminist Analysis of Penality*, London, 1994 for a review of recent literature.

11 A small number were managed by local authorities, notably the London County Council (LCC).

12 A list of eight special industrial schools for the mentally defective was circulated in August 1914 by the Home Office to all industrial school managers. Girls were admitted to Stoke House in Stapleton and Dovecot in Knotty Ash. Protestant boys were sent to Ivy Lodge in Stapleton, Sandwell Hall in West Bromwich or Acre Lane in Brixton. Thurlby House and Pield House in Woodford Bridge and Pontville in Omskirk were for Catholic boys.

13 *Board of Control Annual Report*, 1922, p. 36. Review of the workings of Mental Deficiency Act over 10 years.

14 W. Healy, *The Individual Delinquent*, London, 1915; L. Grimberg, *Emotion and Delinquency: A Clinical Study of Five Hundred Criminals in the Making*, London, 1928; A. Aichhorn, *Wayward Youth*, London, 1936 translation; C. Burt, *The Young Delinquent*, London, 1925.

15 Manchester Education Committee Report on the Operation of the Children and Young Persons Act from its inception to September 1936; *Southend Observer* 24 February, 1937, report by Director of Education for Southend; both quoted in W. Elkin, *English Juvenile Courts*, London, 1938, p. 16.

16 N. Rose, *The Psychological Complex: Psychology, Politics and Society in England 1869–1939*, London, 1985, p. 174.

17 Ibid., p. 173.

18 Ibid., p. 173.

19 GLRO LCC Education Officer's Department Reference Paper May 1927 Juvenile Court Cases and the Mental Deficiency Act 1913 . When industrial and reformatory schools were amalgamated in 1933 numbers of special places decreased. None of the new approved schools created in 1933 catered for young people with special needs and only one borstal accepted boys of 'low-grade mentality'. See W. Elkin, *English Juvenile Courts*, pp. 244–5.

20 *Board of Control Annual Report*, 1922, p. 44. Review of the workings of Mental Deficiency Act over 10 years.

21 *Board of Control Annual Report*, 1936, Part 1, Table 1, p. 62.

22 J. H. Bagot, *Juvenile Delinquency: A Comparative Study of the Position in Liverpool and England and Wales*, London, 1941, p. 52.

23 *The Board of Education Juvenile Organisations Committee Report on Juvenile Delinquency*, London, 1920, p. 12.

24 *Howard Journal*, 1921, vol. 1, no. 1, October 1921, pp. 80–1. Figures refer to those examined during the year ending 31 August 1920.

25 See D. Thom, 'Wishes, Anxieties, Play and Gestures: Child Guidance in Interwar England', in R. Cooter (ed.) *In the Name of the Child: Health and Welfare 1880–1940*, 1992.

26 *Board of Control Annual Report*, 1915, Part 2, Appendix C, pp. 72–85. The total of 107 was made up of 76 certified institutions (including 30 Poor Law institutions certified under Section 37 of the Act), 9 certified houses, and 22 approved homes.

27 GLRO LCC/CH/D/1/3 LCC Education Officer's Department Special Schools Branch. Draft of evidence to be presented to the Departmental Committee on Industrial and Reformatory Schools 1911.

28 GLRO LCC/CH/D/12/8 25 June 1942 notes of a conference held at the Stamford Remand Home.

29 Aichhorn, *Wayward Youth*, p. 38.

30 Ibid., p. 38.

31 Elkin, *English Juvenile Courts*, p. 16.

32 Rev. W. Fowell Swann succeeded Rudolf as secretary in October 1919.

33 For other histories of The Children's Society, see *The First Forty Years: A Chronicle of the Church of England Waifs and Strays Society 1881–1920* [no stated author], London, 1922; M. de Montjoie Rudolf, *Everybody's Children: the Story of the Church of England Children's Society, 1921–1948*, Oxford, 1950; J. Stroud, *Thirteen Penny Stamps*, London, 1971; H. Ward, *The Charitable Relationship: Parents, Children and the Waifs and Strays Society*, PhD thesis, University of Bristol, 1990.

34 Ch Soc case 1. August 1915 matron's general report.

35 Ch Soc case 1. 26 April 1916 from Society to Charles Russell at Home Office.

36 Ch Soc case 1. 11 May 1916 from chief education officer of Willesden urban district council to Rudolf.

37 Ch Soc case 1. 14 July 1916 from Eliot to Rudolf.

38 Ch Soc case 1. 21 August 1916 from G. Aitken, Under Secretary at the Home Office, to Rudolf.

39 For wider discussion of these issues see again Howe, *Punish and Critique*; L. Gelsthorpe, 'The differential treatment of males and females in the criminal justice system', in G. Horobin (ed.) *Sex, Gender and Care Work*, London, 1987; L. Gelsthorpe and A. Morris (eds) *Feminist Perspectives in Criminology*, Milton Keynes, 1990; R. Harris and D. Webb, *Welfare, Power and Juvenile Justice*, London, 1987.

40 For histories of sexual abuse see G. K. Behlmer, *Child Abuse and Moral Reform in England 1870–1908*, California, 1982; C. Hooper, 'Child sexual abuse and the regulation of women: variations on a theme', in C. Smart (ed.) *Regulating Womanhood: Historical Essays on Marriage, Motherhood and Sexuality*, London, 1992; V. Bailey and S. Blackburn 'The Punishment of Incest Act 1908: A Study of Law Creation', *Criminal Law Review*, 1979, pp. 708–18; J. Demos, 'Child abuse in context: an historian's perspective' in his *Past Present and Personal*, Oxford, 1985.

41 Ch Soc case 2. 6 February 1912 matron's comments paraphrased in a letter from the Society to the Guildford Guardians.
42 Ch Soc case 3. 19 September 1900 from C. Fitzgerald of Mumbles Home to Rudolf.
43 Ch Soc case 4. Ibid.
44 Ch Soc case 5. 8 and 10 November from matron to Rudolf.
45 Ch Soc case 6. 1915–16 correspondence.
46 Ch Soc case 7. 16 December 1914 from matron of St Mary's, Cold Ash to Rudolf.
47 Ch Soc case 8. September 18 1915 assessment by Dr Parson.
48 Ch Soc case 8. November 1915 Rev. H. N. Burden's remarks quoted in letter from Maxwell at the Home Office to Rudolf.
49 GLRO EO/PS/12/SP/124/1 26 January 1918 LCC inspection report by L. Collard on Dovecot School, Knotty Ash.
50 Ch Soc case 9. April 1917 from Ethel Driver of St Ursula's to Rudolf.
51 Ch Soc case 2. 18 December 1913 from Guildford Guardians to Rudolf.
52 Ch Soc case 10. 6 September 1915 from Society to D. O. Holme, Norwich education committee.
53 Ch Soc case 11. 1 March 1910 from Rudolf to LCC education officer.
54 Ch Soc case 11. 2 March 1910 report by Dr John Parson, Shipton medical officer.
55 Ch Soc case 12. 1912–1918 correspondence.
56 D. Garland, *Punishment and Modern Society: A Study in Social Theory*, Oxford, 1990.
57 For example, the 1930 annual report of the Royal Eastern Counties Institution shows that inmates produced 540 tailored suits, 1,300 pairs of boots, over 5,000 socks and stockings and nearly 3,000 brushes. Profits in that year amounted to £8,000, representing almost 10 per cent of the institution's total income.
58 A. Scull, *Decarceration: Community Treatment and the Deviant: A Radical View*, Cambridge, 1984, especially ch. 2.
59 Ch Soc case 13. July 1920 from Rose's uncle to the Society.
60 The responsibility for administering the 1913 Act was shared by several agencies; the Board of Education, the Home Office, the Prison Service, the Ministry of Health, Poor Law Authorities and Local Authorities. Communication between them was often poor.
61 Ch Soc cases 2, 8 and 14.
62 Ch Soc case 14. July 1916 report on Ellen sent to Brackley Union by the Society.
63 Ch Soc case 14. 1 January 1917 from G. Aitken, Under Secretary at the Home Office, to Rudolf.
64 21 August 1914 circular letter from the Home Office to all industrial school managers.
65 Aichhorn, *Wayward Youth*, pp. 224–5.

10

FAMILY, COMMUNITY, AND STATE

The micro-politics of mental deficiency

Mathew Thomson

INTRODUCTION

Histories of twentieth-century British social policy focus, almost exclusively, on the 'high politics' of parties, parliament and central government. Accounts of mental deficiency policy have followed this pattern. Considerable attention has been paid both to the passage of the 1913 Mental Deficiency Act and to the unsuccessful campaign for voluntary sterilisation of defectives in the 1930s. By contrast, there has been little work on the implementation of the 1913 legislation. In much of the historical literature on mental deficiency there is an underlying assumption that the sterilisation debate emerged due to the limited realisation of segregation under the 1913 Act. This chapter aims to show how the Act reached beyond institutions to cover mental defectives in the community. The chapter will also attempt to redress the exclusively high-political focus of policy-making histories. It is only through supplementing the study of legislative politics with analysis at the point of provision that we can fully assess the nature of policy. In an era of 'adjustment to democracy' it is important to consider the roles of patients, families, and local communities in policy-making. Finally, analysis of policy at the point of implementation will be used to illuminate the attitudes and socio-economic factors which shaped the problem of mental deficiency.[1]

The micro-politics of mental deficiency will be addressed through an analysis of a series of fifty-five detailed case history files of the London County Council (LCC). The case histories all start in the early years of the Act but are made more representative by their length – many extending to the 1950s. The sample seems to have been randomly selected for conservation by the LCC (cases progress evenly through the alphabet). Despite the small size of the sample, it is worthwhile to attempt to produce some quantitative data from the material, but this will take second place to the qualitative nature of the data as one of the main things which the data show is how 'snapshots' are misleading: an individual may well enter the data as an 'institutional case', or a 'supervision case', but the records reveal how cases evolved and moved from one category to another according to changing circumstances.[2] Much of the most important data, such as attitudes towards the home conditions and behaviour of defectives, or attitudes of the family or defectives, is unquantifiable. This type of data is, by its rare nature, particularly valuable and consequently will be referred to in detail in an attempt to reveal how the politics of the family and home contributed to the problem of mental deficiency.[3]

THE TARGETING OF THE ADMINISTRATION

Distribution of defectives by age, sex, and grade

Unfortunately, national statistics of mental deficiency were not differentiated by age and sex until the 1950s. The first clear statistics come from the Registrar General's Office in 1949. According to these statistics, there was a greater number of male than female defectives resident in institutions. This was especially pronounced at younger age groups. Above the age of 45, female defectives outnumbered males.[4] This might be due to a slightly greater life expectancy among women, but this explanation alone is inadequate. The disparity is also an indication that defective women were being kept in institutions for longer than men. This is supported by the higher median stay of female defectives of 9 years and 7 months, in contrast to 7 years and 9 months for males, and the higher number of women resident in an institution for over ten years, outnumbering men by 273 to 210.[5]

The relationship between gender and certification can be illuminated through an analysis of the sample of fifty-five London cases. A mental certificate recording grade of deficiency survives for forty-seven cases. From high to low grade of intelligence the sample contains: two moral imbeciles, twenty feeble-minded, twenty-four imbeciles, and one idiot. This is a higher proportion of imbeciles and a lower one of idiots than would be representative of a normal population and reflects the fact that since the mid-nineteenth century many London idiots had been placed in the Metropolitan Asylums Board (MAB) institutions, enabling the LCC to concentrate upon an atypically high-grade defective population.[6]

The distribution of grade according to sex reveals a link between higher intelligence and female cases: among the feeble-minded there were fifteen female compared to just five male cases, and the two moral imbeciles (certified for moral rather than intellectual inadequacy) were also females. These ratios partly reflect the greater number of females in the sample (31:24). However, male imbecile (lower intelligence) cases did outnumber females (14:10). There was also a gender difference in the age at which cases were taken up by the LCC. Under the age of 9 there was an approximately equal proportion of boys and girls; at the 10–14 age range the number of boys rose to 7:5 and this continued in the 14–17 range with a ratio of 6:3; but in the 18–25 age group the balance was dramatically reversed with women now outnumbering men in a ratio of 3:13. These distributions reflect the different reasons for the certification of male and female defectives.

Defective girls and sexual control

An examination of two case histories will indicate how young women of dull but not debilitating intellect could be certified. Born in 1894, Ada D. only came to the attention of the authorities at the age of 20.[7] She had not been recognised as defective at school and had been able to gain paid employment. She came to the notice of the authorities only when she went into the workhouse to give birth to an illegitimate child. The mental certificate of the Westminster Infirmary doctor was not that of an 'expert'. He certified her as feeble-minded reporting that she was 'dull and tells me she has had several situations and refused to work but does not know why. Appears morally defective.'[8] The mental deficiency expert, Dr Shrubsall, enforced this by his certificate which noted the result of specific tests: she could not add sums of money in shillings and pence, nor could she give differences between a dog and a cat, although it was acknowledged that she could read to Standard III.[9] The statement that she 'couldn't remember' may have been because she was confused, upset, and uncooperative as a result. Moreover, the report that she could not deal with money was inconsistent with her working in a shop in Regent Street, at a lodging house, or as a labeller in a factory.[10] These doubts are supported by the fact that when she was released on licence, after thirty years of institutional care, she was again able to support herself in work.

Kathleen W. was born in 1903 and notified at the age of 14.[11] She had previously, in 1911, been excluded from special school as 'ineducable'. Her parents, upset, had wanted her to be given another trial.

This had led to a second examination where she was certified as being a moral imbecile: she was said to be unfit to be with other children, punishment having no effect on her. The head teacher reported her as having no concentration, of stealing, of talking indecently, and of eating food off the street.[12] The enquiry officer complained, '[she] has invented stories [in offensive language] as to what boys have been doing to her on the Common, also of the behaviour of her father and step mother'.[13] There is no sign of consideration that the girl might have been telling the truth. Even if she had, this was likely to have been seen as proof that she needed to be placed in a 'protected environment'. The Enquiry Form concluded: 'Altogether the child seems a very serious source of moral danger to all the children of the neighbourhood and a danger to herself also unless under adequate control.'[14] It was felt that certification was urgent as control had to be found for Kathleen during the holiday. She was not discharged until after the passage of the Mental Health Act of 1959.

These cases indicate how the imprecise nature of mental testing and the category of moral deficiency enabled the Act to be targeted for social reasons. This was reinforced by the statutory forms which directed attention to the social and hereditary history of cases.[15] The persistence of forms and regulations which had been designed in the first years of the Mental Deficiency Act meant that even though concerns over problems such as eugenics may have lessened, the administration had an inbuilt bias which continued to orientate it towards these issues.[16] In total, eleven of the thirteen female cases aged 18 or older were linked to sexual concerns: seven of these were feeble-minded, three were imbeciles and one was a moral imbecile.[17] In at least five of the cases, as described above, there are grounds to question the assessment of serious intellectual deficiency. In the other cases, where some degree of handicapping intellectual deficiency was more obviously present, sexual factors were still vital in leading to an institutional solution.

The passage of the Act coincided with a heightened concern over the control of sexual behaviour. Whereas in the late nineteenth century concern had centred upon protection of the 'weaker sex' from moral vice, the discourse of sexuality in the early twentieth century shifted towards seeing the individual as a potential danger to the body of the community.[18] War heightened fears over venereal disease; the defenceless female defective was now seen as a potentially dangerous vector of infection to the home-coming troops.[19] In the early years of the Act in London, although venereal disease itself was not taken as evidence of mental defect, the continuation of behaviour which was deemed to have placed one in danger of contracting or spreading the disease did encourage such a diagnosis.[20] The problem of prostitution was also associated with mental deficiency; local authorities were ordered to pay special attention to defectives if 'a prostitute[;] or lodges or resides with prostitutes[;] or otherwise lives in circumstances calculated to cause, encourage or favour her seduction or prostitution'.[21] Alarm at this link was diminishing by 1926 when research by Cyril Burt claimed that just 1.8 per cent of prostitutes were hereditarily defective. On the other hand, he also stated that a disproportionately high percentage of prostitutes were dull and backward, lacking full control of their sexual instincts.[22] The idea of sexual profligacy among the dull and backward provoked fears that the middle class would be swamped by the progeny of the less able. Therefore, although the prostitute and venereally diseased woman were gradually depathologised, this did not mean the end of sexual fears; in fact, the problem widened to addressing the sexual behaviour of the population as a whole. The machinery of the Mental Deficiency Act made the female feeble-minded, dull and backward a target population for sexual control. By contrast, there was less concern to control the sexuality of male defectives, even though they were more often involved in sex offence cases.[23]

The gendered nature of the system was reflected in the duration and type of care provided. There was a greater likelihood of boys being placed under supervision than girls. This was one of the reasons for the greater number of male cases under the age of 18 in the London sample. Girls were often seen as in need of tighter moral control than could be provided by supervision at home, so a place in a refuge or voluntary religious home, away from the allures of London, was preferred. Of those cases provided with care, the initial form was supervision in 68 per cent of male cases, but only in 35 per cent of female cases. This contrasts with 26 per cent and 44 per cent, respectively, given institutional care. This figure is exaggerated even further if the 5 per cent of male and 22 per cent of female cases under 'place of safety' orders are included.[24] There is a further disparity if the length of this initial supervision is calculated: the average duration for males was 15.7 years, but for females only 11.5 years. Similarly, a sexual disparity appears in the comparison of the length of institutional provision. Once females had been sent to institutions they tended to stay for long periods, often until the reassessment of cases in 1959: of thirteen female cases the average length of institutional care was 32.7 years, spent in an average of two different institutions. There were only four male long-term cases. Moreover, males were more likely to be released on trial after a short stay or to be paroled on licence for long periods.

The delinquent male

In the sample there was a sharp division in which boys under the age of 16 were certified as imbeciles whereas those over this age were judged to be feeble-minded. This distribution stemmed from the use of the Act to help control delinquent boys after the age of 16. In fact, five of the six feeble-minded cases were ascertained because they came before the judicial authorities for committing a crime, and the remaining case was described as 'out of control'. By contrast, in the female sample, just two cases were dealt with due to coming into the hands of the penal authorities, one of whom, as a prostitute, was primarily the object of sexual concern. Figures from 1922 for male and female ascertainment via the Children Act show approximately twice the number of boys ascertained compared to girls. Even more striking are the national figures comparing criminal and non-criminal ascertainment for the period 1913–1927: female cases outnumbered male, 18,219 to 14,930, in non-criminal sources of ascertainment, but among criminal cases men predominated by 2,984 to 770.[25] An analysis of several male case histories will cast light on the links between the mental deficiency and penal systems.

Born in 1901, Frederick B. was charged at Clerkenwell Court with a felony in 1917 and sent by order under the Mental Deficiency Act to Brunswick House.[26] Although he had been slow at school, he had not been notified as defective and certification would not have taken place if he had not come before the courts. Frederick was, in effect, sent to a mental deficiency institute as an alternative to a penal solution, and as a form of preventive control while his father was away on military service. In 1919 his mother applied to the authorities, anxious for his discharge. The Board of Control asked the local authorities to investigate his home conditions which were reported as good. It was explained that the boy had been out of control due to his father's absence. His father was now back, and his uncle, a policeman at this time, was also boarding at the house. The discharge of the boy was consequently approved, the presence of the uncle at home bearing heavily on this outcome. The defective, despite his behaviour, which had led to an arrest for felony, and included an attempted escape, was able to get discharge after just two years. This is especially striking when it is compared to the cases of female defectives. The case history reads more like a penal than medical one, with first the escape, then the two year 'sentence', and then the 'probation' at home under the eye of his police officer uncle and the LCC mental welfare visitors.

A similar pattern is found in the case of William S.[27] Born in 1901, William was recognised as a defective when at Sandwell Hall industrial school. At 16 William was transferred under Section 9 of the Mental Deficiency Act to Brunswick House. This was a way of continuing control beyond the remit of the Children Act. To facilitate this the boy had to be officially charged at Marylebone Police Court. In 1918 the official visitors to Brunswick House suggested that he should be given licence with a view to discharge. He was given a trial leave with his parents for four weeks, this was extended, and three months later he was discharged. The use of the 1913 Act had extended the control over the boy for two more years after Sandwell Hall, but once within the system he had been filtered back out as inappropriate as a charge of the Act. In 1924 William was arrested by the Metropolitan Police. The medical officer asked for a report and discovered William's previous history as a certified defective. He was therefore not criminally sentenced but sent under Section 8 of the Mental Deficiency Act to the Manor Institute. After one week at the Manor, William escaped. He was free for six months before his recapture. Within three months he had again escaped. By the time the authorities could locate him, his original one-year order had expired, and he had to be dealt with instead by sentence to prison. From here he was again ascertained as a defective, this time by the prison medical officers, and sent to Rampton State Institution for dangerous criminal defectives. Subsequently, he was discharged from Rampton and sent, full circle, back to the LCC. This time he was placed in the higher security Farmfield Institution for defectives. He was not discharged until 1946. If William had served his sentence in prison he would probably have been released years earlier. Perhaps if he had not been sent to Brunswick House when he was just 16, he would not have been considered a defective when he was arrested in 1924. It is very difficult to conclude from the skeletal evidence whether there was any benefit to an individual such as William from being sent to a mental deficiency home rather than being dealt with by penal discipline. From his reaction, it seems that he saw the course taken to be punishment rather than care.

From these cases it is apparent that the mental deficiency legislation in London in the early years of the Act was being used to control delinquent behaviour of boys. This coincides with a time when adolescent delinquency was coming to be seen as a considerable problem.[28] The first reason for this was that a new scientific discourse, epitomised by the developmental 'periodicity' theory of Stanley Hall, problematised adolescence in medical terms.[29] The defective, epitomising 'lack of development', was a natural site for these concerns. In the early twentieth century there was also growing alarm over the problem of boy labour.[30] Concerns were exacerbated by the absence of parental control during the war. The fact that defective boys could obtain work during the war was seen as a temporary phenomenon, to last only until the return of the forces. In the meantime the spending power of the boys gave them greater independence and created further alarm over control.[31] The category of moral imbecility, implying a moral but not necessarily intellectual deficiency, was made part of the 1913 Mental Deficiency Act. Not surprisingly, this raised definitional problems and was not adopted on a significant scale.[32] Interest in the relationship of intelligence to behaviour continued, but it was no longer defectives who were viewed as the group for primary concern. In the work of Cyril Burt, the young delinquent was seen as defective in only 7 per cent of cases, but in 30 per cent to be dull, and in 40 per cent to be backward.[33] Delinquency was reinterpreted as merely an extreme example of 'childhood naughtiness', where primitive instincts were not under control.[34] The dull and backward were especially prone to delinquency as they were likely to be frustrated at school, perhaps teased, and consequently were likely to look for alternative outlets. Moreover, they were manipulable, easily exploited by brighter children, and likelier to get caught if causing trouble.

The changing relation between delinquency and mental deficiency was associated with new techniques and strategies to discipline the young. The 1908 Children Act separated children from the adult penal system and shifted child penality from institutional punishment to probationary prevention. However, the war precipitated a new phase of alarm over delinquency.[35] There was a sharp increase in the number of boys sent to Home Office Schools, rising from 4,632 in 1913 to 5,738 by 1916.[36] The new category of mental defective may have alleviated this situation by providing an alternative form of provision. However, since the introduction of psychologists as expert witnesses in the courts was slow, the number of charged children who were certified as defective was low – still only 0.16 per cent of new cases in 1926.[37] On the other hand, defectives were ascertained and relocated after being sent to penal institutions.[38] Others were certified before being charged. For instance, in 1921, 156 defectives (114 boys: 42 girls) were ascertained under the Children Act before criminal charge.[39] Subsequently, the number of defective children notified under the Children Act declined and the ratio of male to female cases equalised: by 1938 just 6 boys and 10 girls were dealt with in this way.[40] This trend was shadowed by the expansion of the new borstals, holding 561 boys in 1926, but 1,011 by 1932. Again this institutional care was directed overwhelmingly at boys, with just 47 girls held in 1932.[41] The impact of psychiatric ideas on social work also offset the use of the Mental Deficiency Act to control delinquency. In the 1930s some high-grade defectives were dealt with by child guidance services. In 1936 figures published from the seven London child guidance clinics, dealing with over 1,000 cases in the year, showed backwardness to be the third highest reason for sending children to the clinics, not far behind nervous disabilities and behavioural difficulties.[42] In summary, the Mental Deficiency Act should be seen, not only as an example of specialisation of welfare, but also as part of the differentiation and specialisation of penality in the early twentieth century.[43] The history of care for the defectives exemplifies the process of 'transcarceration', in which individuals were relocated between penal, medical, and educational areas of the welfare complex.[44]

THE ROLE OF THE FAMILY

The attitude of the authorities towards the family

Mental deficiency provision was also shaped by assumptions about, and regulation of, 'family life'. To a certain extent the control of behaviour and removal of defectives from the home subverted the independence and integrity of the family. Paradoxically, the actions of the authorities were also restrained and shaped by their desire to assert the centrality of family. Even when a defective was removed from a 'neglectful' family, the authorities vigorously tried to maintain some kind of family responsibility by collection of maintenance contributions. This could miscarry and restrict interventionism if families refused to contribute.[45]

The authorities used the concept of 'neglect' to justify intervention in at least one quarter of the sample. Intervention had a preventive mission of control over defectives and a wider one of reforming their families. As one social worker described the situation:

> At first, the personal condition of the defective is often uncleanly – hair uncared for, nails dirty, and appearance generally unkempt. But by tactful management, the Home Teacher is generally able by degrees to give her pupil an appreciation of nicely kept hair and hands, and this new appreciation of cleanliness will permeate the whole family.[46]

Targeting of those defectives perceived to be socially 'neglected' helps to explain why a higher than normal proportion came from lowest social classes IV and V. This class distribution was especially marked among the feeble-minded where cultural bias was likely to have played more of a factor.[47]

Enquiry into home circumstances usually occurred before the mental exam. In London, this enquiry was made by voluntary mental welfare workers who often equated irregular conduct with mental defect.[48] The definition of 'neglect' followed the 1908 Children Act's expansive definition:

> a parent or other person legally liable to maintain a child or young person shall be deemed to have neglected him in a way likely to cause injury to his health, if he fails to provide adequate food, clothing, medical aid or lodging for the child or young person, or if, being unable otherwise to provide adequate food, clothing, medical aid or lodging, he fails to take steps to procure the same to be provided under the Acts relating to the relief of the poor.[49]

It is too simplistic to see 'neglect' as a tool of middle-class social control over working-class behaviour, for ideas of 'respectability' were central to the working-class domestic economy. The main objects of concern were those 'social problem' families who, due to impoverishment or lifestyle, failed to satisfy the conventions of respectability. However, as child care was made into a professionalised science, adopting psychological theories, regulation of neglect extended to the familial emotional environment:

> the type of control exercised in the home, the consistency and severity of any punishments or the nature of rewards and encouragements should be noted carefully … Recreational facilities may be inadequate. In those of older years the occupation may be detrimental to health or morals, unadapted to the individual, or economically inadequate and so liable to encourage disturbances of behaviour. For satisfactory home care the parents or guardians need to have some understanding of the mental condition and needs of the defective and to do their best to provide care, encouragement, occupation, training, and recreation. If, as is often the case, they doubt the fact of deficiency and are content to treat the subject as a normal individual in all ways; still worse if they are always full of complaints in his presence or upbraid him for contributing inadequately to the family exchequer, the control is likely to be faulty and the influence unfavourable.[50]

In such circumstances even the 'respectable' were liable to criticism over the standard of home care.

In the sample, only five homes were given the label of 'good'.[51] These cases, two of them male and three female, were all placed under supervision rather than institutional care. The average duration of supervision was fifteen years, after which three left the records, and two others were forced into institutional care after changes in the ability of the family to care for them. In one of these cases, that of Cherry M., the parents could afford to send their daughter to a private school and subsequently, when care at home became difficult, paid the Brighton Guardianship Association to care for her; the means of the family enabled Cherry to be kept out of the state system. Despite poverty, if a home was considered to be 'good', and the defective was not in one of the groups targeted for control, the authorities were often reluctant to intervene.[52]

Supervision was not a static phenomenon. The reports on home conditions came from the London Association for Mental Welfare (LAMW) which evolved during the period from voluntary to statutory status.[53] This evolution was paralleled by a transition from the moral concerns outlined above, towards a more environmental and economic analysis in the 1930s. A sample of cases from the LAMW in 1930 reveals the growing interest in economic circumstances.[54] A record was made of the rent paid by the parents, the size of the house, and the employment and salary of parents. Defectives were described in terms of employment potential. Note was made of school records, including type of manual training given, the abilities of the defective, and the recommended future employment. Having left school, the visitors recorded the defective's history of subsequent employment, the level of pay, the duration, and reasons for termination of employment. The reports were guided by an attitude which saw self-support, rather than control of moral behaviour, as the central problem. On the other hand, when behaviour was a problem, the link to economic circumstances was still rarely made. For example, a boy who was failing at school must have been affected by working on an early morning milk round, but this link apparently was not made.[55] The tone continued to be moralistic with defectives criticised for their laziness or inadequacies.[56]

The weakening of family responsibility?

The rise in the number of defectives and insane was attributed by the Board of Control partly to a decline in family responsibility in caring for dependent members.[57] Among the sample of fifty-five London cases, in only seven cases is there evidence of families requesting care for defectives, and in three of these the request was for schooling rather than institutional provision. Moreover, there were eleven cases where parents actively objected.[58] This data does not mean that familial opinion was only active in these cases; in other cases the familial role may not have been recorded, or it may have fallen between the two poles, accepting early aid but not the subsequent incarceration. More importantly still, a request for aid is not evidence of a lack of care or responsibility, on the contrary, it may be evidence of those very characteristics. In some cases, it was the parents who accused the authorities of neglect in not providing care. Frederick W.'s mother complained about the lack of provision:

> It was my wish that he should be allowed to attend day school, but by the Council's ruling it seems that he is to be kept almost uneducated until he is of an age when he will find it hard to learn anything. He is at present at home, restless and tiresome because he has nothing to occupy his mind. I think it is a downright shame that the Council, who are responsible for the child's education, should have put this matter off as long as this and then to have come to a decision whereby nothing is done save a visitor calling now and again giving advice which is not practicable.[59]

A further difficulty in discussing the familial role is that it changed over time according to the ageing, retirement, or death of parents, the arrival of new siblings, and the ageing of the defectives. All of these factors could make care more difficult and lead to a reluctant request for institutional aid. Equally, once a defective had been placed in an institution, the family might move to a smaller house or new area, or become economically stretched by unemployment, and thus be inhibited from requesting discharge.[60] The 'family', itself, is not easily definable. From the case histories, there are signs that in a number of families there was an extended network of care. In some cases of maternal 'neglect', defectives may have been cared for by relatives or local friends. Ellen Ross's work on child-minding in London, where mothers combined in 'survival networks', may similarly apply to the care of individuals such as the handicapped.[61] In this respect, it is interesting that a number of the case histories refer to defectives playing with younger children.[62]

The case of Aaron G. demonstrates the involvement of a wider kinship, neighbourhood, and community role in care.[63] Aaron originally became a problem when he was bullied by the boys of his neighbourhood. His rabbi, as a leader of the local community, rather than the 'state' authorities, placed pressure on the family to obtain care for the boy.[64] Institutionalisation was avoided through the assistance of Aaron's kinship network. He was offered a barrow but his mother refused to allow him such unrespectable work. Instead he was kept occupied with errands and visits to relatives.[65] Later, the LAMW reported that Aaron had been given work by a friend of the family and that he and his brother slept at their grandfather's in the same street, as their own house was overcrowded.[66] Evidently, a much wider group than the nuclear family was taking an active and sympathetic interest in Aaron's care. Such communal concern offers an alternative meaning to the idea of 'community care' which was at this time being appropriated by the authorities.[67] Aaron's communal care did not fit into the model employed by the LAMW when judging standards of care. Normally, if the home of a defective had been overcrowded it would have been a reason for replacing supervision by institutional care. Similarly, if a defective had been found not to be sleeping at home with his 'family', it would have been evidence that he was 'out of control', 'abandoned', or even in 'neglect'. Within this Jewish community the idea of 'home' and of 'family' had a different meaning. The authorities seem to have accepted the value of the indigenous form of community care in their assessment that it was a 'good home'. This positive attitude may have been influenced by the fact that this assessment came from the LAMW which had close links to the London Jewish community and may have been sympathetic and understanding of the local culture.[68] However, when the case reached the stage that the laws of the wider community were abused to such an extent that it led to begging and wandering, Aaron was eventually sent to an institution.

A further problem with generalising about familial responsibility is that it ignores intrafamilial differences. In particular, there could be a division in attitudes and roles between fathers and mothers.[69] The sample of fifty-five cases had more fathers than mothers officially complaining to the authorities. This probably reflects a cultural tendency for fathers to act as the voice of the family when dealing with official matters. There is little evidence to support a black-and-white picture of the caring mother in contrast to the brutish father.[70] The fact that the mother was more likely to be referred to in the visitors' reports as caring for the child reflects both the attitudes of the visitors and the probability that fathers were working outside the home at the time of the visit. In cases where a father was permanently at home he too might be centrally involved in care. For instance, Winifred E. was cared for by her home-bound invalid father, and Herbert C. worked alongside his foster father in the latter's music shop.[71]

Although the argument that there was a decline in family responsibility seems to be flawed, and is unanswerable without a survey which compares data over time, the evidence is useful in suggesting some of the motivations which informed this abstract notion of 'family responsibility' in caring for defective dependants. Historians of the family have been divided over whether affection or economic instrumentality bonded the early twentieth-century working-class family.[72] In the case of the mentally defective, one has to look at the additional factor of sentiment towards the handicapped. It is notoriously difficult to gauge popular attitudes and generalisations can be misleading as attitudes differed according to the circumstances. The Board of Control complained about the inconsistency of the public who objected if defectives were kept on licence rather than being discharged, but were outraged if a discharged defective subsequently committed a serious crime and were unsympathetic towards high expenditure on care.[73] Familial sentiment was not necessarily the same as popular attitudes. Although stigmatising hereditary explanations of mental deficiency were common,[74] a survey of parental views reveals that parents looked on the deficiency as an accident.[75] When the National Society for the Prevention of Cruelty to Children (NSPCC) reported that a high proportion of their cases involved defectives, they pointed to the difficulties of caring for such children, rather than reporting on cruel parents.[76] In the London sample there is little evidence of rejection of children due to stigma or lack of love.

To argue that an important part of family relations was economics is not to discount affection as the two are not incompatible. However, economic difficulties were so great in many working-class families that they sometimes naturally had to take precedence over sentiment based upon affection. In the interwar years of high unemployment and housing shortages there was considerable economic pressure pushing the worst afflicted families to find statutory care for non-contributing dependants, such as defectives.[77] If a parent, in order to care for the child, was prevented from going out to work or performing paid labour in the home, this would make the economic impact even more serious.[78] However, the equation was not as simple as this. In the first place, the authorities demanded a contribution in non-pauper cases, usually set at 2s 6d per week, which, although less than the cost of support at home, was so vehemently objected to by parents that it seems likely to have undermined any economic motive for sending a child away. Second, it would be misleading to view the defective as necessarily a financial burden upon the family. In many cases defectives contributed to the family economy with a wage, helped in the family business, or performed housework. In the case of one blind mother, the removal of her defective son would have meant that she herself would have needed institutional care.[79] The authorities, with their middle-class standards of the child's proper role, may have interpreted necessary survival as exploitation and reason for removal of the child.[80]

The familial role in the construction of policy

The Mental Deficiency Act is commonly seen as an example of legislation imposed from above with the aim of control. The case history evidence reveals a more complex picture. Families, too, might use the Act to control the behaviour of defective dependants. The association of mental deficiency with a child-like state made the development of defectives' sexual interests a shock to parents and the physical growth of the child could make them difficult to control if they became agitated. Due to the frustrations of their lives, defectives were probably particularly prone to behavioural problems. Parents may have been at a loss to control delinquency of high-grade children.[81] Parental dissatisfaction with the attitude and ability of a child to work could lead to notification.[82] Concerns over sexual control of adolescent daughters probably contributed to a higher familial notification of female, than male, defectives: in 1922 the figures were 201 and 51, and in 1932 females outnumbered males by 146 to 25.[83] It would be misleading, however, to see familial use of statutory control as simply a negative restrictive action for it might be directed towards making defectives more manageable so that care within the family could continue. In a number of cases, care was requested by a parent to protect the defective from a violent spouse, or bullying from children.[84] Care and control were both inherent parts of coping with defective dependants. In summary, it would be wrong to oppose family and statutory care; families did at times look to the state for aid. Because of this alliance, families had some influence in shaping the implementation of the Act at the local level.[85]

The role of families in shaping provision can be considered by examining the evolution of methods of community care. In supervision, welfare workers had to gain access to households by winning the confidence of the parents. Then, in order to establish effective community control, they had to rely on the families themselves.[86] If supervision was not effective and institutionalisation was necessary, the process was again far easier if parental approval could be gained. After institutionalisation parental cooperation still needed to be obtained to collect maintenance contributions.[87]

The evolution of parental guardianship is a good example of policy being negotiated between family and state. In 1913 the payment of guardians in the community was intended to be the main form of community care. In reality, the authorities struggled to locate 'suitable' guardians who were willing to accept the strict rules and potential fines involved in the guardianship contract.[88] Parents were excluded from guardianship as it was designed to remove the defective from the neglectful home environment. But by the 1930s, parents were being subsidised as guardians. The change in policy was due to the failure of non-familial guardianship, greater awareness of the financial dimensions of care, and the continued lack of institutional accommodation. Guardianship was a cheap option for the authorities. In 1936 institutional accommodation could cost anything between 24s a week, for the cheapest colonies, to 42s, for a small voluntary-run home in the countryside. Guardianship using voluntary agencies would cost between 15s for females to £1 1s for males. It was even cheaper to place defectives with their families at 15s per week.[89] Despite this underlying economic rationale, the policy shift was reluctant and individual families did play an important role in convincing the authorities that they could be used as guardians.

Albert G. was born in 1905 and notified as an imbecile in 1915.[90] Supervision was recommended as his home was said to be 'good', the mother was at home, and the boy was not 'immoral'. The LAMW visited and reported quarterly. The reports were consistently favourable, and so, from 1924 onwards, the reports were made at less frequent intervals. In 1930 the LAMW reported a deterioration in the financial position of Albert's family: his father was not in full-time work, another brother was at home, and out-relief for Albert had been stopped.[91] The LAMW brought this latter point to the attention of the council authorities. As a result, by 1931 the family was again receiving a form of 'out-relief' to help support Albert. However, the father had now been laid off and his unemployment allowance had been reduced. Even when he was back in work in 1933, earning just £2 5s per week, the finances of the family were precarious.[92] In such a situation, a defective was likely to be judged 'in neglect' and in need of institutional care. In this case, however, an alternative of guardianship under the father was recommended, allowing the fee to go to the parents instead.

A second example of negotiation of community care was attendance of defectives at occupation centres. In 1933 Albert G. was encouraged to attend Shoreditch craft centre.[93] Attendance at the centre became an area of tension between family and authorities. In January 1935 the supervising visitor, arguing that Albert needed regular occupation, informed the authorities that he was no longer attending the centre.[94] For twenty years of Albert's life this had not been a problem, but now the authorities were extending their standards to monitor the use of time within the home. Since Albert was under guardianship, the authorities had power to exert control over conduct within the previously private sphere of the home. His mother complained that attendance at the centre was too much strain as travel to the centre involved a train journey and then a ten-minute walk to the centre. Although the authorities thought the parents' objections were unreasonable, the parents' complaints led to a guide being provided from the station to the centre. It was not possible to provide a guide for the whole journey, but the authorities, at a time of more widespread parental pressure to increase assistance, did decide to pay the parents' fares.[95] After the boy had slipped and hurt himself at a football match trip organised by the centre, the family decided that it was safer to keep him at home. The Board of Control were consulted by the LCC and agreed to provide a door-to-door guide on both journeys to satisfy the parents, but still the parents did not send their son along. The authorities were annoyed at this and highly critical of the parents.[96] The standard of care, which had previously been given good reports, was now attacked. The mother was criticised for allowing her son out alone, for his lack of occupation, and his 'thin and nervous' condition.

The mother's side of the story shows the gulf in understanding between the authorities and family. She pointed out that her son had been going to the park on his own for the past twenty years and had never been warned against this. He was always very well behaved and never talked to strangers, except for a couple of pensioners. He was well known in the park and safe under the supervision of the park-keeper. Under such conditions, the boy could hardly be described as 'out of control'.[97] When the visitor had written a critical report on the defective doing nothing in the house except for standing around and looking at himself in the mirror, she failed to realise that the defective did in fact have his own 'occupational regime' at home: dressing and washing himself would take all morning, then the afternoon would be spent walking in the park. The mother argued that the boy was therefore by no means unoccupied and saw the addition of the occupation centre as totally disrupting this proven and congenial routine. Attendance at the centre so upset the boy that it caused the nervousness and enuresis which was complained of at the occupation centre. Albert's mother argued that in other circumstances she would welcome the relief offered by the centre, but in fact attendance produced more trauma than it alleviated. She added that in the past she had always been treated with great respect by the 'lady visitors' and medical officers, and was obviously quite upset by the new interventionist stance of the authorities.[98] The authorities finally conceded defeat over the attendance at the occupation centre, though they considered the mother to be dangerously 'over protective' – an ironic term when one considers the parallel use of 'neglect'.

It is difficult to conclude how far the regime of occupation centres was shaped by the needs of families and clients. The mixture of marches and raffia work, on the one hand, and country dances and games, on the other, indicates both disciplinary and recreational elements. The LCC reported on their early ventures in 1923:

> Parents appear to interest themselves in the work of these centres, and although the attendances of the children are not large, much useful work appears to have been accomplished already. Several mothers have given testimony to the improved deportment and usefulness of the children when at home which has followed their attendance at the centre.[99]

The description indicates that the regime, in an attempt to attract clients, did become attuned to the concerns of parents. Since it was unlikely that cases from 'poor' homes would be allowed to stay in the community, the families using these centres were probably of a higher than average social status, and may consequently have had more influence in negotiating the conditions of the centres. Many mothers were in desperate need of some relief from their constant role of home care. Reflecting these concerns, the Mother's Defence League voiced its support for the occupation centres.[100] One should be careful, however, of accepting these middle-class groups' views as representing working-class mothers. As long as occupation centres were so limited, working-class families were forced to accept what provision they could find. They therefore had little power to shape policy as 'consumers'. As Albert G.'s case demonstrates, the threat of official sanction sometimes coerced parents into using this imposed community care to prove their worthiness as guardians.

It was even harder for parents to take an active role in influencing institutional care, where the realities of conditions were largely hidden. If they did object to conditions they were unable to react by withdrawing their children, but had to proceed through a myriad maze of bureaucracy. Letters of complaint and requests for withdrawal, holiday, or licence could be sent to the institution, the local authorities, or the government, yet action upon this was hampered by administrative confusion over responsibility, by a conservative attitude which mistrusted the motives of the parents, and the restrictive rules and regulations of the administration.[101] In some cases, the family had agreed, perhaps under duress and deference to the expert, to initial care for their child, but often under a misunderstanding that it was only for a short period of time. The father of Elizabeth D. wrote in 1923 when his daughter was 23; 'I am asking if I can have her home as when she first went away she was only supposed to be away for 12 months, and then it was until she was 16.'[102] Families often accepted institutional care on the understanding that their children, having been excluded from school, would get a residential education. On visiting their children and seeing the reality of the conditions, parents, such as the mother of Charlotte T. expressed disappointment:

> I don't think she is being taught anything in particular as regard earning her living as we understood she would be. Could you be so kind as to find out for me if she could come home at the end of her two years.[103]

Parents were often too cautious, for fear of damaging their image in the eyes of the authorities, to openly express their anger, but this was evident in letters to children:

> I suppose you are longing to come home as we are longing for you. If you come home there is no need for you to work you were always very well and happy when you were at Halstead we don't understand why they want to keep you in that place for I suppose they are keeping you for their own use ... It doesn't seem to us as though they are treating you properly if they don't let you home before very long. Father is going up and make them understand that you were in fit state when you went to that place. If they have any children of their own and had any love

> for them as your mother and Father has for you it would make them understand a bit better.[104]

Parents usually lacked the necessary understanding of the Act, or the financial means, to channel their resistance and complaints through the law. Detailed legal records of one London case do survive, in which a philanthropic employer and sympathetic solicitor intervened to help a defective,[105] but this case cannot be taken as typical, on the contrary, it highlights the weakness of legal aid to counter medical bureaucracies at this time.[106] It is not surprising that families sometimes reacted in desperation by attempting to aid the escape of an institutionalised member.[107]

CONCLUSION

It is important to balance the 'high politics' of social policy with analysis of implementation at the micro-level. The London sample reveals the targeting of the Mental Deficiency Act at sexually active females, delinquent males, and 'unrespectable' families. Three factors interacted in the micro-politics of provision: the forms and regulations of the mental deficiency administrative machinery, and changing state policy over other areas of welfare such as the Poor Law, the penal, and the educational systems; the views of the social workers, local authority welfare workers, and psychologists who interpreted the legislation and ascertained defectives; and the roles of the defectives and their families who may have actively requested aid, resisted provision, or encouraged the modification of policy to serve their needs. However, the weighting of power was heavily on the side of the authorities. Families were often coerced into acceptance of care through a combination of deference to medical and bureaucratic authority and confusion about the legislation. In an era of adjustment to democracy, greater 'consumer-power' as welfare recipients was balanced by disempowerment in navigating the increasingly complex and professionalised welfare machinery.

NOTES

1 For an overview which integrates the micro-political level into a broader social policy analysis see M. Thomson, 'The Problem of Mental Deficiency in England and Wales, c.1913–1946', unpublished DPhil thesis, Oxford, 1992.

2 The disadvantage of institutional studies is that they tend to hide the interaction of institutional care and community and family care: M. Ignatieff, 'Total Institutions and the Working Classes', *History Workshop Journal*, 1983, vol. 15, pp. 169–70.

3 L. Gordon, *Heroes of their Own Lives: The Politics and History of Family Violence*, London, 1989, p. 18, despite a much larger sample of cases acknowledges the quantitative problems and concentrates upon a qualitative approach.
4 *Registrar General's Statistical Review of England and Wales 1950–51*, London, 1955, p. 130 for mentally ill; Table M7, pp. 138–9 for defective.
5 Ibid., p. 188.
6 M. Thomson, 'The Problem of Mental Deficiency in Inter-War London', unpublished paper.
7 Greater London Record Office (GLRO), PH/MENT/2/10 Case 1418.
8 Ibid., J. Coulson, 17 August 1916.
9 Ibid., F.C. Shrubsall, 10 August 1916.
10 Ibid., Enquiry Form, 22 December 1915.
11 GLRO PH/MENT/2/12 Case 2112.
12 Ibid., 23 July 1917.
13 Ibid., 20 July 1917.
14 Ibid., 20 July 1917.
15 F. C. Shrubsall and A. C. Williams, *Mental Deficiency Practice*, London, 1932, pp. 295–307.
16 *Minutes of Evidence to the Royal Commission on the Law Relating to Mental Illness and Mental Deficiency 1954–7*, vol. 22, Evidence of NCCL, pp. 832–4.
17 Adelaide B., Francis C., Ada D., Emily E., Winifred E., Laura G., Florence L., Annie M., Ellen S., Winifred T., Winifred W.
18 F. Mort, *Dangerous Sexualities: Medico-Moral Politics in England Since 1830*, London, 1987, pp. 153–209.
19 L. Bland, '"Guardians of the Race" or "Vampires upon the Nation's Health"? Female Sexuality and its Regulation in Early Twentieth-Century Britain', in E. Whitelegg *et al.* (eds) *The Changing Experience of Women*, Oxford, 1982, pp. 373–89.
20 GLRO PH/MENT/1/5.
21 *Board of Control Annual Report for 1914*, p. 51.
22 C. Burt, 'The Contribution of Psychology to Social Hygiene', *Health and Empire*, 1926, vol. 1, pp. 25–33; Burt, 'The Causes of Sex Delinquency in Girls', *Health and Empire*, 1926, vol. 1, pp. 251–71. The work of Burt has been focused upon here as he was the official psychologist for the LCC at this time. See S. Sharp and G. Sutherland, 'The Fust Official Psychologist in the Wuurld', *History of Science*, 1980, vol. 18, pp. 181–208.
23 *Board of Control Annual Report for 1931*, pp. 86–9.
24 Place of safety orders enabled temporary institutional care to be provided in uncertified accommodation. This order was frequently manipulated to provide longer-term care in order to overcome the lack of certified accommodation.
25 *Board of Control Annual Report for 1934*, p. 39.
26 GLRO PH/MENT/2/10 Case 1992.
27 GLRO PH/MENT/2/12 Case 1826.
28 J. Gillis, *Youth and History: Traditions and Change in European Age Relations, 1770–Present*, London, 1974, ch. 4.
29 S. Hall, *Adolescence: Its Psychology*, New York, 1904. Hall's work was taken up in Britain by J. W. Slaughter, *The Adolescent*, London, 1911.

30 H. Hendrick, *Images of Youth: Age, Class, and the Male Youth Problem, 1880–1920*, Oxford, 1990; E. J. Urwick (ed.) *Studies of Boy Life in Our Cities*, London, 1914.
31 Frederick B. Case 1992.
32 S. Watson 'The Moral Imbecile: A Study of the Relations between Penal Practice and Psychiatric Knowledge of the Habitual Offender' unpublished PhD thesis, Lancaster, 1988, p. 177.
33 C. Burt, 'Delinquency and Mental Defect', *British Journal of Medical Psychology*, 1923, vol. 3, pp. 169–78.
34 C. Burt, *The Young Delinquent*, London, 1925, p. viii.
35 G. K. Behlmer, *Child Abuse and Moral Reform in England, 1870–1908*, Stanford, California, 1982, pp. 193–207.
36 V. Bailey, *Delinquency and Citizenship: Reclaiming the Young Offender, 1914–1948*, Oxford, 1987, p. 317.
37 Ibid., Table 1b, pp. 312–13.
38 *Board of Control Annual Report for 1933*, pp. 83–4.
39 Ibid.
40 *Board of Control Annual Report for 1932*.
41 Bailey, *Delinquency and Citizenship*, Table 13, p. 325.
42 *LCC Annual Report, 1936,* III, Part II, 1937, pp. 60–4. This is supported by material for Birmingham: C. L. C. Burns, 'Birmingham Child Guidance Clinic: A Review of Two Years' Work', *Mental Welfare*, 1935, vol. 16, pp. 3–6. Again, however, Birmingham was not typical.
43 D. Garland, *Punishment and Welfare: A History of Penal Strategies*, Aldershot, 1985, pp. 223–4.
44 J. Lowman, R. Menzies, and T. S. Palys, 'Introduction', in *Transcarceration: Essays in the Sociology of Social Control*, Cambridge, 1987, pp. 9–11.
45 GLRO ACC 2201/33/1/19, Speçial Report referring to administration of mental deficiency act, submitted May 1917, Case of E.M.D.
46 M. Anderson, 'The Home Teaching of Defectives', *Mental Welfare*, 1936, vol. 17, p. 36.
47 This is indicated by the higher rates of high-grade mental deficiency found among lower social groups, in contrast to a more equal distribution of lower-grade defectives: *The Registrar General's Statistical Review of England and Wales, 1950–51*, p. 186, Table M.33.
48 Shrubsall and Williams, *Mental Deficiency Practice*, p. 245.
49 Children Act, 1908, 8 Edw. 7, Ch. 67, Section 12 (1); On Children Act, Behlmer, *Child Abuse and Moral Reform*, pp. 193–207.
50 Shrubsall and Williams, *Mental Deficiency Practice*, p. 251. For the imposition of strict and unsuitable standards of care on mothers see: E. Peretz, 'The Professionalization of Childcare', *Oral History Journal*, 1989, vol. 12, pp. 22–7.
51 Herbert C., Winifred E., Aaron G., Albert L., Cherry M.
52 GLRO PH/MENT/2/11 Case 389.
53 Thomson, 'The Problem of Mental Deficiency in Inter-War London'.
54 L. Smith (ed.) *The New Survey of London Life and Labour*, VI, London, 1934, pp. 364–79, Annex 1: 17 cases of 9 boys and 8 girls. For insights into methodology behind selection of cases: New Survey of London Archive, British Library of Political and Economic Science (NSOL), 5/5 Shrubsall to Mr Verdeer, 5 July 1933; and for more case histories, NSOL 5/7.

55 Smith, *New Survey of London*, Annex 1, Case 9.
56 Ibid., Cases 6, 11, 13, 14.
57 *Board of Control Annual Report for 1930*, p. 8.
58 See Table 7.IV for statistics on referrals by relatives.
59 GLRO PH/MENT/2/12 Case 1987, letter from Mrs Wooding to Council 19 April 1917.
60 For example, in Case 1412, Elizabeth D's parents became pensioners.
61 Ellen Ross, 'Survival Networks: Women's Neighborhood Sharing in London before World War II', *History Workshop Journal*, 1983, vol. 15, pp. 4–27.
62 For example Cases 450 Elsie L., 290 Ellen S. As these cases grew older, however, the parents became concerned at their treatment of younger children.
63 GLRO PH/MENT/2/11 Case 389. On indigenous care within Jewish community: L. Marks, 'Irish and Jewish Women's Experience of Childbirth and Infant Care in East London, 1870–1939', unpublished DPhil thesis, Oxford, 1990.
64 E. Black, *The Social Politics of Anglo-Jewry, 1880–1920*, Oxford, 1988, pp. 181–4, 232–6 on interest of Jewish community in such areas of voluntary welfare.
65 Case 389, LAMW 28 June 1927.
66 Case 389, LAMW 30 January 1927.
67 See discussion by E. and S. Yeo, 'On the Uses of Community from Owenism to the Present'. The continuing importance of community and kinship networks is stressed in recent social history: Benson *The Working Class in Britain*, pp. 117–137; especially in poor London areas, as shown by Ross, 'Survival Networks'; and J. White, *Campbell Bunk: The Worst Street in North London*, London, 1986.
68 GLRO PH/MENT/5/1, Mins 22 July, for Jewish representatives placed on Executive.
69 J. Lewis (ed.) *Labour and Love: Women's Experience of Home and Family, 1880–1940*, Oxford, 1986, pp. 106–8. N. Lowe, 'The Legal Status of Fatherhood Past and Present', in M. O'Brien and L. McKee (eds) *The Father Figure*, London, 1982, pp. 26–42.
70 There is little work on the father's role, an exception is T. Lummis, 'The Historical Dimensions of Fatherhood: A Case Study 1890–1914', in O'Brien and Mckee (eds) *The Father Figure*, pp. 43–56. A 'child guidance and fathercraft' group was set up in Kensington, *Journal of Mental Science*, 1927, vol. 73, pp. 443–6.
71 GLRO PH/MENT/2/10 Cases 1943 and 572.
72 M. Anderson, *Family Structure in Nineteenth-Century Lancashire*, Cambridge, 1971; E. Shorter, *The Making of the Modern Family*, New York, 1975.
73 *Board of Control Annual Report for 1934*, pp. 55–6; *Board of Control Annual Report for 1937*, pp. 8–9.
74 E. Goffman, *Stigma: Notes on the Management of Spoiled Identity*, London, 1968, pp. 26–7.
75 *LCC Annual Report, 1930*, III, Part I, pp. 44–5.
76 Public Record Office (PRO) MH58/102, NSPCC evidence to Brock Committee on voluntary sterilisation; *Report of the Departmental Committee on*

Sterilisation (Brock Report), PP, Cmnd 4485 xv 1934, pp. 80–91. On the other hand the NSPCC were active proponents of the Mental Deficiency Act to remove defective children or to remove normal children from defective parents: *NSPCC Yearbook 1913/14*, pp. 46–7.

77 Thomson, 'The Problem of Mental Deficiency in England and Wales', ch. 6: 'The Geography of Mental Deficiency'.

78 On importance of maternal income as a supplement to 'family wage' of male, see E. Roberts, 'Women's Strategies, 1890–1940', in Lewis (ed.) *Labour and Love*, pp. 223–48.

79 GLRO PH/MENT/2/10 Case 572.

80 GLRO PH/MENT/2/12 Case 1414.

81 GLRO PH/MENT/2/12 Case 208 Charlotte T.

82 Smith, *New Survey of London*, VI, pp. 364–78.

83 *Board of Control Annual Report for 1922*; *Board of Control Annual Report for 1932.*

84 Case of Nellie T. (206) where father was worried about drunken mother; Elsie L. (450) who was rough with other children; Aaron G. (389) who was bullied by other children. Gordon, *Heroes of Their Own Lives*, pp. 55–8, 213.

85 Compare Gordon, *Heroes of Their Own Lives*, p. 6.

86 E. Fox, *The Work of the Local Associations for the Care of the Mentally Defective*, London, 1920, p. 8. For discussion on the limitations of supervision see *CAMW Conference 1926*: Miss Darnell, pp. 48–9; Mrs Emmett, pp. 54–5; Mr Wormald, pp. 59–60.

87 GLRO PH/MENT/2/10, Elizabeth D. Case 1412, is an example of non-payment by the parents leading to a court case.

88 *Board of Control Annual Report for 1923*, pp. 49–51; *Board Of Control Annual Report for 1926*, pp. 53–4.

89 *LCC Annual Report*, 1936, IV, p. 46.

90 GLRO PH/MENT/2/11 Case 398.

91 Ibid., LAMW 25 July 1930; 25 August 1931.

92 Ibid., Supervision Section, 28 December 1933.

93 GLRO PH/MENT/2/11, Case 398.

94 Ibid., Board of Control to Mental Hospitals Department, 25 January 1935.

95 *LCC Annual Report, 1930*, III, Part I, p. 47.

96 GLRO PH/MENT/2/11, Case 398, Supervision Section 6 December 1935.

97 Ibid., Mother, 12 May 1936.

98 Ibid., Supervision Section 12 May 1936.

99 *LCC Annual Report, 1923*, III, pp. 51–2.

100 N. Boyle, *CAMW Annual Conference Report 1922*, 22 July.

101 GLRO MAB 238a, 7 January 1930.

102 GLRO PH/MENT/2/10 Case 1412, letter 25 July 1923.

103 GLRO PH/MENT/2/12 Case 208, letter from mother 12 August 1916.

104 GLRO PH/MENT/2/12 Case 1627, letter undated c.1919.

105 On the issue of poverty of legal aid, and inequalities within legal system see *Justice in England*, by a Barrister, London, 1938.

106 *Justice in England*, pp. 140–7, on analogous medico-legal problem of workmen's compensation.

107 GLRO PH/MENT/2/11 Annie M. Case 1614. On resort of families to anti-statist and extra-legal tactics; White, *Campbell Bunk*, p. 158.

INDEX